D1159899

Political Television

Bernard Rubin
School of Public Communication
Boston University

Wadsworth Publishing Company, Inc.
Belmont, California

For

Ruth
Roberta Louise, our daughter
Our parents

319.0230979
B896p-p

© 1967 by Wadsworth Publishing Company, Inc.,
Belmont, California.
All rights reserved.
No part of this book may be reproduced in any form,
by mimeograph or any other means,
without permission in writing from the publisher.

L.C. Cat. Card No.: 66–27584

Printed in the United States of America

Preface

Political Television is an account of the dramatic reshaping of elections and the Presidency by television, the mass communications medium that brings current history into the home.

This story of the five years preceding the general election of 1964 is told in the context of two presidential campaigns, in an attempt to show why and how television has become able to exert such profound political influences.

Major examples of recent influential telecasts have been highlighted. To illustrate, the debates between the nominees of the two major parties were a principal feature of the campaigning in 1960. Therefore, these debates are stressed in the discussion of the 1960 contest. Little is said about the national party conventions of 1960, but a full treatment of the conventions of 1964 is offered. In short, every effort has been made to analyze the essential problems posed by television and the more consequential adventures of leading political figures who have had to learn about the medium. Considerable attention is given to the growing power of television as an administrative tool at the highest executive level of our government. The political ramifications are stressed because of their importance to every alert and informed citizen.

What follows is an introduction to the presidential race of 1968. It is hoped that general appreciation of what has happened in recent years can lead to more constructive political contests in the near future.

My longtime interest in the political ramifications of television was stimulated when I was invited to prepare a research report for the Committee of The American Political Science Association (1963) headed by the eminent Harvard University scholar Professor Carl J. Friedrich. This committee was appointed to study procedures and formats for possible television and radio debates between presidential candidates.

I wish to extend my deep appreciation to three of the people who helped me. Miss Nancy Bernstein, while my student, aided the project by assisting in the assemblage of the endless research source material. Her cheery interest was most welcome. Two young ladies worked industriously on the typing of the manuscript. Miss Ranko Iwamoto labored over the early chapters, and Mrs.

Shirley Laska typed the rest of the material. They have earned my plaudits for willingly tangling with my penmanship.

Finally, I give sincerest thanks to my wife for her invaluable assistance at every stage of the endeavor.

Contents

Preface   iii

1   The Public Be Served   1

General Education   1
Information Sources: Television Compared with Other
   Mass Media   3
Television Motivation: Voting Turnout   4
Television and Political Controversy   5
The Moral Dimension: Network Administration   7
Governmental Controls   8
The Powerful Personalizing Effect: The Kefauver
   Hearings of 1951   10
The Boomerang Effect: McCarthy—Symbol, Idol,
   Mass Media Experimenter   12
Footnotes   16

2   Qualified Political Argument   18

Impact of the 1960 Presidential Debates Upon the
   Election Outcome   18
Origins of the Debate Idea of 1960   20
A New Ritual   22
Equal Time   24
What Is Meant by "Debate"   29
Personality   31
In Person?   37
Footnotes   39

3   Perspectives on the Kennedy-Nixon Debates
   43

The Two Men   44
Preparation for the Debates   48
The Debate Of September 26, 1960   53
The Debate Of October 7, 1960: Reactions   55
The Debate Of October 13, 1960: Reactions   56
The Debate Of October 21, 1960: Reactions   58
Appraisals of the Debates   60
Anticlimactic Telethon   61

v

METHODIST COLLEGE LIBRARY
Fayetteville, N. C.   28087

Sidelights   62
The 1960 Experience: Ramifications   62
Footnotes   66

4   **Television and the New Frontier**   69

Eclipse   69
The Victor   70
Inauguration Day   71
Seeking Cooperation   74
Certain Precedents   74
Televised Press Conferences: JFK's Approach   80
Urgent and Special Television Appearances   86
Television on the Scene   93
Factors of Consequence   94
Managed News   97
Footnotes   100

5   **Those Four Days**   104

Air Force One   104
Those Four Days and Television   104
The Influence of Television   108
Footnotes   109

6   **Let Us Reason Together**   110

Which Lyndon Johnson?   110
Taking Hold: First Days in Office   114
The President in Action   116
The Extent of Presidential Domination of
    Television   118
Of Politics and Government   121
Interested Parties   124
Footnotes   125

7   **Behind the Screens**   127

Congressional Views: Spring 1964   127
Money and the Partisan Objectives   130
The Networks Organize to Report the Campaign   134
Fairness   138
Fair Enough?   139
Footnotes   140

8   **To The Boardwalk and the Golden Gate**   143

Presidential Primaries   143
New Hampshire   145
A Road of Thorns   151
Hypotheses and Opinions   152
Certain Post-New Hampshire Developments   153
Conventions 1964   155

METHODIST COLLEGE LIBRARY
Fayetteville, N. C.

The Republicans Converge   158
The Republican National Convention   160
The Democrats' National Convention   168
Footnotes   172

9   The Best and the Worst of Times   174

Of Proposals and Disposals   174
Extremism: Illustrations   176
Television Enterprise: The Crisis Factor   176
Racial Violence   177
Keeping Racial Tension Down   178
Issues Bandied About during the Campaign   179
Campaigners' Characteristics and Significant
    Campaign Events   180
Goldwater on Television   182
Democratic TV Commercials and a Republican
    Morality Film   185
Pollsters' Conclusions   187
The Voters Turn Out: Television Reports   188
The Big Story of Another Beginning   192
Lessons and Suggestions   192
Television, Education, and Politics   193
Footnotes   194

Index   197

1 / The Public Be Served

Observers of American political institutions and behavior have veered to extremes in deprecating or overemphasizing the influence of television. Such strong diversity of opinion is quite understandable; television is a relative newcomer among the established mass media, and its role in politics has been, until recently, too new to be clearly assessed.

The phenomenal rise of the television industry as a mass media force is traceable from World War II but most of its history in national politics goes back only to the early 1950s. In 1948, when Harry S. Truman defeated Thomas E. Dewey, television was still a novelty found in few American homes. The voters who watched the election-night returns on television that year made up only a very small percentage of the population.

By 1952, because of the rapid physical growth of the television industry and its overwhelming acceptance by a public on a receiver-buying spree, the medium had emerged as a major recreational institution in our society and a developing political force as well.

Today, there is sufficient history on the subject to permit objective analysis. The pattern of the presidential campaign of 1960, which featured the now famous Kennedy-Nixon television debates, made clear the need to take a measure of the medium's impact upon political life in this country. The election of 1964, while less outwardly dramatic, contributes much to our understanding of certain still-novel political processes.

We will deal with what might be tagged "polivision"—the perception of politics as influenced by television. As an introduction to the issues raised in this account, the discussion that follows will highlight several illustrative problems.

GENERAL EDUCATION

How does television affect political life in the United States? First and perhaps foremost, the medium can transmit sounds and sights from the locales where news events are unfolding.

1

Consequently, since television's early days as a mass medium, interest in on-the-spot news reporting has grown tremendously. Before World War II, it was difficult for the average person to picture news events in real-life settings. Today, most Americans can visualize a civil rights demonstration, a political party convention, a Presidential address, or a rocket launching through television presentations. Obviously, television has been educational in this sense. Of course, it can be argued that the quality of television news is not uniformly high. Also, it is clear that television has usually been a poor rival of the print media when it comes to getting at long-range meanings behind events! But on a day-to-day basis, be it the story of a combat patrol in Vietnam or in the Congo, or a report on flood damage in Kentucky or in the Netherlands, television has assumed a tremendous role in civic education.

Granting the general educational influence of television, students of the mass media are most curious about citizen reactions to all this information. Such interest is quite understandable, since all news media devote so much attention to reporting political events and elections. But before we turn to this question, it might be well to point out that scholars have tended to measure the effects of television on politics in those areas where the results of an opinion shift are most tangible. There is, for example, a fixation on comparing election-day statistics with the results of pre-election polls—a comparison that can be carried out by simple ballot-counting. Once we venture beyond such straightforward measures of an opinion shift, it is as difficult to determine how television affects public opinion as it is to determine how books or newspapers ordinarily impress readers.

One thing is certain, however, and it bears directly upon the body politic! A range of information beyond the imaginings of the learned of 50 years ago is available to television viewers today. For all of the tawdry offerings that are so common, when one sifts through program schedules, it is obvious that *important* productions—productions that in some manner foster human rationality—are also abundant.

Television cameras are frequently aimed at scenes that mark shifts in public opinion. In every community, television brings the same package of ideas to all social and economic classes. Television is a highly democratic medium. The programs are beamed without direct cost to all those with receivers, and there are few families too poor to have a set.

It is a matter of the utmost political importance that the sights and sounds of Congress in action, a student demonstration, a civil rights protest march, a race riot, or a political rally can be absorbed by slum dweller and slum lord alike. A program offering a sophisticated exposition on the European Common Market may ultimately be of less influence on adults than on the child who senses through that program and others that the world is a large and wondrous place indeed. Although societal changes are rooted deep in social and economic opportunities, or the lack of them, the easy availability of such dramatically presented information and education has had and will have profound implications for American society.

Information Sources: Television Compared to Other Mass Media

In 1965, 668 television stations were reaching into 52.6 million American homes. The Television Information Office (established in 1959 by the National Association of Broadcasters) released, in March 1965, the results of five studies that had been undertaken between 1959 and 1964 by the polling organization Elmo Roper and Associates. They concluded that, as of 1964, "television [had] replaced newspapers as the public's *primary news source,*" keeping a slight lead —58 per cent to 56 per cent—first achieved in 1963 (55 per cent to 53 per cent).*

One question was aimed at finding which of the mass media—television, newspapers, radio, or magazines—was the public's *most believable source of news.* Television was substantially in the lead in 1964, maintaining a margin first seen in 1961 over competitive media. By 1964, 41 per cent of those interviewed selected television as most believable, against 23 per cent for newspapers, 8 per cent for radio, and 10 per cent for magazines.

In response to the question "Which of the four versions would you be *least inclined to believe*—the one on radio, television, magazines, or newspapers?" newspapers led with 28 per cent, followed by 24 per cent for magazines, 11 per cent for radio, and 6 per cent for television.

The Roper organization inquired into the comparative values of these same media as sources of information about government at the local, state, and national levels.

One poll was taken in June, before the 1964 election, and another in November, after the ballots had been cast. The group polled in the last week of June consisted of a representative national sample of 1,583 people. Between November 16 and 23, a total of 1,996 interviews were conducted.

Regarding the local level of government (city, town, county) the source of information considered most valuable in June was newspapers (48 per cent), followed by television (41 per cent), "people" (18 per cent), radio (10 per cent), and "other" (5 per cent). After the November elections, newspapers were still rated highest (42 per cent), while television dropped drastically (27 per cent). There was no change in the other two categories. The considerable drop in the television category after the elections may have been due to the replacement

---

* Totals exceeded 100 per cent because some respondents named more than one medium as a source of most of their news. Italics added to quotations.

of election-geared special programs by entertainment shows or other non-political presentations.

As a source of information about state-level office seekers in 1964, newspapers registered a small lead over television in June (52 per cent to 49 per cent), but the pattern reversed in November after losses for both media (television down to 43 per cent and newspapers, 41 per cent).

For information about candidates for national office—the Presidency and Congress—those polled in June depended upon television most heavily (65 per cent), with newspapers second (45 per cent) and other sources far behind. As of the November polling, television had dropped only 1 per cent, while newspapers had lost 9 per cent from the previous tally. It is most interesting to observe the television lead in both June and November. Perhaps this lead is due to the fact that national stories involve network enterprise primarily, and the networks have no reason to drastically reduce their Washington and government-centered programming after the elections. The political rivalries that dominated interest before the elections are replaced by news events of equal political importance afterward.[1]

TELEVISION MOTIVATION: VOTING TURNOUT

The Roper organization results on television as a believed-in source of news should not, however, be taken as implied evidence that people *act* in accord with television appeals. For example, "get out and vote" campaigns aimed at the television audience by the American Heritage Foundation, the Advertising Council, and similar organizations during the 1964 presidential campaign met with only limited success. William A. Glaser of the Bureau of Applied Social Research at Columbia University, in his article "Television and Voting Turnout," was cautious about the results achieved. He concluded, "Newspaper reading may be more effective than television watching in affecting turnout and in effecting the fulfillment of intentions to vote." He qualified this conclusion by adding, "When practiced jointly, newspaper reading and television watching are associated with very high rates of turnout," but he reaffirmed that television may "add less to the combination than newspapers."

Glaser reminds us that, even if motivation is increased, television campaigns to encourage voting are tied to the public's need for information about "registration and absentee ballot procedures" and the like. In short, if the appeals do not specifically educate as well as motivate, the turnout will be less than hoped for. He also pointed out that stimulation of interest in voting will not necessarily enable the sick or infirm to vote unless special provisions are made to accommodate them. These factors somewhat reduce the weight of Glaser's general conclusion: "television leaves a more lasting impression than newspapers and radio when conveying reminders to vote."[2]

TELEVISION AND POLITICAL CONTROVERSY

Xerox Corporation and the United Nations

Because television is a prime source of popular information, the medium sometimes draws attacks when strong partisans of one point of view object to its presenting an opposing view. A case in point concerns the Xerox Corporation's sponsorship of a series of television specials on the United Nations. The corporation put up $4 million to underwrite the cost of the series designed to familiarize Americans with the activities of the U.N. The nonprofit Telsun Foundation was created to produce the programs. Xerox was to be given only institutional credit at the opening and close of each 90-minute program.

Before the first program was televised, the John Birch Society's bulletin commented, "We hate to see a corporation of this country promote the U.N. when we know that it is an instrument of the Soviet Communist conspiracy." An "avalanche" of complaining mail was urged against Xerox. Soon after the Birch Society view was published, mail began to flow into Xerox offices, 100 to one against the shows. The Xerox Corporation had the 61,000 or so anti-U.N. letters analyzed and concluded that only about 16,000 people had written the 61,000 letters. Later, some 14,500 approving letters came in to the corporation, and the research conclusion was that they had come from 14,500 people.

To counter the John Birch "avalanche," pro-U.N. individuals and more than 100 organizations (including the League of Women Voters, Hadassah, and the National Council of Churches) had rallied support for Xerox.

After the first two programs had been televised nationally, Xerox commissioned Elmo Roper and Associates to conduct a survey of popular reaction. A cross section of 1500 adults was polled. On the question about Xerox sponsorship of the series, Roper found that "favorable comments outstripped criticism by more than ten to one." Of those who had seen the shows, 54 per cent offered the opinion that it was "an extremely important and worthwhile series."[3]

Fortunately for the general public, the Xerox Corporation had the courage to face the first storm of condemnatory letters and later to commission a nationwide survey to assess public reaction to the programs.

The John Birch Society's mail campaign against the series on the U.N. suggests that the potential power of television is enough to motivate unscrupulous attempts to kill programs by intimidating the sponsors. Strike at the tree by killing the roots!

The National Council for Civic Responsibility

Dr. Arthur Larson, at a press conference on September 22, 1964, announced the formation of the National Council for Civic Responsibility. Larson, Director of the World Rule of Law Center at Duke University (and former Director of the USIA and advisor to President Eisenhower), told why he and other distinguished people* had decided to create the organization. The purpose was, he said, "to bring to the American people, through the mass media, the truth about the John Birch Society and related radical reactionary groups, and about the misstatements on public issues and personalities that they are spreading on a rapidly increasing scale." He continued, "The statistic I personally found most ominous is this: there are now more than 7,000 radio and television broadcasts weekly in 50 states now being aired by groups whose officers are either acknowledged members of the John Birch Society or linked with it in other ways."

At that conference, a listing of the nine leading radical-right broadcasts was provided.

Specifically cited were: *Howard Kershner, Manion Forum, Dan Smoot, America's Future* (R. K. Scott), *Independent American Radio Edition* (Kent and Phoebe Courtney), *Billy James Hargis, Church League of America, Life Lines,* and *Twentieth Century Reformation Hour.* Abetting very extensive radio efforts (examples: *Manion Forum*—30-minute commentary weekly on 240 radio stations; *Life Lines*—15-minutes daily on 325 radio stations) was impressive television involvement. At that time, *Manion Forum* was seen weekly on 30 television stations; *Dan Smoot* weekly on 40 television stations; *Billy James Hargis* daily on 7 television stations; and *Life Lines* daily on 69 television stations.[4]

The public relations firm of Ruder and Finn became associated with the campaign to counteract propaganda from the groups considered "radical reactionary" by the Council. Among other duties taken up by this firm was the task of interesting mass media managers in providing more coverage of far-right-wing activities. Newspaper advertisements were prepared, stressing "six reasons why you should worry about extremism in the U.S. today." A series of five-minute radio recordings was produced, and arrangements were made for daily broadcasts in the eleven states where the Council felt that extremists were most active.

It is reasonable to assume that the battle between the Council and its rivals in 1964 is but a prelude to a future mass media pattern that will see political rivals setting progressively more stock in television propaganda. Television has already become a critical medium in the view of political partisans. For those who are less concerned with elections per se than with ideological opinion

---

* Including: Conrad Aiken, Thurman Arnold, Harry Ashmore, John Mason Brown, Stuart Chase, Benjamin Cohen, J. Lawton Collins, James B. Conant, Erwin N. Griswold, Oscar Handlin, Leon H. Keyserling, George Cabot Lodge, Mrs. Oswald B. Lord, Archibald MacLeish, Ralph McGill, William C. Menninger, Lewis Mumford, Rt. Rev. James A. Pike, Nathan Pusey, Clarence B. Randall, David Riesman, Albert B. Sabin, Rex Stout, Mark Van Doren, Roy Wilkins, Edward Bennett Williams.

display before mass audiences, dependence upon the medium will increase dramatically in the near future. Because of the delicacy of the distinction between liberty and license in the area of free speech, the ramifications of this new trend deserve to be watched by all who advocate responsibility *and* democracy.

THE MORAL DIMENSION: NETWORK ADMINISTRATION

If one reads John Henry Faulk's autobiographical account of his six-year battle to defeat the blacklisters who drove him from a highly successful career as a radio-television personality, one comes away with a sinking feeling that the mass media have been far too susceptible to naked pressure tactics. Faulk's book, *Fear On Trial,* offers dramatic evidence of how the members of a small anti-Communist organization called Aware, Inc., posed as "consultants" to the industry and managed to be paid for their efforts to use innuendos, half-truths, and meaningless "research" to defame and ruin the professional careers of artists, commentators, and managers.

With the help of the celebrated attorney Louis Nizer and at enormous personal sacrifice, Mr. Faulk won a legal battle against Aware, Inc., and its founder and director, Vincent W. Hartnett. Faulk returned to work in the industry, and to some extent, the whole affair bucked up the courage of those who felt that the mass media should not be subject to any sneaky group or kangaroo court. However, this episode could be repeated if the leaders of the communications industry are not better able to handle their responsibilities in the future and, thereby, protect the public interest and the interests of their employees.[5]

Other cases of moral breakdown in the industry have also been revealed in recent years. In 1959, the Congressional investigation of television quiz shows uncovered the many contestants and several producers who had connived to rig certain programs. One fact brought out was that many so-called contestants were made aware of the questions and answers before the *live* programs went on the air—before those contestants seemed to squirm, so visibly, on camera.[6] During 1960, the same committee went into the "payola" situation and showed that "commercial bribery" had become "a prime factor in determining what music is played in many broadcast programs and what musical records the public is surreptitiously induced to buy."[7]

More recently, in 1965, the dismissal of James Thomas Aubrey, Jr., from his post as head of the Columbia Broadcasting System's television network suggested that the highest executive chiefs of the industry have not been as alert as possible to the consequences of program manipulation (primarily in the entertainment category). Such manipulation allows a handful of officials of the three major networks to determine which program proposals will be selected and which will not. The end results of such centralized and sometimes capricious controls have too often been programs that are below the professional capabilities of the industry and below the mean intellectual level of the general public.[8]

Aubrey was virtually unchallenged at CBS when he judged which entertainment programs would or would not be selected for a season's run. After his downfall it became public knowledge that many of his vital decisions were unduly influenced by personal friends with much to gain from the exercise of his power on their behalf. Too often, these friends gained, and CBS presented programs considerably less ingenious than their advertisements.

If television is such a believable source of information and such a powerful force upon politics, then the Aubrey case, with all of the alleged manipulations based upon an overwhelming concern for audience "ratings," must not be repeated. At least, the high moral and intellectual standards publicly advocated by the leaders of the industry must relate to operational decisions. As Charles A. Siepmann put it:

> I believe that one measure of the health of a society is the proximity between the standards a man honors in his private and his public life, and that consequently he who fixes a quiz program, doubles his income by payola, or provides a call-girl for an influential client on a Saturday, and on a Sunday takes his children by the hand and goes to church, represents the house that, divided against itself, cannot stand.[9]

GOVERNMENTAL CONTROLS

When should governmental pressure be brought to bear on the private enterpreneurs in electronic mass communications? That question is answered in part by the fact that federal rather than state authority dominates in this area. Controls, such as they are, have been largely in the hands of the Federal Communications Commission (FCC) since the passage of the Communications Act of 1934. The FCC decides, on the basis of certain standards, who will be licensed and who will not be licensed to operate radio and television stations. When certain technical changes are proposed or are in the offing, the FCC studies the developments and decides whether the innovations (usually of a far-reaching nature) will be allowed. The law restricts, and the FCC's own organizational tradition inhibits, FCC intervention in controversies surrounding program content unless some clear violation of public service is involved.

On March 7, 1946, the FCC issued a report entitled *Public Service Responsibility of Broadcast Licensees* and commonly referred to as the "Blue Book." The report, which was largely devoted to program content and public service, contained a citation of a stand taken by the FCC's administrative ancestor, the Federal Radio Commission.

> Broadcasting stations are licensed to serve the public and not for the purpose of furthering the private or selfish interests of individuals or

groups of individuals. . . . If . . . the station performs its duty in furnishing a well rounded program the rights of the community have been achieved.[10]

This 1946 report of the FCC, issued just in the infancy of commercial television, forecast the problems inherent in the developing ties between the electronic media and political affairs. The following are several leading questions selected from the long list found in the report:

> Shall time for the presentation of one point of view on a public issue be sold, or shall all such presentations be on sustaining time* only?
> If time is to be sold for presentation of a point of view, what precautions are necessary to insure that the most time shall not gravitate to the side prepared to spend the most money?
> Are forums, town meetings, and round-table type broadcasts, in which two or more points of view are aired together, intrinsically superior to the separate presentation of points of view at various times?
> How can an unbiased presentation of the news be achieved?
> Should news be sponsored, and if so, to what extent should the advertiser influence or control the presentation of the news?
> Should commentators be forbidden, permitted, or encouraged to express their own personal opinions?
> The Federal Communications Commission is forbidden by law to censor broadcasts. Should station licensees have the absolute right of censorship, or should their review of broadcasts be limited to protection against libel, dissemination of criminal matters, etc.?
> Should the "right to reply" to broadcasts be afforded; and if so, to whom should the right be afforded, and under what circumstances?[11]

Securing a "balanced interpretation of public needs" as against private purpose in terms of program content, a task self-imposed by the FCC, is no easy assignment. Its Blue Book bared many abuses by license holders—advertising excesses, partisan presentations, and the like—but only a moderate amount of preventive official action followed. As late as 1956, Professor Robert E. Cushman reported, "No station appears to have been denied a license for any violation of the programming standards set out in the Blue Book."[12]

Those standards include laudable statements in support of laudable causes. We cannot argue over statements such as: "the Commission concludes that one standard of operation in the public interest is a reasonable proportion of time devoted to sustaining programs"; "reasonable provision for local self-expression still remains an essential function of a station's operation"; there is a "crucial need for discussion programs, at the local, national, and international levels alike"; and "the public interest clearly requires that the amount of time devoted

---

* The Blue Book defines a sustaining program as "any program which is *neither* paid for by a sponsor *nor* interrupted by a spot [commercial] announcement."

to advertising matter shall bear a reasonable relationship to the amount of time devoted to programs."[13]

One can understand governmental timidity in this field, in part because of our heritage stressing fear of official intrusion upon our privacy and the destruction of our freedom by the exercise of government controls in the world of ideas. At any rate, despite the courage implied in the FCC report of March 7, 1946, little has actually been done.

There have been some glimmers of hope, however. Miss Frieda B. Hennock, a former FCC Commissioner, charged that radio and television appeal "to the lowest common denominator in taste and intelligence." Editorially supporting Miss Hennock in 1950, the *New York Herald Tribune* commented,

> Broadcasters can, of course, reply that they are in business to make money, and that you make money by reaching a mass audience. But there is also a public responsibility involved, and when it is ignored completely, F.C.C. members aren't the only ones who begin to stir uneasily.[14]

Warren E. Baker, then general counsel to the FCC, declared in 1954 that Congress, in granting power to the agency in the Communications Act of 1934, "denied it one important but not easily definable power—censorship." Mr. Baker argued that, while "Congress intended to prevent the Commission from becoming a group of government officials primarily concerned with wielding their heavy blue pencils over every prospective script," he did not believe "that one can be said to be censoring when in the process of determining whether it is in the public interest for a particular person to be, or continue to be, a licensee, past or prospective program policies, rather than specific programs, are evaluated. . . . This function of periodic evaluation, properly exercised, is not tantamount to censorship of programming. Improperly exercised, it can become censorship."[15] If ever there was a ticklish situation, this is it.

By virtue of this twilight zone between the jurisdiction of the FCC and the self-policing of responsible broadcasters, there have been instances where action was needed *from some source* but was absent. For example, when the National Association of Educational Broadcasters tabulated the results of a week-long monitoring of seven New York television stations (January 4–10, 1951), the organization reported that "10 per cent of the program time on the air was given over to adult crime drama," while *public issues and public events occupied but 3 per cent of the air time during that period.*[16]

THE POWERFUL PERSONALIZING EFFECT: THE KEFAUVER HEARINGS OF 1951

Television has now become a major instrument of American political campaigning. Especially since 1951 and the televised hearings of the Senate's Special Committee to Investigate Crime in Interstate Commerce, commonly known as the "Kefauver Investigation," the impact of this new form of public contact has dominated the political scene. Estes Kefauver, as chairman of the committee looking into the activities of organized crime in the United States, was raised by the magic eye from the status of just another United States Senator to the very verge of the Presidency, from being an interesting "comer" from Tennessee to a pinnacle of national popularity and international interest.

Senator Kefauver, in his own story of the lively, camera-covered days of his elevation, wrote:

> Toward the end of the hearings under my chairmanship, the twentieth century phenomenon of television became a major factor in our operations. . . . In New York and in the last few days in Washington the programs joined the network and were seen by an audience estimated at between 20,000,000 and 30,000,000 persons. . . .
>
> A public hearing is a public hearing, and to me it makes no sense to say that certain types of information-gathering agencies may be admitted but that television may not, simply because it lifts the voices and faces of the witnesses from the hearing rooms to the living rooms of America.[17]

The parade of the alleged leaders of what were labeled "syndicates" for popular consumption may not have led to great advances in the battle against crime and corruption, but the proceedings did set the parade's marshal in a very favorable spot. Kefauver and his Senate colleagues appeared as valiant crusaders deployed to defeat the black-hearted knights of the underworld. The question of whether or not legislation beneficial to the public would result from the testimony was somehow lost in the kaleidoscopic patterns that mixed just enough evil and just enough virtue to provide a spirited study in contrasts. John Mason Brown phrased the modern problem of leadership beautifully, saying, "By obstructing the horizon, those we follow seem somehow to replace it, since they are as far as we can see. The nearer they are to us, the greater our natural interest in them as individuals and personalities."[18]

The groundwork for televising the Kefauver hearings was laid in 1948, when the embryonic television audience was treated to the Congressional hearings on the affairs of Alger Hiss, Whittaker Chambers, and others, and in 1950, when the United Nations summer sessions on the Korean War crisis were televised. Just as Orson Welles, unmindful of the trigger effect upon public emotions,[19] electrified the nation in 1938 with his radio production of H. G. Wells' *The War of the Worlds,* so Senator Kefauver caught the popular imagination because of high public interest in the news; the perennial fascination with evil-doers and evil-doing; a new technique for on-the-spot reporting; and the combination of facts and natural theater that made a Congressional hearing a highly dramatic event.

It is important to realize that neither Orson Welles nor Senator Kefauver realized the potency of the mass media at the outset. After the lighting struck, however, both took advantage of the penetration of the public's imagination. We must recognize their talents in learning to use what was placed before them. Henry Ford may not have discovered the automobile, but he quickly learned how to produce it; others may have foreseen the impact of television upon politics, but it was Senator Kefauver who first found the new flower of mass communications in full bloom.

Critics of the Kefauver hearings of 1951, though disagreeing on many of the motives behind the participants and events, were unanimous in the opinion that the presence of television changed the tone of the proceedings. Some observers felt that hearings held under the unblinking stare of the cameras violated the elementary right to a fair trial. Frank Costello (who testified only on the condition that he would not be made a spectacle, and won the concession that his privacy would be protected to the extent that only his hands would be televised), William O'Dwyer, Virginia Hill, Joe Adonis, and the others who testified openly or under pressure were subject to the bar of public opinion as well as to the questions of the Senators and their legal assistants.

Senators Estes Kefauver, Herbert R. O'Conor, Lester C. Hunt, Alexander Wiley, and Charles W. Tobey, and legal counsel Rudolph Halley soon were transformed from committee workers into personalities. Each had his own particular offering for the great unseen audience. Every participant sensed that fate and television had cast him (or her) upon a gigantic stage in front of an audience such as the world had never known before. For each participant, the new dimension of television became the tail that wagged the dog. The quiet simplicity of Senator Kefauver, the registering concern of Senators O'Conor and Wiley, the wrath and literary prowess of Senator Tobey, and the relentless lisp and shrewdness of Rudolph Halley all became trademarks of the hearings, as did the personal characteristics of the witnesses.

Thus, despite the worries of some critics that trial by television was not as good as trial by jury in a court of law,[20] the indisputable fact emerged that television had become a source of political power. Out of the hearings came much information about individuals tagged with alleged "syndicate" connections, and the first man ever to be raised to political heights by television—Estes Kefauver. Whether he deserved it is beside the point and subject to political partisanship; that he benefited from the smile of the Cyclops is beyond dispute. The ubiquitous magic eye was here to stay in politics. It would make some politicians, and it would break others. But never was it to be completely trusted, for it soon showed it could destroy those who threw their weight behind its power.

THE BOOMERANG EFFECT: McCARTHY—SYMBOL, IDOL, MASS MEDIA EXPERIMENTER

Senator Joseph R. McCarthy's place in recent American political history is too well known to bear further descripton, but his activities are important for students of mass communications. The relationship between his elevation and his televised eclipse requires that certain aspects of his story be reviewed.

At the time of the U.S. Senate debates over whether to censure Senator McCarthy, *The New York Times* took its measure of the junior Senator from Wisconsin in a stinging editorial. The editorial challenged McCarthy's thesis that his purpose was to warn America against Communist infiltration of our government and society. Declaring that anti-Communist activities had begun long before McCarthy took the field, the *Times* branded him "a camp follower who has brought confusion and dissension into the ranks of fighters for democracy."[21]

Senator McCarthy, for his own part, observed during those proceedings, "It is not easy for a man to assert that he is the symbol of resistance to Communist subversion—that the nation's fate is in some respects tied to his own fate. It is much easier, I assure you, to be coy, to play down one's personal role in this struggle for freedom." He added, "Self-effacement is always a comfortable posture. But I take it that you would rather I be frank than coy; that you would rather I acknowledge and accept the fact that McCarthyism is a household word for describing a way of dealing with treason and the threat of treason. And so I shall."[22]

The background factors responsible for the rise and the fall of Senator McCarthy and the growth of McCarthyism between 1950 and 1954 were many. Americans, disillusioned again in their hope for peace after they had shed their blood to win another world war, were worried about the new threat from the Soviets. Fears were widespread that the nation was in grave danger of Red subversion. Indications of serious lapses in our internal security system were enough to convince many citizens that the threat to our freedom had not been fully described to the public. The warnings against Communist treachery and power, so widely circulated by Senator McCarthy beginning in February of 1950, seemed to many to be confirmed by the outbreak of the Korean War in June of 1950.

Senator McCarthy declared himself the leader of the battle against the evils of Communism at home and abroad, with special emphasis on domestic problems. Support for the Senator was obtained indirectly from sources who, though disapproving, could not attack him because they were using his tirades as ammunition against the Truman Administration. Some politicians, while privately shuddering at the McCarthy escapades, preferred to take the public position that, if Senator McCarthy was in error in respect to methods, his objectives were still worthy. Other politicians grew more and more afraid of the growing power of the irrepressible solon from Wisconsin, and limited their opposition to very indirect and abstract oratorical defenses of fair play for all. McCarthy's slashing attacks, aimed directly at individuals, had destroyed sufficient of his opposition to take the heart out of the fickle or cowardly. His tactics of hitting hard and then galloping to new sets of facts and figures confused all who tried to argue with him. When driven to extremes, he would accuse opponents of furthering the Communist cause. As Chairman of the Senate Permanent Subcommittee on Investigations, the Senator gained a reputation for securing headlines about what witnesses did—and did not—tell his committee.

Since he was the self-propelled center of controversies tearing at the whole society, McCarthy was subject to intense news coverage by the mass media. After a while, one began to feel that the junior Senator from Wisconsin had staked his entire political future on a single issue and that he needed to make news in order to survive. In the absence of definitive answers from more moderate quarters to the highly complex questions at issue, McCarthy's pose of infallibility was successful. There can be no doubt that television, the new medium for mass communications, aided his success by its capacity to emphasize the dramatic.

Thus, a combination of circumstances, natural abilities, and national frustrations and fears worked to create an "ism" where there had been only a man. McCarthy has been called "the most unprincipled man in public life since Aaron Burr and the most successful demagogue since Huey Long."[23] He became a symbol of anti-Communism for multitudes who demanded simple answers to a complex problem and found satisfaction in McCarthy because he rarely went beyond thundering.

Senator McCarthy was, above all, an experimenter between 1950 and the days of his tribulations in 1954. He experimented with the media for mass communications, particularly television, in a manner that few politicians had ever tried before because his senatorial adventures and the medium's infancy coincided. "There have always been rabble-rousers in the nation, but they can be more effective now because of the new means of communication available to them."[24]

In his role as an experimenter with the impact of the media, Senator McCarthy contributed an important lesson to all who study propaganda—*the media that create personalities can destroy personalities*. Nothing proved this point so well as the long, drawn-out proceedings of the so-called Army-McCarthy dispute.

At 10:35 A.M. on April 23, 1954, an investigation began under the authority of the Senate Permanent Subcommittee on Investigations. Senator Karl E. Mundt presided at what proved to be one of the most distressing episodes in the history of American legislature. What started out as an investigation of the strained relations between the Army's civilian bureaucracy and the Senator and his assistants turned into no-holds-barred duel between the Senator and almost everybody not directly on his side. Rules of procedure were so flexible that one wondered whether the Senate's committee was examining McCarthy's relationship with the Army or whether Senator McCarthy was examining the committee.

At every session of the more than month-long hearings, television cameras,

motion picture cameras, and photographers' flash cameras scanned the participants in the affair. From the first session to the last, the participants were as
much concerned with the unseen audience of millions as they were with the
official representatives of any group in the room. And with good reason. On
Friday, April 23, 1954—the opening day—63 per cent of the television sets in
New York were tuned in to the hearings.[25]

Each important figure at the hearings became a personality in what looked as
though it might become the longest show in television history. The moves and
countermoves rivaled those of Hollywood dramas.

Senator McCarthy, no less than his friends and tormenters, was unable to get
out of the range of the spotlight long enough to rest and collect his thoughts.
Finally, he led the way in abandoning almost all pretense at objectivity and
began to lash out wildly at everyone who bothered him. In doing this, he played
almost exclusively to the unseen audience. Soon, every newly made television
personality at the hearings was doing the same thing, though McCarthy was
almost alone in the peculiarities of his approach to the battle for publicity.

Senator McCarthy was never the same after that long siege on television.
Even Senate censure, cast upon him after a long investigation and debate (not
televised), was just another event in the dramatic decline that began at the
Army hearings.

No one at those hearings escaped the revealing power of the television
camera. Senator McCarthy, Secretary of the Army Robert T. Stevens, Roy M.
Cohn (McCarthy's aide-de-camp), John G. Adams and Joseph N. Welsh (Army
counsels), Ray H. Jenkins (counsel to the Committee investigating the countercharges), Senators Mundt, Dworshak, Potter, Dirksen, McClellan, Symington,
Jackson, and all of the other protagonists in the lengthy drama shared a
dilemma. Evasive tactics, even the ones thought most useful in politics, were
clearly shown up as such on television. Furthermore, when every eye twitch and
finger tap sped across the land, the trivial became important, and the important
became seemingly trivial. No mystery or aura of dignity withstood the klieg
lights. McCarthy's great crusade, represented by his roars at the hearings,
seemed more entertaining than significant; the Army's pleas of self-defense
seemed quite inadequate in the light of the testimony of the Secretary of the
Army and others, which described a less-than-courageous administration whenever Senator McCarthy's influence was felt; the committee's square-jawed counsel appeared determined but without any understanding of the plot; and the
committee's Senators tried to be judges, at least in appearance, but the great
political scenario quickly geared them for partisan roles.

Only those with wit, charm, and personality survived untarnished. A case in
point is Joseph N. Welsh. His animated face and ready brilliance was a relief to
all, against the depressing backdrops of mediocrity or histrionics.

Wisconsin's junior Senator, long used to playing the game by his own rules,
attempted to do so at the Army hearings. He was superficially successful in

winning his way by sheer bravado and dogmatic audacity, not to mention the timidity of the chairman's rulings. The participants remembered McCarthy's power before the hearings, and they were all a little frightened. Who wanted to tangle with a self-propelling social and political force in the form of a man?

Because the participants were so close to the action at the hearings, they could not have the detached perspective of television viewers. Of these, many McCarthy boosters were dismayed to find that he was earth-bound like the rest of us; many McCarthy opponents were dismayed to discover the caliber of those responsible for governmental activities; all saw the mystery stripped from their favorites. But the participants failed uniformly to recognize the destructive power of the cameras. Perhaps they did not remember that, while Senator Kefauver was a smash hit in 1951, he and his committee had the advantage of foiling witnesses who wanted to hide anyway. The Senators, since their own integrity was not at issue, could be very dignified and aloof in dealing with the witnesses from the underworld.

Since the Army-McCarthy affair, politicians are aware that the television cameras have the power not only to build, but also to destroy. In the light of reports that there were, in 1956, approximately 38 million television sets in the United States (80 per cent of the world's supply at the time) and the estimate that, as of January 1961, "47 of our 53 million homes had one or more sets,"[26] one wonders how many public figures will be created by television and how many will be ruined. For the student of government, it is even more important to know why the "powerful personalizing effect" of television produces certain results under certain conditions. If an unscrupulous politician ever discovers how to master the medium and secures the time he wants on it, he may be well on the way toward destroying our liberties.

FOOTNOTES

1. Elmo Roper and Associates, "The Public's View of Television and Other Media, 1959–1964" (New York: Television Information Office, 1965).
2. William A. Glaser, "Television and Voting Turnout," *The Public Opinion Quarterly*, Vol. 29, No. 1 (Spring 1965), pp. 71–86.
3. "Xerox and the UN," *The Public Pulse*, No. 21 (October 1965), Elmo Roper and Associates, New York.
4. Press Kit issued on September 22, 1964, by the National Council for Civic Responsibility of the Public Affairs Institute. Especially note: "Who's Who in the Council for Civic Responsibility"; release on the nine radical-right broadcasters; "Statement of Dr. Arthur Larson, Chairman" (New York: National Council for Civic Responsibility, 1964).
5. John Henry Faulk, *Fear On Trial* (New York: Simon and Schuster, 1964).
6. Hearings, Part I, Subcommittee, Committee on Interstate and Foreign Commerce, House of Representatives, 86th Congress, *Investigation of Television Quiz*

Shows, Part I, October 6–10 and 12, 1959 (Washington: U.S. Government Printing Office, 1960).

7. Hearings, Part I, Subcommittee, Committee on Interstate and Foreign Commerce, House of Representatives, 86th Congress, *Responsibilities of Broadcasting Licensees and Station Personnel,* February 8–10 and 15–19, and March 4, 1960 (Washington: U.S. Government Printing Office, 1960), p. 1.

8. Richard Oulahan and William Lambert, "The Tyrant's Fall That Rocked the TV World," *Life,* Vol. 59, No. 11 (September 10, 1965), pp. 90, 92, 94, 96–98, 101, 102, 105, 107.

9. Charles A. Siepmann, "Moral Aspects of Television," *The Public Opinion Quarterly,* Vol. 24, No. 1 (Spring 1960), p. 12.

10. *Public Service Responsibility of Broadcast Licensees* (Washington, D.C.: Federal Communications Commission, March 7, 1946), p. 12.

11. Ibid., pp. 39–40.

12. Robert E. Cushman, *Civil Liberties in the United States* (Ithaca, N.Y.: Cornell University Press, 1956), p. 43.

13. *Public Service Responsibility of Broadcast Licensees,* pp. 55–56.

14. Editorial, "Television's Real Problem," *New York Herald Tribune,* November 17, 1950.

15. Warren E. Baker, "Problems of the Radio and Television Industry," in *Communication Media Legal and Policy Problems, 1954* (Ann Arbor: University of Michigan Law School, 1954), pp. 142–143.

16. "Monitors Criticize Seven TV Stations," *New York Times,* January 24, 1951. See also, "Radio and Television: A Warning," *New York Times,* September 24, 1954, and "Monitor System Checks TV and Radio for False Ads," *New York Times,* March 14, 1956.

17. Estes Kefauver, *Crime in America* (Garden City, N.Y.: Doubleday and Company, Inc., 1951), pp. 313–314.

18. John Mason Brown, *Through These Men* (New York: Harper and Brothers, 1956), p. 4.

19. John Houseman, "The Men from Mars," in E. Schuler, D. Gibson, M. Fiero, and W. Brookover, eds., *Outside Readings in Sociology* (New York: Thomas Y. Crowell Company, 1953), p. 295.

20. See John Havas, "Trial by Television—Trouble in the Air," *News Workshop,* Vol. 3, No. 1 (New York University Publication, December 1951).

21. Editorial, "Senator McCarthy's Elbow," *New York Times,* November 19, 1954.

22. "Text of McCarthy Speech for Delivery Today in Censure Debate," *New York Times,* November 10, 1954.

23. Arthur S. Link, *American Epoch* (New York: Alfred A. Knopf, 1955), p. 645.

24. Statement issued by the Public Affairs Committee of Freedom House, reprinted under the title "The Evils of McCarthyism," *New York Herald Tribune,* January 7, 1952.

25. "TV Coverage Cut Arouses Protests," *New York Times,* April 27, 1954.

26. "TV: Giant in Seven League Boots," *The UNESCO Courier,* Vol. 9, No. 1 (July 1956), p. 14. See also, Gary A. Steiner, *The People Look at Television* (New York: Alfred A. Knopf, 1963), p. 4.

2 / Qualified Political Argument

The outcome of the Presidential election of 1960 was dramatically influenced, if not determined, by the *debates* between Richard M. Nixon and John F. Kennedy. Those televised confrontations between the candidates of the major parties personalized the rivalry to a degree and in a manner never before achieved in American political history.

IMPACT OF THE 1960 PRESIDENTIAL DEBATES UPON THE ELECTION OUTCOME

A number of astute and experienced political observers contend that Mr. Nixon lost the election because of his performance before the television cameras. These same commentators suggest that the victor of the 1960 election fought his most important battles for popular support before the unblinking eyes of those cameras. That opinion has great importance in light of the *almost* 50–50 split of the electorate that year.

In his widely heralded study of that campaign, *The Making of the President 1960,* Theodore H. White phrases the judgment cautiously. He writes that, when the debates began, "Nixon was generally viewed as being the probable winner of the election contest and Kennedy as fighting an uphill battle; when they were over, the positions of the two contestants were reversed."[1]

Many others are more blunt. Robert Kennedy, the Democratic candidate's brother and his campaign manager in 1960, declared immediately following the victory, "It wouldn't even have been close without the debates. Jack's appearance on TV and the way he handled himself was the big factor in our victory."[2]

Richard Nixon in his autobiographical book, *Six Crises,* reasons that his opponent gained more from the debates than he did. He agrees with and quotes the views of two Scripps-Howard newsmen, Charles Lucey and Jack Steele: " . . . on balance, the four debates . . . left Mr. Kennedy with a big political plus."[3]

A tone somewhat critical of Mr. Nixon's decision to debate at all is taken by

Emmet John Hughes in *The Ordeal of Power*. Hughes was an adviser to Dwight David Eisenhower in the campaigns of 1952 and 1956 and served that Chief Executive as speechwriter and assistant in the White House. According to Hughes, "If any one specific and deliberate decision contributed fatally to his [Nixon's] defeat, this was his personal readiness ever to appear in televised debate with Kennedy." He adds, "The mere fact of the closeness (and frequent diffuseness) of the debate between the two men sufficed, of course, to destroy any presumption of superior wisdom or greater maturity on the part of Nixon."[4]

On the eve of the balloting, *Broadcasting* magazine argued, after viewing the pro-Kennedy trend in the public opinion polls conducted by Sindlinger and Company of Philadelphia, that " . . . if Richard Nixon is elected, it will be despite his four face-to-face appearances with John Kennedy on television."[5]

A similar opinion was expressed by Earl Mazo, head of the Washington bureau of the *New York Herald Tribune*. In a summary entitled "The Great Debates," which he prepared for the Center for the Study of Democratic Institutions, he says flatly, "My own view, based upon an analysis of surveys and polls I consider reliable and on a first-hand acquaintanceship with much of the campaign and its participants, is that if there had been no debates on television, Nixon would have been elected President."[6]

Rarely does a student of the debates discover an opinion that plays down the factor of personality in 1960. Stanley Kelley, Jr., has said that "personality does not seem to have played anything like the role in the 1960 election that it did in the elections of 1952 and 1956."[7] Nevertheless, he has also written of the "facts" that "the Nixon-Kennedy joint television appearances aroused an extraordinary amount of interest among voters, [and that] they were widely believed to have had a crucial part in deciding the outcome of the 1960 election. . . ."[8]

Elihu Katz and Jacob J. Feldman, in their 1962 article, "The Kennedy-Nixon Debates: A Survey of Surveys," extracted important findings from the results of 31 independent public opinion studies of reactions to the encounters. The authors concluded that these 31 efforts made available for analysis the "largest number of studies of a single public event in the history of opinion and attitude research." According to their "conservative" estimate, "at least 55 per cent of the total adult population watched or listened to each of the debates and, altogether, . . . upwards of 80 per cent of the [adult] population saw or heard at least one of the debates."

At least thirteen studies attempted to find out *who won* each of the debates. Conclusions were that the majority of respondents gave a clear victory to Kennedy on the first; that the second and the fourth were "very close"; and that Nixon won the third.

It is unfortunate that the many polls have not given us reliable information, based upon more than political speculation, as to whether the outcome of the election itself was affected directly by the debates. But, according to Katz and Feldman, such information is "very elusive . . . , primarily because of important built-in inadequacies of the polling procedures." It is clear, nevertheless, that, when respondents were asked if the debates influenced their voting decisions, they tended to say yes.[9]

ORIGINS OF THE DEBATE IDEA OF 1960

Credit for the 1960 presidential debates, permitted by Congress's temporary suspension of certain provisions of Section 315 of the Federal Communications Act, can be given to the individuals who prompted interest in such a suspension; to the broadcasting networks that offered their facilities to the two major candidates; and to the previous political debaters who had imprinted the debate concept on our national history.

The late Senator Blair Moody (Democrat–Michigan) proposed such debates in July of 1952. Among other leaders making similar suggestions were National Broadcasting Company (NBC) chairman Robert Sarnoff and Columbia Broadcasting System (CBS) president Frank Stanton.[10]

Adlai Stevenson suggested, in a March 1960 article entitled "Plan for a Great Debate," that from Labor Day to election eve there should be a 90-minute program each week featuring the two major-party candidates. Each program would deal with one broad issue. Each candidate would be allowed 30 minutes to present his case, and the other would be allowed 15 minutes for rebuttal. Interesting propositions offered by Stevenson included the following:

> The central idea is that in some manner the candidates appear together at the same prime time each week for a serious presentation on public questions.
> TV is today the most powerful medium of communication to candidates for public office. It owes an obligation to serve the public good . . . such a useful means of mass communications must be conserved for the improvement of the democratic dialogue. . . .
> . . . I don't mean "debate" in the literal collegiate sense of the word, but a sustained discussion. Only TV can establish such a forum. I suppose that it provides a quadrennial clearing of the air by the use of the air.
> Sustained, serious discussion on all networks would reach all the people directly. It would require effort on their part, mental effort, and I know of no better cure for apathy. It would end the financial problem that TV now presents to the parties. It would end the tendency to reduce everything to assertions and slogans. It would diminish the temptation of politicians to entertain, to please and to evade the unpleasant realities.[11]

Landmarks

Historically, American electorates have been eager to have rival candidates and political leaders meet one another over issues. Landmarks include the 1830

Webster-Hayne debate in the United States Senate, when the nature of the Union and the validity of nullification were argued; the three-cornered Senate debate on the Compromise of 1850 in February and March of that year, featuring Henry Clay, Daniel Webster, and John C. Calhoun (Calhoun was dying and asked Senator Mason to read his speech for him); and the Lincoln-Douglas debates of 1858, occasioned by Lincoln's challenging Douglas for his seat in the Senate, dealing with such burning questions as slavery, the nature of the federal Union, and the meaning of the Dred Scott decision.

Stanley Kelley, Jr., in his *Political Campaigning,* quotes a very interesting comment by a veteran Mississippi politician, Reuben Davis. In 1889, Davis lamented the decline of debates, saying:

> Forty years ago, constant practice had made our public speakers so skillful in debate that every question was made clear even to men otherwise uneducated. For the last twenty years this practical union between politicians and people has not existed. Only one party is allowed to speak, and the leaders of that party no longer debate, they simply declaim and denounce. . . . In my judgment, this state of affairs is fatally injurious to our institutions, and dangerous to our liberties. . . . The evil of mischievous assertion is greatly lessened when free discussion is allowed, and error exposed and combated by the unsparing vigor of an opposing party.[12]

These argumentative sessions called debates have been ingrained in our pattern of social and political thought. Debates have not always been ordinary and routine elements of politics, but the concept of face-to-face debates has firm historical precedent in American political life and, thus, is not novel or surprising to the American voting public.

Other landmarks of the debate concept appear in our more recent history. The 1948 radio debate, originating in Portland, Oregon, between Thomas E. Dewey and Harold Stassen, both then aspiring to the presidential nomination of the Republican Party, is one example. The subject of the debate was whether the Communist Party should be outlawed in the United States. The result of that encounter, in which Stassen had a difficult time, did much to clear the way for Dewey's second presidential nomination.

On May 21, 1956, Senator Estes Kefauver and Adlai Stevenson discussed campaign issues in a nationally televised debate originating in Miami.

During the 1956 New York contest between Jacob Javits and Robert Wagner, for a United States Senate seat, the issues of civil rights and foreign policy were debated face to face.

Another very meaningful aspect of the development of public receptivity for the 1960 Nixon-Kennedy debates was the talk about national goals during the Eisenhower Administration. A definition of social, economic, and political objectives was encouraged by President Eisenhower, who appointed a number of eminent people to his Commission on National Goals. With the help of philanthropic foundation grants, the critical studies were administered by the American Assembly, Columbia University. A report in book form was published in 1960, accompanied by tremendous publicity on the "every-American-should-read" theme. The mass media provided fine public service by bringing the report, dealing with major problems facing the government and the people, to the attention of the citizenry.

More specific were the reports prepared by the Special Studies Project of the Rockefeller Brothers Fund. Over 100 prominent business, media, government, cultural, educational, political, and social leaders contributed to these reports, which dealt with subjects ranging from foreign policy to individual liberties and civil rights.

An "urgent summons" for "America in crisis" came from *Life* magazine, which ran a series of articles entitled "The National Purpose" prior to the general election of 1960. Contributions by John K. Jessup, Adlai Stevenson, Archibald MacLeish, David Sarnoff, Billy Graham, John W. Gardner, Clinton Rossiter, Albert Wohlstetter, James Reston, and Walter Lippmann dealt with subjects of great public interest. "Turn the Cold War Tide in America's Favor" by David Sarnoff; "Can We Count on More Dedicated People?" by John W. Gardner; "Our History Suggests a Remedy" by James Reston; and "National Purpose" by Walter Lippmann indicate the approach taken in this thoughtful series. The *New York Times* carried the series.[13]

Kennedy vs Humphrey in West Virginia

Senator John F. Kennedy debated against Senator Hubert H. Humphrey, rival candidate for the Democratic Party presidential nomination, on May 4, 1960. The debate originated from WCHS-TV, Charleston, West Virginia, and reached a vast audience through connections with other television stations in West Virginia and in Pittsburgh (KDKA-TV), Boston (WBZ-TV), Cleveland (KYW-TV), Baltimore (WJZ-TV), Chicago (WIND-TV), New York (WNEW-TV), Detroit (WWJ-TV), Washington (WTOP-TV), and Canada. Taped portions of the encounter were later shown on the NBC-TV program *Today,* which has a national network audience, and on ABC-TV's *Open Hearing* program.

The audience-impact potential of that debate prompted GOP chairman Senator Thruston B. Morton (Republican–Kentucky) to declare, "Between the two candidates there was no debate, no difference of opinion." He went on, "This was a carefully planned Siamese-twin attack on the Republican Adminis-tration." Morton demanded equal time and got some degree of satisfaction by forcing the networks to study what practical "fairness" involved.[14] Meanwhile, these debates between Democratic rivals had further whetted public interest in interparty debates.

A NEW RITUAL

Following the presidential debates of 1960, the debate idea caught on all over the nation, and a new ritual was added to the ceremony of American politics. Literally hundreds of political debates were held in 1962. Notable among the many confrontations, most of which were televised, were the four debates between George Romney and his rival for the governorship of Michigan, John Swainson; and the on-again, off-again proposed debates between Nelson Rockefeller and Robert Morgenthau, contenders for the governorship of New York. They never agreed to debate, but, on the Sunday before the election, the two men met for what was termed a "joint appearance." This appearance developed into a good deal of acrimonious exchange over who was telling the truth and who had good motives. Very little of importance was said, but the two rivals had at last shared a platform.

Another "joint appearance" took place between gubernatorial rivals Richard Nixon and Pat Brown in California in 1962 after both camps bickered over formats for some two months. The results of this appearance were as inconclusive as those of the New York encounter between Rockefeller and Morgenthau. The opponents hurled charges and countercharges of a personal nature, but the meeting provided little real clarification of issues for the California electorate.

In Massachusetts, there were the widely publicized television debates between Edward Kennedy and his rival for the Democratic Party's senatorial nomination, Edward McCormack.[15] Following Kennedy's success in attaining the nomination, he refused to appear on platforms with the nominees of the other parties entitled to a place on the ballot. The Republican nominee, George Lodge, agreed to argue the issue with all opponents (including Professor H. Stuart Hughes of Harvard, who ran as an Independent), and he did so with television and radio coverage. But Kennedy's seat was always empty during these interparty debates.

Kennedy's decision not to debate the other contenders proved wise from his point of view. By standing aloof and campaigning hard alone, he avoided direct personality and opinion confrontations from which he might have carried political scars. However, the solution of the Edward Kennedy group raises hard problems for students of government. It is reasonable to assume that Kennedy wanted to avoid the minority-party candidates and the Republican Lodge as much as possible. One cannot force a candidate to debate. But, how effective is a debate carried on, as in this case, without a leading contender in the election? One is reminded of President Franklin Roosevelt's casual treatment of Thomas E. Dewey during the campaign of 1944. Not only did Roosevelt not debate, he habitually failed to personalize the situation by mentioning his opponent by name. Dewey, it was reported, disliked that tactic and developed a strong distaste for his opponent because of it.

Of course, as the ritual becomes more established, it will become more and more difficult to refuse to debate. However, backing away from the debate situation still may be practical politically!

Does one debate with minority-party candidates and run the risk of being forced into very tight corners by contenders who have little or no chance of victory at the polls? There is an important question of responsibility that distinguishes the leading candidate, who will likely have to "make good" on his proposals, from the minority-party candidate, who is not victory-oriented but rather issue-oriented. Or again, the minority candidate may be interested primarily in a special crusade such as banning the bomb, or alcohol, or meat-eating. He can reduce the hope for a clear and broad debate of the major issues to a limited series of parries and thrusts on matters dear to the hearts of very few voters. How do we reconcile the rights of the majority candidates with the interests of the minority candidates?

An aspect of the Kennedy-McCormack Democratic primary debates that deserves attention is the criticism by some observers of their failure to include the Independent candidate, H. Stuart Hughes, who was very much interested in arguing the nuclear-weapons problem. On the other hand, Professor Hughes himself suggested to the public that, while *he* deserved to be heard with the Democratic and Republican candidates for the Senate, "splinter candidates" (Socialist Labor and Prohibition) did not deserve the same right because there was "no massive demand from the citizens of Massachusetts."[16] For the FCC, problems of this sort are compounded by the rules that provide for "equal time" on the air for all candidates.

The ritual of television debating, now becoming increasingly popular, demands a full consideration of what the rules should be and what the general interest requires.

EQUAL TIME

Certain ground rules regarding the rivalry between candidates for political office are set down in the Communications Act of 1934. Section 315 of the Act is most significant. First, if a station licensee gives or sells time to any legally qualified candidate for any public office, "he shall afford equal opportunity to all other such candidates for that office in the use of such broadcasting stations." A candidate is considered legally qualified if he meets the standards of the state in which he announces his candidacy; then, whether or not he has any real chance of winning, he is entitled to equal air time with his opponents. Thus, the station licensee can either deny air time to all candidates or provide equal time for all candidates. Of course, there is nothing in the rules to preclude any faction's purchase of more time than its opposition. If opposition parties, following the period for nominations, demand equal time, and can afford to pay for it, then they are entitled to it.

Several flaws in the equal-time system are immediately apparent. A political party with millions of members may be given the same amount of time as a political party having membership in the thousands or less. The major parties, which have been directly responsible for government administration for long periods of time at local, state, and national levels, and which vie for the right to lead again on the basis of mass support, are put into a position of equality with political organizations whose membership is scanty and whose histories show no record of public responsibility.

Dr. Frank Stanton, president of the Columbia Broadcasting System, suggested in 1955 that the Communications Act should be amended so as to reflect more fairly the standings of major and minor parties.[17]

Speaking in January 1960 about the licensing woes of the Federal Communications Commission, chairman John C. Doerfer said that the 28 years of failure to resolve "consistently and conclusively" the license-renewal problem indicated to him "not laxness, nor an abandonment of duty, nor lack of courage, but reasonable doubts and practical difficulties of reconsidering some of the fundamental conflicting views." Vital questions were, he said, "Will the F.C.C. become a supreme board of censors? How far can it go to achieve balance in program? How can it aid the industry to do more public service programming and still observe the fundamental law of the land?"[18]

His successor, Newton N. Minow, in his celebrated opening barrage to the National Association of Broadcasters (May 9, 1961), declared, " . . . you are free to communicate ideas as well as relaxation. You must provide a wider range of choices, more diversity, more alternatives. It is not enough to cater to the nation's whims—you must also serve the nation's needs."[19]

In 1959, Congress amended Section 315 to exempt candidate appearances on bona fide news programs from the equal-time restriction. Then, in 1960, Congress suspended Section 315 as it applied to the two major-party candidates for the Presidency and their running mates. The 1960 action was designed "to obtain information for considering permanent change" in the Communications Act.[20]

It should be noted that the easement of 1960 came after the conventions. Therefore, in the words of *Freedom of Communications,* the final report of the Senate's Committee on Commerce: "Despite claims to the contrary, the exemption from Section 315 . . . did not give us a comprehensive picture of what would happen if the exemption were made permanent. The 1960 exemption became effective . . . *after* both national conventions of the two major political parties."[21]

These two constructive enactments—the 1959 amendment of Section 315 and the 1960 suspension of it—resulted from a long period of agitation in which the representatives of the broadcasting networks and others took leading roles. *The changes in the equal-time provisions were not caused by any sudden flurry of activity but were the product of much careful thought.*

For example, Charles A. H. Thomson suggested in his *Television and Presidential Politics* (1956) that certain changes of Section 315 would "improve the chances of full political use of television."

> As a first step, amend the Communications Act so as to define a *major party* and to make the equal-time provision apply only to candidates of such parties or their authorized representatives, and to leave to the

discretion of stations decisions on how far their general responsibilities for giving balanced treatment to controversial issues require them to give time to other political parties. The second step would be to amend the act further to define a *leading candidate* and to restrict the benefits of the equal-time provision to leading candidates of major parties in the case of pre-nomination campaigns.[22]

But who wanted to step forward to administer, for example, Mr. Thomson's second proposal? It would have been exceedingly difficult to suggest to a contender at the prenomination stage that he was not a leading candidate.

In 1952, Senator Robert A. Taft of Ohio was openly annoyed by the time given to his leading opponent for the Republican presidential nomination. All three major radio-television networks covered the homecoming of Taft's rival, General Dwight D. Eisenhower, from his NATO command. At Abilene, Kansas, Eisenhower announced his candidacy. Senator Taft demanded equal time on the networks, and, when refused, asked the FCC to protect his rights under the law.[23] Senator Estes Kefauver of Tennessee, a Democratic contender, also asked the FCC to take action in his behalf. He wanted the agency to force the Columbia Broadcasting System to put him on the air immediately following Eisenhower's candidacy speech.[24]

Complicating the imbroglio was the decision of the FCC, two weeks previous, in the case of *CBS v. William Schneider*. This peculiar ruling of the FCC, awarding equal time to a poller of less than 600 votes in two presidential primaries, was consistent with the letter of the law as it then read, and the agency took the legal position that it could not determine which candidate was most likely to succeed.

Contributing indirectly to the 1959 change in Section 315 were the activities of Mr. Lar Daly who often ran for the Presidency dressed in an Uncle Sam suit. In that year Daly announced himself a candidate for mayor of Chicago. He demanded equal time after Mayor Richard J. Daley, a candidate for re-election, had been seen on regularly scheduled news programs. The Mayor had been seen greeting the visiting President of Argentina and opening a March of Dimes Campaign.

By a vote of 4 to 3, the FCC granted Daly equal time. The chairman of the FCC, Mr. Doerfer, voted with the minority and openly proposed repeal of Section 315. He gave his views at the annual convention of the National Association of Broadcasters. Salient arguments of his included the following:

> An informed public is indispensable for the continuance of a democratic society. If every presentation of a duly elected public official, who happens to be, at a given time, a qualified candidate for an office, must be matched by an equal amount of free time by all other such candidates, then the essence of Governmental news will be emasculated during campaign periods. The broadcaster will be shorn of any journalistic judgment during this critical period.[25]

Before the lifting of the equal-time handicap on presidential candidates, in 1960, this observer saw a good example on television of the ridiculous consequences of the law. Lar Daly demanded and received equal time on Jack Paar's nationally televised program because Paar had proposed to display John F. Kennedy and Richard Nixon on the program. Daly cavorted, almost without touching upon American politics as responsibly practiced. Attired in his Uncle Sam suit, he advanced the cause of responsible government solely by attracting considerable attention to one of its problems.

Dr. Frank Stanton proposed in 1955 that the Communications Act be amended so that his network, CBS, could present the two major-party presidential nominees in a series of "Lincoln-Douglas" debates without affording the same privilege to the Vegetarian, Prohibition, and other minor-party candidates.[26]

Plainly, Dr. Stanton was aware of the practical realities facing the television industry at the time of its political coming of age. Robert L. Moore, a correspondent for the *New York Times,* set the scene nicely in an article of May 1956.

> In 1956, with the maturity of the electronic age, there would be a minimum of whistle-stopping; from here on it's campaign by television.
>
> Back in 1858, some 75,000 fortunate Americans heard the Lincoln-Douglas debates. This year the spoken words of the candidates will be audible to an estimated 115,000,000 persons by television, 140 million by radio. And with 40,000,000 TV sets expected to be in American homes by convention time, it is no wonder that the political parties, the broadcasters and the commercial sponsors are going all-out to take full advantage of the situation.[27]

Dr. Stanton, following the 1959 decision of the FCC upholding Lar Daly's demand for equal time in the Chicago mayoralty case, struck at the decision with all the power of his conviction and caused newspaper editors around the country to think the problem through. The overwhelming majority of editorials and news articles that resulted supported his position. Attracting further attention to the Stanton position was the reaction of President Eisenhower to that ruling. He called it "ridiculous" and asked Attorney General Rogers to look into the matter to see what could be done about it.

The press reaction to the ruling constituted another major step forward on the road to the suspension of Section 315 in 1960. (See references for key examples of press reactions.)[28]

Following by only a few hours the Stanton attack on Section 315, NBC board chairman Robert W. Sarnoff, in a speech to the National Association of Broadcasters, appealed for a unified effort by all in the industry to acquaint the public and the lawmakers with the problems of television. He wanted a general awareness and understanding of the broadcasting situation.[29]

By the time of the 1960 presidential debates, release from the equal-time restrictions was even more important than before because of the numerical growth of the television audience. A substantial portion of the voting public were now television viewers. "The best estimates place the audience for one or all the debates at 115 to 120 million persons, the greatest listening audience ever assembled for any program of any type."[30]

Effective August 24, 1960, Congress did suspend Section 315 as it applied to the presidential campaign. Then, following the election, the Subcommittee on Communications of the Senate's Committee on Commerce, under the chairmanship of Senator Ralph W. Yarborough, held extensive hearings to study the possibility of permanent change in the equal-time provision. In its final report of April 17, 1962, the Subcommittee declared that in its opinion:

> . . . consideration of a permanent statute to qualify Section 315 of the Communications Act along the lines of the Presidential and Vice Presidential candidate exemption of 1960 is premature at this time, but [the Subcommittee] recommends a review of this matter early in the next (the 88th) Congress.

The sentiment of the Subcommittee about the roles of mass media representatives was clearly not enthusiastic.

> The drive for suspension of Section 315 permanently has some curious overtones. There seems to be a feeling on the part of some proponents of this type of legislation that those who are eminently qualified in the field of entertainment are better able to judge the format and content of political programs designed to enlighten the public than the candidates themselves. Those who test the public response and rate programs accordingly for entertainment value or the sale of commercial products may not be the best judge to analyze the citizen's quest for information or his taste for political controversy. Programs of a political nature in our society are a paramount public service responsibility of licensees. And the interposition of the public does not mean that the licensee is to act as a filter, substituting his judgment for that of the candidate as to what the American people want to know.
>
> A very substantial part of the public's acceptance of a candidate rests on the public's concept of the candidate's judgment; and the candidate's judgment is ofttimes best expressed in his exercise of that judgment as to what tactics and strategy would best serve his campaign. The exercise of editorial judgment by licensees can very easily be used by them in political programming to direct a political campaign the way they think the campaign ought to go.[31]

Certainly this rather tart appraisal expressed the lingering doubts of many political professionals both within Congress and without.

Television-Station Editorializing

The view of the Subcommittee on Communications dealing with "the exercise of editorial judgment by licensees" brings up a closely related problem—television-station editorializing.

In 1963, two studies were made by the National Association of Broadcasters (NAB) and the Television Information Office (TIO) of television stations' editorial work. It was determined from these investigations that approximately one-third of the television stations in the United States broadcast editorials and have a daily editorial schedule. Approximately one-half of the stations that prepare editorials broadcast them on a regular weekly schedule. The remainder deliver them on an irregular basis.

Most of the editorials deal with subjects having some connection to public affairs and government. Results of the TIO research highlight local subject material, which accounted for 87 per cent of all editorial time. Of the stations responding to the TIO inquiry, 59 per cent reported that they devoted their editorials to local subjects exclusively, 26 per cent replied that they editorialized on international topics occasionally, and 41 per cent said that they handled national themes from time to time.

As for the political ramifications, the NAB asked, "Do you editorialize on political issues?" One hundred and two stations (53 per cent) replied in the affirmative. On the question "Do you editorialize for or against political candidates?" only twelve television stations (6 per cent) told the NAB that they did.

The present editorial trends have developed since 1949, when the FCC reversed its 1941 Mayflower decision forbidding broadcasters to editorialize. Today there is much confusion in the industry, compounded by (1) the FCC doctrine that the stations should be "fair" to all legitimate interests and (2) the alleged inconsistencies that the broadcasters see in FCC rulings on the question.[32]

We can expect the editorial work of television stations to bring increasingly intense reactions from individuals and groups who disagree with the views presented. A particularly difficult matter is the business of backing candidates for political office. In analyzing the relative merits of legislative action or executive action, the cry that the stations are politically partisan will be heard more and more. So far, by sticking to local topics and by avoiding most sensitive areas, the stations have kept controversy to a minimum. It is well to note, however, that television editorializing may become a *major* political topic soon.

WHAT IS MEANT BY "DEBATE"

One of the most humorous and perceptive commentaries about presidential candidacies is Charles Ellis's and Frank Weir's *I'd Rather Be President,* brilliantly illustrated by Walt Kelly. This tongue-in-cheek effort offers us an interesting observation about debating, which the authors classify as a "hallowed campaign maneuver": "Throw down the gage (observing the no-name rule) to the 'other candidate' and insist that he meets you 'on the same platform' to thresh out the issues. Mention the Lincoln-Douglas debates, which have a nostalgic appeal in no way diminished by the fact that Lincoln and Douglas were not contesting for the Presidency at the time."

Ellis and Weir go on, advising, "You will be pretty safe in thus daring your opponent. Since there is no reason why he should let you run *his* campaign he will almost certainly decline. When he does, your staff of interpreters can scoff that he is afraid."

Finally, "If he beats you to the draw with a challenge of his own, observe loftily that such a debate 'would serve no useful purpose.' Add that you see no reason why you should lend the use of your name to give him free publicity."[33]

Few students of political affairs would advocate that debates be made mandatory. After all, the ideal debate situation requires arguments of conviction delivered with a degree of enthusiasm by the debaters.

George Hamilton Combs, the news commentator, offered the Subcommittee on Communications his opinions about what makes an "illuminating debate."

> . . . an illuminating debate must presuppose a willingness on the part of both debaters to explore each others' minds—to probe and to submit to probing in complete good faith—not just fencing, but excavation. It means a deep examination of all the relative views, emotions, and philosophies of the two men. The discussion of even one issue might take an hour, or a day. That sort of deep personal engagement simply can't be accomplished under arbitrary time limits or even in the panel formula.[34]

Stanley Kelley, Jr., suggests that "debate occurs when two parties advocating alternative courses of action bring their dispute before a common audience and ask that audience to favor one of the two proposals." Note Kelley's language, which connects the idea of alternatives with the presence of a dispute. It may be that his language is too strong and that debaters can offer alternatives without implying that one another's proposals are wrong. This question raises the issue of whether, in a debate, argument must be continuous or whether discussion can alternate with dispute. If rivals are diametrically opposed in thinking or if they distrust each other or if there is a record of hostility between the contenders, then discussion will probably be a minor element of the debate. Otherwise, it would probably be unwise for one side or the other to claim infallibility or to patently reject all arguments proposed by the opposition. Audiences inspired by the democratic concepts of reason, fair play, and objectivity would possibly resent such stubborn inflexibility in a debate.

On the other hand, Kelley is on very firm ground when he says:

The debater is under a compulsion to challenge those parts of his opponent's arguments that express aims or assumptions different from his own and must answer similar challenges from his opponent. If he does not, he risks a conclusion by the audience that his opponent's arguments cannot be challenged or that his own cannot be defended. If the debater replies to a challenge with too many obvious hedges, the audience may infer that his case is too weak to be frankly discussed.

There remains a shadow of uncertainty about the absolute reliability of the next proposition, however.

It is not advisable for a debater to misquote his opponent or to give an obviously distorted version of what his opponent has said. Members of the audience have heard his opponent's words for themselves and the opponent can be counted upon to call attention to the distortion.[35]

Kelley tends to underestimate the factor of emotional play that has dominated certain political debates in the past. What guarantee do we have that the audiences can sense "obvious" distortions? How can we assume that audiences will remember all previous points raised by the contenders?

Long before the advent of television as a medium for mass communications, Ralph D. Casey commented on the propaganda factor, outlining the elements of a classic political problem. "As political action on the part of thousands of voters is based upon traditional voting, prejudice, and irrationality, candidates and their propaganda chieftains do not scruple to make use of sentiment and suggestion propaganda. The *honest debate* of really significant issues is subordinated to *specious appeals that will capture votes.* The propagandist works on emotional attitudes, pays little attention to logical arguments. . . ."[36] Isaiah Berlin, in an article on "Political Ideas in the 20th Century," warned that a *new belief,* in this century, "consists not in developing the logical implications and elucidating the meaning, the context, or the relevance and origin of a specific problem . . . but in *altering the outlook* which gave rise to it in the first place."[37] Robert K. Merton, in his article devoted to "Mass Persuasion: The Moral Dimension," attacks the same problem with an eye to *manipulation.* "Mass persuasion," he says, "is not manipulative when it provides access to the pertinent facts; [but] it is manipulative when the appeal to sentiment is used to the exclusion of pertinent information."[38]

PERSONALITY

Arthur Krock, that canny observer of the Washington scene and of national political developments, estimated,

The judgment of history . . . has been more favorable to Presidents who were elected on the basis of the personality choice which is epitomized in the campaign of 1960 than to the Presidents who owed their victories to the popular strength of their parties at the time or to the subordination of their personalities to the abstract issues then dominant.[39]

Dwight David Eisenhower appealed to the winning combination of ballot casters primarily because of his personality. He instilled confidence that, if he were elected or re-elected President, programs would be as he promised. Leonard Hall, the GOP national chairman (1953–1957) who steered massive campaign efforts and who was devoted to Eisenhower, has assessed several past Presidents and presidential hopefuls from the angle of personality. Here are some of his opinions.

> President Coolidge wouldn't be a good candidate today. Nowadays a candidate must be able to get through to the people, to the individual voter.
> Al Smith . . . would be terrific. Al was very articulate. Maybe he would use "ain't," but that gave him color. It was part of his personality and background.
> Herbert Hoover would get through to the people as a man of sincerity and dignity.
> . . . Franklin D. Roosevelt, of course, would probably have been even better on television than he was on radio, and on radio he was one of the greatest. With his smile, his manner and his voice, F.D.R. would have been great political drama on TV.
> For the 1950's it is hard to imagine a better candidate than President Eisenhower. He does the natural thing as well as any man I've ever seen. With most candidates, you tell them to do things that will help them. This fellow Ike will do them naturally. It is instinct with him. He's a natural candidate simply because he's a great fellow.[40]

Typical of Eisenhower's approach is the following excerpt from one of his campaign speeches in October of 1952. He reminded his audience that "the only way I know how to talk is to talk plain. But I thought and I still think that the American people prefer honesty to distortion . . . that the American people prefer integrity to corruption . . . that American people are honorable and decent in their dealings with each other and that they want honor and decency in their government."[41]

According to James Reston, "Instead of the old-fashioned emphasis on what a candidate thinks, or what he says, the emphasis now seems to be on how he looks, especially on television, and on what kind of personality he has."[42]

Reston may be a bit oversatisfied with "old-fashioned" politics and perhaps carried away by his sincere desire to point out an obvious problem. But he is correct in warning us that, because of mass electronic communications, the candidate with the ability to convey "polivision" charm to vast audiences can use his own personal appeal to distract attention from substantial issues.

Learned commentary on these problems is largely devoted to worry about the impact of "polivision" imagery. In their *Going into Politics* (1957), Robert E. Merriam and Rachel M. Goetz tell why, in their opinion, the "old-style operator" is at a disadvantage. They observe that television can accomplish what no other form of mass communications, including radio, can. Television can communicate "a sense of immediacy that is peculiarly, and some say devilishly effective." For the "scores of millions" in the living-room audience, "personal qualities come across in a way no other medium can match; at the same time distance is narrowed and time condensed. Showmanship can be used to define or illustrate issues, or to confuse them."[43]

According to the well-known television commentator, Eric Sevareid, "This is the age of appearances, when the wrapping seems more important than the contents." He explains, "Wrappings can be seen at a glance, while contents require digging, and that requires time. Our political campaigns are the longest in the world, much too long in many respects, but still too short for the full unfolding of a public man's private nature."[44]

There is little argument to contest the point that Harry Truman, the last of the pretelevision Presidents or the first of the new breed, if you stretch effects a little, owed much of his success in 1948 to his ability to project his personality. On the other hand, his opponent in 1948, Thomas E. Dewey, lost small but crucial percentages of the popular vote in key midwestern and other states because he failed to convey *warmth*. Dewey seemed too slick and too aloof.[45]

Alice Roosevelt Longworth, in her warning to Republicans in 1936, called Franklin D. Roosevelt a "golden voice" able to convince the electorate. Mark Sullivan, the very able journalist and historian, remarked that the President "could recite the Polish alphabet and it would be accepted as a plea for disarmament."[46] One who remembers the impact of F.D.R. on the radio (his "fireside chats" in particular) and the forceful image of a vibrant, adventurous personality brought to public attention in motion-picture newsreels must be curious about how he would project in the television era. Could the opposition do any better today against that broad smile, that cigarette holder, and that phrase that drove terror into Republican hearts, "My friends, . . ."?

The supporters of Adlai Stevenson during his two tries for the Presidency were vastly impressed with his intellect, manifested in his ability to deliver the grand speech or to produce the artful turn of phrase. Many gave him their allegiance with some emotion. On the other hand, he had certain limitations that stopped him just short of the broadest public appeal—the kind necessary to win. First, his personality could not distract the electorate from the substantial point that he was another Democrat after the long Roosevelt-Truman era. Eisenhower was able to direct his 1952 appeals to the theme "it's time for a change," a theme simple and broad enough to fit his personal quality of sincerity about *basics*. The campaign of 1952 matched Eisenhower's personality in many ways because of the dominance of general and often abstract issues.

Eisenhower's celebrated TV "spots" on the themes of corruption; high prices and high taxes; and war were most effective. These 49 "spots" (each only a few minutes in duration) for television and the 29 prepared for radio hit the themes simply and directly. Produced by Ted Bates and Company and managed by the Batten, Barton, Durstine and Osborne advertising-public relations agency retained by the Republican National Committee, these "spots" carried forth the plan conceived by Michael Levin. He recommended a three-week saturation campaign utilizing such "spots," and in his original proposal to the Republican National Committee he suggested:

> The spots themselves would be the height of simplicity. People from each of . . . 49 areas would each ask the General a question. . . . The General's answer would be his complete comprehension of the problem and his determination to do something about it when elected. Thus he inspires loyalty without prematurely committing himself to any straight-jacketing answer.

Candid interest and uncluttered involvement were highlights of these "spots," which registered, first and foremost, Eisenhower's personality. For example, one "spot" showed a very sincere nominee. A voice asked, "Mr. Eisenhower, what about the high cost of living?" He answered straightforwardly, "My wife, Mamie, worries about the same thing. I tell her it's our job to change that on November 4."[47] This time it was the Democratic Party that bit its collective fingernails over the problem of the man who could deliver the "my friends" theme so effectively.

In contrast, Adlai Stevenson seemed to many observers to be "more concerned with the literary quality of his speeches than with the projection of himself over television. . . . Stevenson, master of artful prose and the well-turned phrase, never made a wholly successful adaptation to these demands of television."[48]

Joseph and Stewart Alsop called Eisenhower's personality "the greatest political asset which has been made available to the Republican Party in many years." Stevenson appealed to the intellect and Eisenhower to the emotions, at least for a vital segment of the electorate. We all remember such exchanges as that occasioned by the young politician who remarked that many intelligent people admired Stevenson. "Sure," was the reply, "all the egg-heads love Stevenson. But how many egg-heads do you think there are?"[49] Stevenson fell short of convincing a majority of the electorate that he was "a happy combination of the man and the hour."[50]

Mr. Nixon's 1952 Speech

Without television, it is likely that Richard Nixon's career would have taken a drastically different turn in 1952 than it did. The medium gave him the opportunity to explain himself to the American people and to his immediate associates in the leadership of the Republican Party, following the disclosure that he had taken $18,235 from a group of California Republicans to pay his political expenses.

The affair burst out to captivate public interest and partisan concerns on Thursday, September 18, 1952, with a *New York Post* story.

The effects were predictably severe. The Democratic National Chairman called Eisenhower to demand the resignation of the vice-presidential candidate; Eisenhower was tremendously disturbed and asked Nixon to explain; crowds on Nixon's whistle-stop campaign train tour began to heckle him; some Republican leaders called for the candidate's scalp; Nixon suddenly became the *cause célèbre* of the presidential campaign, and Eisenhower was thrust into the position of deciding whether to retain his running mate.

Hurried and harried meetings were held between Nixon and his advisers. A key adviser, Murray Chotiner, gave his opinion. "Every time we get you before an audience, you win them. What we have to do is to get you before the biggest possible audience so that you can talk over the heads of the press to the people."[51]

Eisenhower telephoned Nixon after four days of the sensation. He told him, "You know, this is an awfully hard thing for me to decide. I have come to the conclusion that you are the one who has to decide what to do. . . . I think you ought to go on a nationwide television program and tell them everything there is to tell, everything you can remember since the day you entered public life." In answer to Nixon's question about whether a decision would be announced after the program, Eisenhower replied, "Maybe after the program we [can] tell what ought to be done."[52]

The vice-presidential nominee went before a national television audience on September 24, 1952, and delivered a speech and radiated an appeal that not only saved his place on the ticket but also transformed him from a sudden campaign liability into a campaign asset.

> Within twenty-four hours the entire Republican hierarchy was singing hosannas, including the leaders who felt the program's emotional pitch to be revolting. His success sent the Republican campaign soaring, establishing him as a national figure and the best-known largest-crowd-drawing vice-presidential candidate in history.[53]

Presidential nominee Eisenhower watched the broadcast with great interest and, at a meeting with Nixon shortly thereafter, gave him his full support. Eisenhower told a campaign crowd at Wheeling, West Virginia, that Nixon had been "completely vindicated."[54]

In that now famous speech, Nixon stressed his almost Horatio Alger rise as a fulfillment of the traditional American dream; he remarked on his own very high standards of personal morality and defended his use of the campaign money in the tone of a man appealing for support of the underdog (another

American folk custom); he told about his family, his parents, and the family grocery store in East Whittier, California; he talked about working his way through college, about his devoted wife Pat, and about his war record; he told the audience about the strains of starting a law practice, about his modest manner of living, and about his personal debts; he made reference to his dog, Checkers; he recalled his active efforts in the Alger Hiss affair and commented about the fight against Communism; he struck out for ethics and against corruption; and he suggested that he did not feel that he should withdraw from the Republican ticket, but concluded that he willingly left the decision to Eisenhower because he would not want to hurt the General's chances. He said, "Because folks remember a man that's to be President of the United States, a man that's to be Vice-President of the United States must have the confidence of all the people."[55]

The Religious Issue of 1960 and Implications

"Majority Voice No Objection to Catholic Nominee for President" headlined the Gallup poll released for publication on December 9, 1959. According to that poll, "The great majority of American voters today would have no objection to a Roman Catholic being elected President. Behind this viewpoint is the general belief of many voters that questioning a man's qualifications for office on religious grounds would be a violation of an American tradition of religious freedom." Sixty-nine per cent of the people polled said they would vote for a Catholic, 20 per cent said that they would not, and 11 per cent said that they did not know whether they would or not. This reported 31 per cent against or undecided indicated the presence of a serious religious issue for the coming 1960 election if a Catholic were nominated.[56] When the Democratic Party chose John F. Kennedy to be its standard bearer, the issue was joined.

Televised meetings between nominees can serve the function of education as well as of argument. The awkward experience of 1960 shows that, when an issue like that of religion is vital to the electorate from the beginning of a campaign, we need to provide both candidates with a suitable opportunity to give their full opinions on that issue freely and objectively. The communications industry, in conjunction with the learned societies of scholars, should propose a televised discussion program that would be clearly identified as a discussion and not a debate.

In 1960, Mr. Nixon's position on the religious issue was most commendable. He opposed bigotry as firmly as he could, but he faced a handicap in not having had the early opportunity to venture deeply into the question with Mr. Kennedy at a time when both men could have stated their common resolves and philosophies as citizens and as leaders of opinion.

The issue remained serious during the whole campaign because it was such a personal subject for the electorate and because no way was found to neutralize it politically for both Democrats and Republicans.

Perhaps Nixon wanted to warn the public more forcefully about the dangers of allowing religion to become an issue but could not see a way to do so. Neither, probably, could his advisers. Thus, the underdog situation was produced again.

John Kennedy's head-on assault on the bigots, the fearful, the doubters, and the undecided was also commendable, but the religious issue was the kind of a problem that deserved to be put at the feet of *both* candidates—in fact, of all responsible candidates in any election of this sort.

A series of discussions, sponsored as suggested and following the original meeting proposed, could have cleared the air. The underdog factor was stronger than necessary in 1960. It is an unhappy fact that a great many voters got bogged down in the "religious issue" despite the worthy intentions of both candidates.[57]

IN PERSON?

"The most notable triumph of the broadcasting industry," according to Gilbert Seldes, is that "it has made itself indispensable to public discussion, so that the entire nation turns on its sets with absolute confidence when information without prejudice is wanted, or the clash of opinion on any conceivable subject."[58]

Al Smith regarded the impact of radio very highly. He argued, on the basis of his experiences as a presidential candidate in 1928, that his personal appearances were not very effective.

> There are still some places at which a candidate must actually show himself, where perhaps there may be such doubt as to his personality or his convictions that he and his advisers may honestly feel that the only way to gain votes and change sentiment in his favor is to circulate in person, shake hands with the proper people, and show himself in a large hall to as many of the citizens as possible.
>
> But when the campaign is all over and the candidate sits back in his easy chair and looks back over his experiences, he will usually find that ninety per cent of the political committees who urged him to appear in their town or states, and whose requests were granted, were really more eager for local glory and the benefit they might gain for their individual organizations, than they were for the ultimate success of the party in the nation.[59]

During the course of the 1960 campaign, Richard Nixon fulfilled a campaign promise to visit all 50 states. His decision, carried out at great physical cost to him, proved to be less important than John Kennedy's decision to face the religious issue squarely by a dramatic personal appearance before the Greater Houston Ministerial Association in September of 1960. Kennedy chose a personal appearance to focus national attention upon a topic he wanted to bring into the open. Texas television carried the dramatic meeting and his careful presentation of his personal credo. Later, national television networks carried the message. Still later, the Democratic National Committee and the Kennedy campaign organization used segments of the *tape* as "spot" material for television. Radio as well carried his words widely.

Would Kennedy have risked so much before the Ministerial Association if he had not counted on the electronic mass media to deliver his message to the American people—to carry his tactful elucidation of liberalism beyond the ministerial conference to the vast publics the ministers represented?

For both nominees, the mass media for electronic communications provided a way around the burden of personal appearances that seemed more imposing to them than it had to politicians of the whistle-stop vintage. In 1960 air travel was so speedy that it had to be countered by highlighting key speeches on the subjects at issue.

A study of the campaign itineraries points up the problem. For example, between September 12 and 26, 1960, Mr. Kennedy visited audiences in New York, Pennsylvania, Tennessee, West Virginia, North Carolina, Virginia, New Jersey, Ohio, Illinois, South Dakota, Montana, Wyoming, Colorado, Utah, Nebraska, Missouri, Texas, and Maryland. Nixon's itinerary for the same period of time was even wider geographically.

Two theories plagued the candidates. One was that there is wisdom in choosing special places of importance to visit personally. The other was that the "scatter" technique (delivering several versions of the same speech in different areas of a state in order to make local *news*) is indispensable in order to stimulate local press, radio, and television coverage. Both are valid tactics, and both require travel.

Thus an argument in favor of future television debates is that, if we are to wear the nominees out by having them race about the country, we must also provide them with some relief from the burden of personal appearances. What better way than national television, and what better reason than a scheduled, generally anticipated series of debates near the end of the campaign? When we are all tired of all the news about all the speeches, it would be good to see and hear debates that functioned as fit summations for the views of both men.

As Robert Bendiner has so aptly said:

> Given a role in keeping with its power, its nature and its demands, TV can serve to distill the essentials of campaign debate from the mass of flummery and empty rhetoric. It can establish a greater rapport between the nation and its potential leaders.[60]

FOOTNOTES

1. Theodore H. White, *The Making of the President, 1960* (New York: Atheneum Publishers, 1961), pp. 290–291.

2. "Kennedy Asks for Aid of All," *Boston Herald,* November 10, 1960.

3. Richard M. Nixon, *Six Crises* (New York: Pocket Books, Inc., 1962), p. 385.

4. Emmet John Hughes, *The Ordeal of Power* (New York: Atheneum Publishers, 1963), p. 323.

5. "Debate Score: Kennedy Up, Nixon Down," *Broadcasting,* Vol. 59, No. 19 (November 7, 1960), p. 27. For an important experimental study of bias as a factor with viewers who watched the 1960 debates with a strong commitment to the Democratic or Republican Parties, see Ralph L. Rosnow, "Bias in Evaluating the Presidential Debates: A 'Splinter' Effect," *Journal of Social Psychology,* Vol. 67 (1965), pp. 211–219.

6. Earl Mazo, "The Great Debates," in *The Great Debates* (The Fund for the Republic, Inc., 1962), p. 2.

7. Stanley Kelley, Jr., "The 1960 Presidential Election," in Ivan Hinderaker, editor, *American Government Annual 1961–1962* (New York: Holt, Rinehart and Winston, Inc., 1961), p. 72.

8. Stanley Kelley, Jr., "Campaign Debates: Some Facts and Issues," *The Public Opinion Quarterly,* Vol. 26, No. 3 (Fall 1962), p. 351.

9. E. Katz and J. J. Feldman, "The Kennedy-Nixon Debates: A Survey of Surveys," *Studies in Public Communication,* No. 4 (The University of Chicago Press, 1962), pp. 127–163.

10. "A Little Debate over Big Ones," *Broadcasting,* Vol. 59, No. 15 (October 10, 1960), p. 33, "Originator of Debates," *New York Times,* October 14, 1960, p. 21.

11. Adlai Stevenson, "Plan for a Great Debate," *This Week Magazine,* March 6, 1960.

12. Stanley Kelley, Jr., *Political Campaigning* (Washington, D.C.: The Brookings Institution, 1960). Kelley quotes from Reuben Davis's *Recollections of Mississippi and Mississippians* (1889), p. 153.

13. President's Commission on National Goals, *Goals for Americans* (New York: The American Assembly, Columbia University, 1960); The Rockefeller Panel Reports, *Prospect for America* (Garden City, N.Y.: Doubleday & Company, Inc., 1961); or, *The National Purpose* (New York: Holt, Rinehart and Winston, 1960). See also *New York Times* treatment of the "National Purpose" series, for example, John K. Jessup, "National Purpose: Start of a Debate," *New York Times,* May 19, 1960; Hans Meyerhoff, "U.S.A. 1960—The Case of the Missing Purpose," *The Nation,* Vol. 191, No. 5 (August 20, 1960), pp. 85–89.

14. "Beginnings of a Problem" and "One Debate Starts Another," *Broadcasting,* Vol. 58, No. 19 (May 9, 1960).

15. R. W. Apple, Jr., "The Little Debates," *The Reporter,* Vol. 27, No. 10 (December 6, 1962), pp. 36–38; also "A Small State Takes the Limelight," *Life,* Vol. 48, No. 18 (May 9, 1960), pp. 24–29.

16. "A 'Political Clinic' Program?" *Saturday Review,* Vol. 45, No. 46 (November 17, 1962), p. 38.

17. James Reston, "Radio, TV and 1956," *New York Times,* May 26, 1955.

18. "F.C.C. Chief Cites Licensing Woes," *New York Times,* January 9, 1960.

19. "Excerpts of Speech by Minow," *New York Times,* May 10, 1961.

20. Federal Communications Commission, *26th Annual Report* (Washington, D.C.: U.S. Government Printing Office, 1960), p. 40.

21. Committee on Commerce, U.S. Senate, *Final Report: Freedom of Communications*, April 17, 1962 (Washington, D.C.: U.S. Government Printing Office, 1962), p. 10.

22. Charles A. H. Thomson, *Television and Presidential Politics* (Washington, D.C.: The Brookings Institution, 1956), p. 129.

23. "Taft Demands F.C.C. Get Him Free Time," *New York Times,* June 6, 1952.

24. Jack Gould, "Squabbles among Presidential Candidates for Time Indicate Importance Attached to Video," *New York Times,* June 6, 1952. See also editorial, "The Equal Time Folly," *New York Times,* June 18, 1959.

25. Val Adams, "F.C.C. Head Asks 'Equal Time' End," *New York Times,* March 18, 1959. See also, "F.C.C. Puts Out Primer on Politics," *New York Herald Tribune,* September 12, 1954; "Big Headache," *New York Daily News,* September 2, 1952.

26. James Reston, "Radio, TV and 1956," *New York Times,* May 26, 1955. See also, Jack Gould, "TV: Campaign Air Time," *New York Times,* June 18, 1956; Richard F. Shepherd, "Humphrey Scores Equal-Time Curbs," *New York Times,* July 18, 1959.

27. Robert L. Moore, "Politics vs. Radio and TV: The 'Equal Time' Headache," *New York Herald Tribune,* May 20, 1956.

28. "CBS Will Fight Ruling on Political Equal Time," *Washington Sunday Star,* March 15, 1959; editorial, "Distorting the News," *Washington Post,* March 17, 1959; editorial, "Congress Must Spell Out TV-Radio News Freedom," *San Antonio Express,* March 18, 1959; editorial, "A Bad FCC Decision," *Minneapolis Morning Tribune,* March 17, 1959; John C. O'Brien, "Broadcasters Opposing Equal TV Political Time," *Philadelphia Inquirer,* March 19, 1959; editorial, "Minutes Don't Measure Events," *Phoenix Gazette,* March 18, 1959; editorial, " 'Equal Time' Nonsense," *Washington Daily News,* March 17, 1959; editorial, "Editing by Bureaucrats," *Chicago American,* March 17, 1959; editorial, "Newscast 'Equal Time' Rule a Dreary Bore," *San Francisco Chronicle,* March 18, 1959; editorial, " 'Equal Time' Farce," *Knoxville News-Sentinel,* March 17, 1959; "Stanton in Fighting Mood over Equal Time 'Monstrosity' as He Plans Taking It to the People," *Variety,* March 18, 1959; "Sec. 315: Journalism Body Blow," *Broadcasting,* March 16, 1959; editorial, "Equal Time Abuses," *Christian Science Monitor,* March 20, 1959; editorial, "Where 'Equal Time' Has No Place," *New York Herald Tribune,* March 19, 1959; editorial "Equal Time on the Air," *New York Times,* March 22, 1959; "Free, Equal and Ridiculous," *Time,* March 30, 1959.

29. See Leo Mishkin, "Sight and Sound," *New York Morning Telegraph,* March 18, 1959.

30. Ogg and Ray, *Essentials of American National Government,* 9th edition, as edited and amended by William H. Young, (New York: Appleton-Century-Crofts, 1963), p. 175.

31. Subcommittee on Communications, Committee on Commerce, U.S. Senate, *Final Report,* April 17, 1962 (Washington, D.C.: U.S. Government Printing Office, 1962), pp. 9–10.

32. John E. McMillin, "New Voices in a Democracy," *Television Quarterly,* Vol. 3, No. 3 (Summer 1964) pp. 27–52, esp. pp. 29, 34–36.

33. Charles Ellis and Frank Weir, *I'd Rather Be President* (New York: Simon and Schuster, 1956), pp. 127–128.

34. Subcommittee on Communications, *op. cit.,* Part IV, p. 410, for testimony of George Hamilton Combs.

35. Stanley Kelley, Jr., *Political Campaigning,* pp. 19–20.

36. Ralph D. Casey, "Party Campaign Propaganda," in Harwood L. Childs, editor, *Pressure Groups and Propaganda, The Annals of the American Academy of Political and Social Science,* Vol. 179 (May 1935), pp. 102–103; italics mine.

37. Isaiah Berlin, "Political Ideas in the 20th Century," *Foreign Affairs,* Vol. 28 (April 1950), p. 371; italics mine.

38. Robert K. Merton, "Mass Persuasion: The Moral Dimension," in Bernard Berelson and Morris Janowitz, editors, *Reader in Public Opinion and Communication* (Glencoe, Ill.: The Free Press, 1953), p. 466. For an exposition of standards for the establishment of rules for competitive propaganda, see Harwood L. Childs, *An Introduction to Public Opinion* (New York: John Wiley & Sons, Inc., 1940), p. 132.

39. Arthur Krock, " 'The Man Who'—Not 'The Issue Which,' " *New York Times Magazine,* October 16, 1960.

40. Leonard Hall, "An Old Pro Describes How Politics in U.S. Has Changed," *Life,* Vol. 48, No. 16 (April 25, 1960), p. 130.

41. "Text of Eisenhower's Speech at Buffalo in His New York Campaign," *New York Times,* October 24, 1952.

42. James Reston, "Laugh, Politician, Laugh," *New York Times,* October 30, 1958. For other pertinent views on the personality factor, see Russell Baker, "Where Is a Candidate?" *New York Times Magazine,* November 1, 1959; Sidney Hyman, "The Log Cabin Myth Comes to an End," *New York Times Magazine,* September 21, 1958; Raymond H. Bateman, "How to Lose an Election," *New York Times Magazine,* October 1, 1961; James A. Michener, "What Every New Candidate Should Know," *New York Times,* September 23, 1962.

43. Robert E. Merriam and Rachel M. Goetz, *Going into Politics* (New York: Harper & Brothers, 1957), p. 123.

44. Eric Sevareid, editor, *Candidates 1960* (New York: Basic Books, 1959), p. 10.

45. Editorial remarks, "Political Propaganda: American Election Campaigns," in Reo M. Christenson and Robert O. McWilliams, editors, *Voice of the People* (New York: McGraw-Hill Book Company, Inc., 1962), p. 349.

46. W. Norwood Brigance, "Effectiveness of the Public Platform," *The Annals,* Vol. 250 (March 1947), p. 71.

47. Stanley Kelley, Jr., *Professional Public Relations and Political Power* (Baltimore: The Johns Hopkins Press, 1956), pp. 187–190.

48. Walter Johnson, *1600 Pennsylvania Avenue* (Boston: Little, Brown and Company, 1960), p. 255.

49. Joseph and Stewart Alsop, *The Reporter's Trade* (New York: Reynal & Company, 1958), pp. 187–188.

50. Robert E. Lane, *Political Life* (Glencoe, Ill.: The Free Press, 1959), p. 25.

51. Richard M. Nixon, *Six Crises* (New York: Pocket Books, 1962), p. 101. See also, the complete Nixon version of "The Fund," pp. 77–138.

52. *Ibid.,* pp. 105–106.

53. Earl Mazo, "The $18,000 Question," in Andrew M. Scott and Earle Wallace, editors, *Politics U.S.A.* (New York: The Macmillan Company, 1961), p. 257.

54. *New York Times,* Section 4, Sunday, September 28, 1952. See also, Sherman Adams, *First-Hand Report* (New York: Harper & Brothers, 1961), pp. 37–44.

55. "Text of Senator Nixon's Broadcast Explaining Supplementary Expense Fund," *New York Times,* September 24, 1952.

56. "Majority Voice No Objection to Catholic Nominee for President," public

opinion poll issued for release not earlier than December 9, 1959, American Institute of Public Opinion, Princeton, New Jersey.

57. Leo Egan, "The Religious Issue," *New York Times,* September 18, 1960; John Wicklein, "Vast Anti-Catholic Drive Is Started before Election," *New York Times,* October 16, 1960; John W. Finney, "Jesuit Rules Out Church Control over a President," *New York Times,* September 28, 1960; "Test of Religion," *Time,* Vol. LXXVI, No. 13 (September 26, 1960), pp. 21–22; Committee For Fair Play, "An Open Letter about the 'Religious Issue' in This Campaign," advertisement in *Chicago Daily Tribune,* November 4, 1960.

58. Gilbert Seldes, *The Public Arts* (New York: Simon and Schuster, 1956), p. 278.

59. Alfred E. Smith, "Backstage in a National Election," in A. N. Christensen and E. M. Kirkpatrick, editors, *The People, Politics and the Politician* (New York: Henry Holt and Company, 1941), p. 323.

60. Robert Bendiner, "How Much Has TV Changed Campaigning?" in Evron M. Kirkpatrick and Jeane J. Kirkpatrick, editors, *Elections—U.S.A.* (New York: Henry Holt and Company, 1956), p. 71. See also, William R. McAndrew, "Broadcasting and Politics," in NBC News, *1960 Convention Handbook* (New York: Davis Publications, Inc., 1960), pp. 14–15.

3/Perspectives on the Kennedy-Nixon Debates

NECESSARY QUALITIES OF A PRESIDENT

When Richard M. Nixon and John F. Kennedy debated in 1960, the efforts of each nominee were primarily directed at persuading the electorate that the requirements of the Presidency, at that crucial time, demanded a certain *fitness* that his opponent did not quite embody. Behind their responses to the newsmen's questions and behind their careful analyses of various political issues was the candidates' recognition that the people were searching for a man to be the Chief Executive of the most responsible and burdened democracy on earth.

Programs, policies, proposals, and quickly assembled ideas were presented by the two major contenders with the magnetic pull of election day always in mind. Under our system of government, the citizenry listens to the arguments of those who would govern in order to determine which man has the best plans for future action, and to try to sense which plans are backed up by the man best suited to lead.

The President, says Clinton Rossiter, should be "honest, clean, kind, manly, industrious, sincere, frugal, reverent, loyal, intelligent, dignified, eloquent, affable, courageous, efficient, high principled. . . ." Such a paragon of virtue should also have political skill—the art of "persuading men to do what they ought to do without persuasion." He should be "cunning," a "master of the delicate art of manipulating men," and have a sense of history and a sense of humor.[1]

John F. Kennedy, early in that fateful year of 1960, summed up his views on the Presidency before the members of the National Press Club. He observed that "the times—and the people" demanded

> . . . a vigorous proponent of the national interest—not a passive broker for conflicting private interests. They demand a man capable of acting as the commander-in-chief of the grand alliance, not merely a bookkeeper who feels that his work is done when the numbers on the balance sheet come out even. They demand that he be the head of a responsible party, not rise so far above politics as to be invisible—a man who will formulate and fight for legislative policies, not be a casual bystander to the legislative process.[2]

During the postconvention campaign period, Richard Nixon advised the voters:

> I know from experience that when a President speaks, when a President makes a decision, it is for keeps. He doesn't get a second chance. He can't call a bullet back after he shoots from the hip. It goes to the target. In these critical times we cannot afford to have as President of the United States a man who does not think first before he speaks or acts.[3]

THE TWO MEN

The principal contenders in the 1960 presidential race met for the first time in a debate situation in 1947, at the invitation of Congressman Frank Buchanan. They traveled to McKeesport, Pennsylvania, to debate the merits of the Taft-Hartley Act before an audience of (according to Nixon) less than 200 people. Nixon favored the bill, and Kennedy took a stand against it. "We both," says Nixon, "presented our points of view as vigorously as we could."[4] The two debaters of 1947 were just as vigorous in 1960.

As preface to our discussion of the debates, some comments about the public personalities of Nixon and Kennedy are in order. Of direct bearing are the *style* and *approach* of each man.

Richard M. Nixon

The former Vice-President of the United States has many facets to his public personality and several widely recognized, dominant traits. During his eight years with Eisenhower, he did much to maintain and to enhance the dignity and prestige of his office and to impress the public with his forceful character. He served diligently in his ex officio role as presiding officer of the Senate and was "popular among his former colleagues."[5] As confidant to the President, as emissary of the President on state visits abroad, as a key Republican leader, and as a potential candidate for the highest office in the land, he was certainly one of our nation's most important political figures.

Richard Nixon does not shy away from difficult situations. He has, seemingly, an inner compulsion to meet head-on whatever opposes him; his autobiographical *Six Crises* reinforces this observer's opinion on that score. He says that he had certain doubts about debating with Kennedy because "I was better known than he and our joint appearances would simply build up an audience for him." Also, "Kennedy had the advantage that he was attacking a record and I was defending it." But being cast in the position of defending the Eisenhower Administration, which he had served in as Vice-President for eight years, made Nixon feel that he had to accept the challenge to debate. In his own words, "I felt it was absolutely essential that I not only agree to debate, but enthusiastically welcome the opportunity. Had I refused the challenge, I would have opened myself to the charge that I was afraid to stand on our record."[6]

Commenting on his famous debate with Soviet Premier Nikita Khrushchev at the kitchen display of the American Exhibition in Sokolniki Park, Moscow, in July of 1959, he remarks that he had to give suitable answer to the offensive tactics utilized by the Russian leader in private talks during the preceding days. After one Khrushchev blast aimed at the United States, Vice-President Nixon had concluded that "it was imperative that I find the opportunity to strike back so that the record could be set straight publicly."[7]

His dogged display of grit against leftist agitators, ruffians, and mobs during his 1958 state visit to Caracas, Venezuela, also attests to the fact that Mr. Nixon will not use a side door because the front door seems blocked. He tends to plow on through to his destination no matter how much personal travail is involved.

He also prefers the intimate approach, with a good deal of audience participation, and likes off-the-cuff broadcasts rather than formal speeches. In 1955, he railed against written texts or the use of prompters in air-wave campaigning. Speaking to a luncheon meeting of the Radio and Television Executives Society of New York, he gave advice as to how a political candidate should handle television.

> Be sure the candidate is at his best, not worn out after a breathless day's campaigning.
> Do not tie him down with canned news releases, for once a candidate is committed to a statement, it must be read.
> Stick to a subject he knows, never use television to bring up something new.
> Remember that once he gets before the cameras, he will be worried enough as it is; so let him alone for a reasonable time before he goes on the air.[8]

Mr. Nixon followed most but not all of his own advice in 1960's debates.

As is usual with prominent figures in American political life, Nixon's personality has been studied objectively and in a partisan manner by members of the Fourth Estate and others. Here are several views about the man.

The Nation magazine displayed venom in an August 1960 editorial.

> One of the most revealing portraits . . . shows Nixon not only as master politician but as one of the most adroit hidden persuaders in the country who, if he fails to achieve the Presidency, might well find his true metier as head of a great advertising agency, preferably one specializing in corn.[9]

Russell Baker of *The New York Times* showed Nixon more respect in September 1960. "For connoisseurs of the political art he is a delight to watch for the sure-footed professionalism with which he pursues the occult business of getting elected." Also, "the method with which he pursues the ultimate goal is always fascinating for its precision and single-mindedness of execution."[10]

Reviewing Nixon's *Six Crises,* Tom Wicker of the same newspaper called Nixon a "Kafkaesque figure so prominently and yet so elusively in the public eye."[11]

To a certain extent, Nixon is an elusive personality for those who like to label everything exactly and permanently. The former Vice-President defies such labeling because he is, from the public view, a very complicated man. Throughout his governmental career, he displayed not one mood, but a variety of moods. The only certain facet of his personality is that which both friend and foe admit—his deep-rooted sensitivity to persons and situations he faces. A collateral aspect of his public personality is the instinct that he has for throwing himself wholeheartedly into a campaign. For Nixon, it is always the all-out effort that is worthwhile. In his now famous lecture to the press corps after his defeat in the California gubernatorial campaign of 1962, he observed, typically, "I would have liked to have won. But, not having won, the main thing was that I battled—battled for the things I believed in."[12]

One is led to the conclusion that any estimate of Nixon must include his qualities of independence and bluntness when the going gets rough. Richard H. Rovere expressed the opinion in 1960 that Nixon had a "talent for conciliation and accommodation which has often been most impressive" but that he was known to put forward "his nerve, his iron, his toughness in debate, his dogged-ness, his preference for action over inaction. To some extent, obviously, he must play it this way because he must use his strengths, not another man's."[13]

Richard Nixon's imprint on this observer's mind is of a figure who steers his course through life not only by the advice of others, but by the "distant drummer" he alone hears. Virtually all of the modern critics of politics study Nixon for himself and not as a fragment of an organization. Nixon is both the Horatio Alger of twentieth-century American politics and an introspective personality with a certain Hamlet quality. He is no organization man!

John F. Kennedy

In one respect, Kennedy and Nixon had something in common, they both started in politics in 1946, rose quickly to high positions, and reached for the highest rung on the political ladder after significant careers in the national Congress. Until election day of 1960, it was common for reporters to comment on the swift rises to prominence of the two men. Douglas Cater wrote that "Kennedy has come further and faster than any of his contemporaries except perhaps Richard Milhaus Nixon. . . ."[14]

Kennedy was self-disciplined, bright, concerned with the objectives he had set for himself, and willing to listen to the carefully drawn advice of intimates he trusted. He appreciated the value of the team or organization effort and was able to distill what he wanted or needed from the results of group activity.

He was known for his humor, his ambition, and his willingness to take risks if he deemed that the situation required a plunging-forward approach.

To a certain extent, Kennedy struck this observer as a less involved personality than Nixon at the time of their debates. John Kennedy focused on his goal while Richard Nixon had his attentions roving from his goal to Mr. Kennedy who had the advantage of the man with much to gain as against the man with much to lose.

Writing about Senator Kennedy in 1959, Douglas Cater observed:

> . . . he shows a restraint of manner that is unusual among politicians. Both in public and private conversation he eschews cliché with the contempt of a man for whom words are precise instruments. He does not retreat behind the high wall of pomposity that most politicians erect on occasion to protect themselves from interlopers.[15]

Another trait of John Kennedy, so striking in the 1960 campaign, was his self-confidence. Contesting for the party nomination with very active rivals, or standing up podium-to-podium during the debates, he impressed both partisan friends and foes with his ability to argue confidently.

John Kennedy, in 1960, had glamour to offset political handicaps like the religious problem. He was blessed with rugged good looks and a family that could not have been better suited to convey a cheerful picture to the public at large. In ready support of his efforts, that family provided financial assistance, political experience, and political talent.

Not the least of his assets was one he shared with his rival, Mr. Nixon. He was able and willing to exhaust himself on the campaign trail.

One of his objectives in 1960 was to convince the American people that he had maturity. Nixon was also determined to convince the electorate on the "maturity score." But Kennedy had a more difficult task in his effort to look dignified and wise. Typical pithy comments on the maturity issue were written by Cabell Phillips in 1958, in an article about Kennedy's schedule as a U.S. Senator working on "How to Be a Presidential Candidate."

> Maturity . . . —that vague hallmark of virtue which a prospective President is required to exhibit—is not conspicuous among Kennedy's gifts. His youthful look and a certain glibness of speech and manner are against him on this count. And so is the fact that nothing in his background reveals any particular talent for leadership or executive management. The fact that he has never had to hold down a job, meet a payroll, or run a city or a state government—his entire professional life has been spent in Congress—marks him as deficient in the sort of rounded experience with which maturity is equated.[16]

On the subject of his "platform manner" during the predebate months of the campaign, one observer reported that ". . . he much prefers to speak extemporaneously, discarding the unsatisfactory prepared texts his battery of speech writers turn out for him. Sometimes these texts serve as notes on a special theme utilized to develop a major sectional theme, but on other occasions they are thrown away altogether."[17]

The other aspects of the Kennedy personality and background are too well known to bear repetition here. The deluge of material about Kennedy the war hero, the historian, the "Irish Brahmin," and so on, began pouring out long before his presidential effort of 1960. Much of it was absorbed by the public as early as 1956, when he made an unsuccessful stab at the Democratic vice-presidential nomination.

Nevertheless, Kennedy was not as well known as Nixon was before the debates. Kennedy lacked the vantage point of vice-presidential experience, and his record in Congress, though satisfactory, was not sufficient to elevate him to national leadership. Kennedy's name became more familiar as the campaign of 1960 progressed, but it was the debates with Nixon that gave the citizenry a really good look at this "tough-grained and tough-minded man . . . willing to face the hardest of questions."[18]

PREPARATION FOR THE DEBATES

Perhaps the most significant background for the four debates—held on September 26, October 7, October 13, and October 21—was provided by the candidates themselves, who refined the issues into four major subject areas. These four areas of controversy were: (1) the federal government's appropriate role in public welfare; (2) the federal government's obligations and role in economic growth; (3) foreign policy, with special emphasis given to the question of who was better qualified to deal with Khrushchev; (4) the subject "Where Does the United States Stand Today?"—with much talk about the "needs of the sixties," "moving forward," and national "prestige."[19]

To set the mood of public questioning at that time, let us examine sample positions on issues then in vogue. A selected group was provided on June 13, 1960, by *U.S. News and World Report.*

Johnson:

> It seems to me that the real issue of the 1960 election will be the kind of leadership that America seeks in the challenging decade of the 1960's.

Kennedy:

> The great issue is whether the power, prestige, and influence of the United States is increasing or decreasing in relation to the Soviet Union and the Communist world.

Symington:

> [The problem is] . . . to decide which party will give the most
> effective leadership for attaining our two most important objectives:
> (1) permanent world peace (2) domestic economic stability and
> growth.

Goldwater:

> . . . the issue of the 1960's, is whether we are to continue toward
> entrenched centralized government.

Humphrey:

> The restoration of leadership . . . on the domestic front [is essen-
> tial] in order to place priorities on the rise and development of our
> political, economic and spiritual resources in such varied fields as
> education, economic expansion, social welfare. . . . [and] on the in-
> ternational scene—[we need] leadership in safeguarded disarmament
> and a systematic attack on hunger, sickness, illiteracy, and poverty.[20]

Nixon, in a speech in Greensboro, North Carolina, spoke of civil rights.

> I . . . recognize that law alone, while necessary, is not the answer
> to the problems of civil rights . . . that law is only as good as the will
> of the people to obey it. . . . It is the responsibility . . . of those of
> us in positions of leadership . . . to promote . . . the desire and the
> will to keep the law and to make progress in the solution of these
> difficult problems.[21]

Getting Set

A Gallup Poll, issued for release on September 18, 1960, estimated a
"Record 58,000,000 Looking Forward to TV's great debate." The Gallup
organization called the awaited series of "Great Debates" the "new 'X' factor"
of the campaign.[22]

Public anticipation had risen with the first news of the debate idea being
accepted by Nixon and Kennedy. In telegrams of July 28, 1960, to the two
candidates, Robert W. Sarnoff of NBC invited them to appear together on "The
Great Debate," a series of eight full hours of prime evening time on the NBC
radio and television networks. The series would be "dedicated to a dignified,
genuinely informative airing of the candidates' positions on the issues confront-
ing our country."

Kennedy accepted the invitation by telegram and said that he felt that NBC
was performing a "notable public service in giving the American people a
chance to see the candidates of the two major parties discuss the issues face-to-
face." He appointed an aide to work out "suitable arrangements."

Nixon also accepted, noting characteristically, "In general it is my position that joint television appearances of the presidential candidates should be conducted as full and free exchange of views without prepared texts or notes and without interruption." He reminded Sarnoff that similar proposals had been made by ABC and CBS and suggested that their representatives also be present so that the proposals could be "coordinated." Nixon's suggestion was followed, and the three networks quickly agreed to collaborate on the series.

Arrangements for the televised confrontations were made by the candidates' representatives and executives of the broadcasting networks in a September 1960 meeting at the Waldorf-Astoria Hotel in New York. It was agreed that there would be four debates. CBS would produce the first from Chicago, the second would be handled by NBC from Washington, and the third and fourth would be under the production control of ABC—the third to emanate from New York and Los Angeles, and the fourth from New York.

The first debate was restricted to "internal or domestic American matters"; the second was based on an agreement of the nominees to answer "questions on any issue of the campaign"; the third—presented on a split-screen basis, switching back and forth from Nixon in Los Angeles to Kennedy in New York—dealt with subjects suggested by a panel of correspondents; the fourth was confined to foreign policy issues.

At the opening session, each man made an opening statement of approximately eight minutes and a closing statement of approximately three minutes. Between these statements, the candidates were to "answer or comment upon" questions put by a panel of correspondents. Howard K. Smith moderated, and representatives of NBC News, Mutual News, CBS News, and ABC News made up the panel. For the subsequent debates, other organizations represented by newsmen were United Press International, *Newsday,* the *New York Herald Tribune,* and *The Reporter.* These other reporters were selected by lot by the candidates' press secretaries.

The programs were one hour in length, with variations on the original pattern. For example, the second debate omitted the opening statements and the closing statements and devoted the full hour to questions, answers, and comments. That format was repeated for the third debate. The last debate reverted to the format used for the first.[23]

Kennedy and Nixon prepared for the first debate in somewhat different ways.

A team of Kennedy political advisors assembled at a Chicago hotel in order to distill the vast amount of material they had gathered on the campaign issues —their "Sears Roebuck Foot Locker of Documents." After 24 hours of intensive work, they had prepared a 15-page paper subdivided into some 13 general subject areas. In their opinion, their candidate could handle most of the probable questions and have a good deal of the relevant factual material after a careful study of this paper. Kennedy had several tutorial "skull sessions," said to be in the Harvard style. At the end of his training period, Kennedy took a nap, had dinner, and ventured forth to the television studio.[24]

Nixon had spent the day of the debate, preceding his trip to the studio, resting in his hotel room; he was trying to refresh himself physically after the two weeks of campaigning that had followed a midcampaign session in the hospital. He was not available to his advisors for briefings, and he was given only about ten minutes of last-minute advice as he went to the studio by car. That advice was largely devoted to the television advisor's opinion that he should take the offensive from the start of the proceedings.[25]

General Debate Impressions: Assets

Perhaps the most significant feature of the debates was the audience impact. The communications industry estimated that approximately 75 million people watched the first debate. (Some pollsters reduced that figure by about 5 million.) It is agreed that between 51 million and 62 million persons watched the second debate. The third debate occurred before 48 million to 60 million viewers. The last drew between 48 million and 70 million. These figures do not take into account the vast audience overseas who saw excerpts of the debates and who were, perhaps, impressed by these demonstrations of democracy.[26]

As for the debates themselves, there is no question in this observer's mind that the net result advanced the level of public political education that year. Each candidate was literally forced to prepare for these sessions by honing his arguments and proposals until they were in shape to be cast side by side with those of his opponent. What the nominees said or did not say made sharp impressions on the watching electorate. As an example of the fine American tradition of political rivalry without rancor, the television debates were a definite boon.

General Debate Impressions: Problems

This observer was privileged, after each of the debates, to share a half-hour radio program over WBZ (Westinghouse, Boston) with Professor George Black-wood. We appraised the television debates and concluded that, generally, Kennedy was more at ease than his opponent. He was able to spout figures and percentages and could muster facts and opinions handily. We reported that, in our opinion, Kennedy came out on top in the first debate.

After that first debate, people who had listened on the radio and had missed the visual side of the situation reported that Nixon came over quite well. He seemed assured, cautious, and dignified. Apparently television and radio can create quite different impressions of the same event. The radio listener, one is tempted to think, concentrates almost too much on the words of a speech or a debate, while the television viewer concentrates too little on the words and too much on the appearance of the speaker. *Would Mr. Nixon have won the Presidency if the debates had been restricted to radio?*

Theodore White is properly accepted as one of the wisest observers of the 1960 campaign. He was greatly disappointed by the treatment given to *issues* in the debates. In part he blames television's tendency to demand constant action and in part he criticizes the format of the series. Here are some excerpts from *The Making of the President, 1960.*

> All TV and radio discussion programs are compelled to snap question and answer back and forth as if the contestants were adversaries in an intellectual tennis match. . . . The most thoughtful and responsive answers to any difficult question come after long pause, and . . . the longer the pause the more illuminating the thought that follows it, [but] the electronic media cannot bear to suffer a pause of more than five seconds; a pause of thirty seconds of dead time on air seems interminable. Thus, snapping their two-and-a-half-minute answers back and forth, both candidates could only react for the cameras and the people, they could not think. And, since two and a half minutes permit only a snatch of naked thought and a spatter of raw facts, both candidates, whenever caught out on a limb with a thought too heavy, . . . a thought seemingly too bold or fresh to be accepted by the conditioned American mind, hastily scurried back toward center as soon as they had enunciated the thought.
>
> . . . the TV debates did little to advance the reasonable discussion of issues that is the dream of unblooded political scientists. . . .[27]

Is there not a built-in disadvantage to the debate formats of 1960 that tied the candidates so closely to the clock? If issues are the major *raison d'être* of the debate idea, why treat major-party nominees as if they were salesmen on television commercials?

A proper debate between presidential candidates should probably be conducted with no one-hour time restriction. Of course, it is "prime time" from the network's point of view, but at stake is the most important office in the land. Should the debates be restricted, more reasonably, to *two* hours (or more), and should not the candidates' wishes be of paramount importance to those who arrange the formats? The debates of 1960 were too much concerned with formats and not enough with the nominees themselves.

For example, television has quite a tradition of question-and-answer panel shows devoted to public affairs. It is almost rude to suggest, perhaps, that panel shows are not the be-all and end-all of public affairs presentations. But the reporters were a problem as they hopped from subject to subject, forcing the candidates into positions where they were not so much debating with one another as competing with one another to give effective answers to the questions. Fewer questions, more carefully considered by their creators and less directed towards the "hot news" approach, would have been more helpful to the candidates and more constructive for the public.

Reporters do *not* have an unshakable right to take part in these debates. They are not the only representatives of the public interest available. If questions are to be asked, perhaps a more careful search for other participants should be conducted—a search for persons issue-oriented as well as news-oriented. The debates *are* news; the panelists need not feel such a frantic desire to *make* news. Release the candidates from the tension of the rapid-fire questioning, and we will be closer to a real debate situation.[28] Certainly, there was a disconcerting choice of words displayed in the news item entitled "TV Panel Chosen to Quiz Nominees" that appeared in *The New York Times* of September 23, 1960. It reported, "A high official at CBS said that despite the presence of panelists on the Show, it would be a pure debate. 'The panelists will be cross examiners, setting up questions for the candidates to discuss briefly,' he explained."[29]

Finally, there is the question of *what the political parties mean by a debate.* If it is to be a "pure debate," then it could, conceivably, be restricted to the nominees and a moderator. Without such basic agreement on politically acceptable ground rules, it is likely that the news-panel approach will persist by default. Perhaps the two candidates could make opening and closing statements and, in between, truly debate with each other. Such an affair, covered by television, could replace the situation that finds the television factor dominant, with the candidates in attendance at what is, primarily, a television meeting.

THE DEBATE OF SEPTEMBER 26, 1960

Political observers' reactions to the first debate generally followed a pattern. There was appreciation that the nominees had finally met together to argue before the public, and there was a lukewarm acceptance of the format. James Reston was disappointed, feeling that the event "was not great and . . . not a debate." He strongly opposed dealing with so considerable a variety of subjects with such quick answers. However, Reston saw several improvements over what had gone before in the campaign—the "frantic rushing about the nation, roaring at great howling mobs at airports and memorial halls." Also, in Reston's opinion:

> The immense size and importance of the audience . . . [tended] to raise the level of dialogue and discourage the use of shallow or misleading debating tricks that are so prevalent before the local audience. . . .
> It did not make or break either candidate. . . . It surely helped break the apathy and malaise in the country about the election and it showed that there is a way to inform the electorate and campaign for the Presidency without killing or exhausting both candidates in the process.[30]

Russell Baker commented that the two men "argued genteelly" and that their "exchanges were distinguished by suavity, earnestness and courtesy that suggested that the two men were more concerned about 'image projection' to their . . . television audience than about scoring debate points."[31]

The New Republic editorialized, "The Vice-President seemed throughout to be hemmed in as might any man appear who must both defend the past and insist that we have not done as well as we could and should do better." As for Kennedy, the editorial was favorably disposed, saying, "On the central point, Senator Kennedy knowingly and concisely defined the issue: the future of freedom in the world will depend in large part on how imaginatively, how energetically, this society solves its own problems. . . ."[32]

Writing in the *Manchester Guardian Weekly,* Alistair Cooke said:

> On its face it was excessively genteel, Kennedy never blanched when Nixon assured the audience that their only quarrel was over "means not goals." But Nixon was under a strain, Kennedy boxed him in and people began to wonder if after all the young Senator . . . was not as crafty and knowledgeable as Nixon.[33]

The New York Times claimed that a "nation-wide survey" noted "a general reaction that Nixon was ill."[34] On the day after the debate, that newspaper ran a story containing the view that "most of the audience made one of two basic decisions: their vote preferences remained unchanged, or they were still very much undecided."[35]

On one score, the first debate reaped a harvest for Kennedy. Ten Southern Democratic governors (Ellington, Almond, Patterson, Faubus, Vandiver, Tawes, Hodges, Hollings, Combos, and Daniel) sent him a telegram. "We the undersigned Governors . . . wish to congratulate you on your superb handling of Mr. Nixon and the issues facing our country. It is the consensus of the Governors . . . that the masterful way in which you controlled this debate further accelerates the movement to the Kennedy-Johnson and Democratic ticket."

Douglas Cater has written that, from his vantage point "backstage," he felt that the nominees were more concerned about their "images than their arguments." In his opinion, the rapid-fire situation was to the candidates' liking, as was the presence of reporters. He called both men "marvels at extemporization" who wasted no "precious media time in reflective pauses" or to "grasp for the elusive word." They could switch topics easily and could "discuss anything within the allotted two and a half minutes for reply and one and a half for rebuttal."

Kennedy was at the top of his form in the first debate. His opening statement was a plea for the country to "move ahead" more rapidly, tied with many suggestions on social and international problems. In his opening statement, Nixon was attuned to Kennedy's remarks and spent much time picking on the themes just set by his opponent in order to show how Kennedy was wrong. He defended the Eisenhower Administration's record and said he differed with the

Democratic candidate on "means"—"I think that the means that I advocate will reach the goal better than the means that he advocates."

Sander Vanocur, one of the network reporters, queried Nixon on the "experience" claim that he had been making for himself. Vanocur remarked that President Eisenhower was asked on August 24, 1960, "to give one example of a major idea of yours that he adopted. His reply was, and I am quoting, 'If you give me a week I might think of one. I don't remember.' "[36]

Nixon was thrust on the defensive, not by Kennedy, but by a reporter, who was throwing a lighted firecracker rather than asking an issue-oriented question. In a debate between two presidential candidates, when so much is at stake, the debating points should be made by the nominees and not by the newsmen. If reporters are diligent, they can uncover all sorts of incendiary material to heave forth! Nixon could not properly handle the real issue—experience—because he had to dodge the razor-sharp covering put around the issue by Vanocur.

There is no doubt that the first session was most interesting. The questions and answers were usually bright, if sometimes superficial when read in cold print later. But the reporters were far too intrusive.

Each of the nominees presented much material, and each had his style. Nixon seemingly tried to debate more than Kennedy did. In any case, the word "debate" was stretched that night on several counts. As *debaters,* the candidates would have done better alone.

THE DEBATE OF OCTOBER 7, 1960: REACTIONS

In the opinion of Arthur Krock, the second meeting was better than the first. He called it the first "real 'debate.' " Nixon appeared more aggressive and the candidates, wrote Krock, "differed vigorously." He objected to the panel format "which prevents the debate from developing the incisiveness that appears only when the principals ask the questions of each other and can press them home."[37]

Reston found the second debate "more informative, more aggressive and more personal." Also, "this performance helped clarify the essential difference between the two candidates. . . . Nixon . . . concentrated on what was right with present policies, while . . . Kennedy emphasized what was wrong." Reston did not agree with much that Nixon said—he felt it was "definitely not supported by most well-informed observers"—but he thought that the Vice-President scored the most debate points.

Fulton Lewis, Jr., who is not an easy commentator to please, was satisfied that "the performance generally was greatly improved over the first one, particularly the presence and manner of Mr. Nixon. In behavior and poise the two played to an even draw," he thought.[38]

The debates were more polite than the campaigning that took place before and after the sessions. On October 10, 1960, *Life* commented, "The final drive for election opened politely when Kennedy and Nixon tested the new techniques of TV debate. Then, on the road again, they began striking more sharply."[39]

This observer feels that the second debate was more revealing of the true qualities of the men than was the first. Nixon was physically fit for the second, and the exchanges were sometimes sharp. Nixon denied Kennedy's claim that Cuba was "lost"; Kennedy had to take pains to defend a statement that he had made the previous May on the U-2 affair; Nixon struck out at his opponent's charge that the U.S. had lost international prestige; Kennedy hit at Nixon's views about the image of this nation overseas; Kennedy asked for the citizenry to choose moving ahead faster than the Eisenhower Administration had; Nixon said that Kennedy offered "retreads of programs that failed." There was quite a brawl over the defense of Quemoy and Matsu. Kennedy declared he would draw a defense line around Formosa and avoid the risk of "being dragged into war which may lead to a world war over two islands which are not strategically defensible." Nixon snorted in reply, "These two islands are in the area of freedom," and later accused his adversary of "the same kind of woolly thinking that led to disaster for America in Korea."[40]

After the red lights on the television cameras went off, Nixon commented to newsmen, "I thought we had a good exchange." He added, "The difficulty is that two and a half minutes is not enough to discuss the issue. I had some loose ends to tie up, and I'm sure Senator Kennedy did too. I thought there was more clash in this."[41]

"Neither man," noted Russell Baker, "smiled at any time during the hour long show."[42]

THE DEBATE OF OCTOBER 13, 1960: REACTIONS

Some critics, this observer included, could put up a good argument to support the proposition that debaters should be together—in the same place—when they debate. Granted that television technique has advanced to the point where "split-screen" and other electronic means dissolve actual distances! Nevertheless, an intangible something is lost when a look into the opponent's face travels over thousands of miles of cable, as was the case when Nixon and Kennedy were a continent apart, physically, on October 13, 1960.

Would it be fair if one candidate were treated to air conditioning that made him more comfortable than the other? Lighting is never exactly the same; it only seems to be. Camera crews are never coordinated in their movements when separated. One director or producer may say or do something that affects his situation and that does not affect the situation at the other end of the cable. The atmosphere is different under these conditions even if the "sets" are the same.

Among the "small disagreements" of the second debate were differences of opinion about lighting and temperature. "Democrats were the complainers in both instances, contending that steps taken to improve Mr. Nixon's television appearance were unfair to Senator Kennedy." The temperature was raised from 64 degrees to 70 degrees, and the lights were changed.[43]

Media executives may balk at these remarks and argue that, even when the candidates are in the same place for a debate, proximity does not erase the problems faced by television producers. ABC, for the fourth debate, went to great lengths to try to assure equality of treatment for both men. Two identical cottages were constructed in their New York studio. "Decoration and painting were carried out completely. The interior shows even the pictures on the walls were original; the fact that the pictures were not identical was commented on by several reporters during a preview."[44] Perhaps the reporters worried about the artistic impact of the paintings on the debates! Think of the possible effects of two paintings displayed prominently before the contenders' eyes just prior to a debate. What impact would a Jackson Pollock have compared with a Franz Hals? What if a Dali, with dangling and limp timepieces, was seen by one nominee and not the other?

Such fine points aside, the candidates should, on debate nights, share a near-identical experience from the time they enter the precincts of the same studio. Future presidential debates should be strictly on an "in person" basis. The men not only react to each other's ideas; they also react to each other!

The third debate started out with a continuation of the argument over Quemoy and Matsu. Nixon answered the first question, which was about whether Kennedy had, the day before, termed the Vice-President's position "trigger happy." Nixon was quite resentful and said so in no uncertain terms— for example, "I would remind Senator Kennedy of the last fifty years. I would ask him to name one Republican President who led this nation into war."

Later on, after further Nixon comments about the two islands and the Korean War, Kennedy sniped, "I do not think it's possible for Mr. Nixon to state the record in distortion of the facts with more precision than he just did."

An interesting sidelight of the third debate dealt with former President Truman and Nixon's comments about the Presidency. One of the reporters (Von Fremd) asked whether Kennedy should not apologize for some "strong charges" made by Truman, "who bluntly suggested where the Vice-President and the Republican party could go."

Kennedy replied that Truman had his own style and that, since the former President was 76 years old, Kennedy did not think that he could cause Truman "to change his particular speaking manner."

Nixon then seized this opening to wax eloquent on the subject of the Presidency.

> . . . when a man's President of the United States, or a former President, he has an obligation not to lose his temper in public. One thing I've noted as I've traveled around the country is the tremendous number of children who come out to see the Presidential candidates. I see mothers holding their babies up, so that they can see a man who

might be President of the United States. I know Senator Kennedy sees them, too. It makes you realize that whoever is President is going to be a man that all the children of America will either look up to, or will look down to. And I can only say that I'm very proud that President Eisenhower restored dignity and decency and, frankly, good language to the conduct of the Presidency of the United States. And I only hope that, should I win this election, that I could approach President Eisenhower in maintaining the dignity of the office; in seeing to it that whenever any mother or father talks to his child, he can look at the man in the White House and, whatever he may think of his policies, he will say: "Well, there is a man who maintains the kind of standards personally that I would want my child to follow.[45]

Those homilies were approved of by many viewers and caused others to cry out in deprecation of Nixon's approach. James A. Michener, the novelist who was in 1960 Bucks County (Pennsylvania) Citizens for Kennedy chairman, wrote that the Nixon remarks advanced "the father image in place of the political leader."[46]

Summarizing his impressions of the third debate, James Reston characterized the Nixon presentations as "general and often emotional." Kennedy, he thought, "Seldom generalized, plunging into his answers with factual illustrations, and made no appeal to emotions." He concluded that Kennedy, after the third debate, was not necessarily the "underdog" contending against "the champ."[47]

The New York Times stated on October 15, 1960, that a poll taken by its correspondents of some 325 voters in 24 cities gave a "slight edge to Nixon in Thursday's debate." Those same reporters had found the second debate "a draw" and the first debate a "victory . . . for Senator John F. Kennedy. . . ."[48]

Clashes between the two men during the third debate covered a broad range of subjects, including labor, civil rights, the U-2 incident, inflation, balance of trade, national prestige, the space race, and national economic growth.

The next day, Nixon declared that he was shocked that Kennedy had brought "notes" to use during the debate. He called their use a violation of the ground rules agreed on before the series began. Speaking for the Kennedy camp, Pierre Salinger replied that he knew of no agreement "on notes—or on television makeup."[49]

On the whole, the third debate gave the voter a good display of the two men. With the exceptions already taken to format, it revealed much of interest and importance about them as personalities.

THE DEBATE OF OCTOBER 21, 1960: REACTIONS

For the last debate of the series, the discussion was limited to foreign policy and was, despite one or two sharp exchanges, a relatively tame affair. Nixon opened with about eight minutes on the United States' situation in the world and what the Eisenhower Administration had accomplished. Kennedy followed, again picking up a thread of Nixon's remarks on Quemoy and Matsu. His opening statement was also pitched to a wide angle on foreign affairs. Both men repeated themes heard during the earlier debates.

In his closing statement of about four minutes, Kennedy said,

> I believe it my responsibility as the leader of the Democratic Party in 1960 to try to warn the American people that, in this crucial time, we can no longer afford to stand still. We can no longer afford to be second best. I want people all over the world to look to the United States again, to feel that we are on the move, to feel that our high noon is in the future.

Nixon said, in his closing statement,

> . . . in the years to come it will be written that one or the other of us was elected and that he was or was not a great President. What will determine whether Senator Kennedy or I, if I am elected, was a great President? It will not be our ambition that will determine it, because greatness is not something that is written on a campaign poster. It will be determined to the extent that we represent the deepest ideals, the highest feelings and faith of the American people."[50]

Writing before the debates, on August 6, 1960, Eric Sevareid had commented about the future debaters.

> Many of us remain uneasy about them because neither one has acquired a true identity; their faces and voices are familiar but their meaning as men escapes us. . . .
> . . . the washable, wrinkle-proof Brooks Brothers garb of these new and skilled practitioners of the Leadership Business—what is it made of?
> How much is real, how much synthetic?
> Where are the deeds, where the inspiring ideas or rebellious words?[51]

It is probable that Mr. Sevareid was more satisfied after the debates than he was before. Certainly the debates gave an identity to each of the nominees.

The Kennedy camp seems to have become more and more satisfied with the debates as they progressed. On October 11, before the third debate, Kennedy expressed the hope that Nixon would agree to a fifth encounter. Before the last meeting, he announced his willingness to debate for a two-hour period. Nixon said that he could not accommodate a fifth debate because of his crowded campaign schedule.

Frankly, four debates in 1960 were enough. By the last session, each man was forced to spend a good deal of time repeating himself. Facing each other at different ranges (20 feet for the first two debates; 3000 miles for the third; 6 feet for the last), they reloaded some of the original ammunition from time to time.[52]

APPRAISALS OF THE DEBATES

Critics generally considered the four debates, taken as a series, constructive in their over-all impact on the citizenry. Even Max Ascoli, the editor of *The Reporter* magazine, who saw a great many shortcomings in the series, said, "It has been the greatest experiment in direct democracy ever attempted in this country."[53]

Philip M. Stern wrote in *The New Republic,* "The unique provision of the debaters was the opportunity for the voters to get 'the feel' of the two men. . . . Those who viewed . . . were treated to an unusually candid and accurate portrait . . . [of] the two standing on their own feet, without benefit of ghost-written script. . . ."[54]

Also writing for the same magazine, Saul E. Halpert was more impressed with limitations than assets, citing "a preoccupation with trivia, a slighting of matters for manner," and a "predilection for how the debates *look* as a 'show' rather than for full elucidation of the candidates' views. . . ." But he ended his critical article by saying, "Never before has such a large percentage of the American community been assembled for a public discussion of the great issues of the day. Why not do it more often—and in the 200-odd weeks between Presidential elections?[55]

Alan Harrington saw the debates as "the first great, nationwide personnel interview in history." He reasoned, "In dual loneliness, Kennedy and Nixon have to deal with us."

> Until this year, most of the electorate has had to judge the Presidential candidates' fitness by hearsay, press reports, the sound of a radio voice, or their TV appearance *under controlled circumstances.* A political speech made before an admiring audience that will surely applaud the candidate, or a cozy chat issuing from his library, has never given us an approximation of the whole man. Now, thanks to the Kennedy-Nixon TV confrontations, we are appreciably closer to the valid, intuitive "take," the wholly human—even though sometimes mistaken—feeling we have about someone whom we are going to accept or reject for a job.[56]

The presidential debates of 1960 were far better than we had any right to expect in view of the fact that they constituted a television "first." In this observer's opinion, the campaign was more significant to the voters than it would have been without the debates.

By and large, the debates elevated the level of campaign oratory that year. The four sessions added appreciably to the attainment of the democratic ideals of honest argument and considered balloting. This nation has experienced far less salutory Presidential campaigns in its history than that of 1960. To an important extent, the debates were most helpful in securing and maintaining the political atmosphere that existed for Nixon, for Kennedy, and for the rest of us.

ANTICLIMACTIC TELETHON

On the Monday preceding election day of 1960, Richard Nixon attempted to enhance his chances by a four-hour "telethon" on the ABC network. One senses strongly that he felt the need for a comeback after the debates with Kennedy.

Nixon opened the program by reminding the audience that "for the first time in the history of American politics, the American people . . . [can] question a candidate for the Presidency; and consequently we have scheduled four hours of telethon today." He went on, "I understand that they [the announcers] will indicate to you where you can call and how you can get your questions in to our moderators, so they will be asked of me during the course of the program."

That telethon, emanating from the ABC affiliate in Southfield, Michigan, displayed a Nixon better able to provide well-rounded answers than was sometimes evident in the famous debates with Kennedy. Aided by the presence of Henry Cabot Lodge, his running mate, Nixon was more at ease than he had been during the debates. He dealt skillfully with extremely difficult questions pertaining to the United Nations and the problem of Red China; the American policy on purchase of Cuban sugar; his attitude on big government; the prestige of the United States; his ideas on how to avoid an economic depression; Social Security; the Tennessee Valley Authority; Fidel Castro; Negro sit-in demonstrations; and federal aid to education. When asked why Kennedy had refused to buy television time for a similar telethon, he said, in reply to Mr. and Mrs. Earl V. Fisher of Monroe, Louisiana, "I don't know what was in his mind for not buying the telethon time, but I would only suggest that this is the first time I ever heard that Senator Kennedy didn't have the money to get what he wanted. I would suggest that's not the real reason."

When responding to Mr. Eugene Jerkowitz of Melvindale, Michigan, who asked how Nixon could find time for a four-hour telethon when he could not find time for a fifth debate with Senator Kennedy, Nixon gave his evaluation of the decision-making situation in the Kennedy camp. He described a "comedy of errors."

> I had set aside the day, Monday the 31st; had no schedule whatever for that day. That was the day we were talking about for a fifth debate. I had assumed that we were going to have one.
> I also had suggested, and the networks had agreed, that the public wanted to see the vice-presidential candidates on the debate as well. Well, for some reason Senator Kennedy's representatives, and apparently he himself, were very reluctant to have Senator Johnson with them on the program. They indicated finally that they might be willing to have him but the moment then that we started to move to the final

METHODIST COLLEGE LIBRARY
Fayetteville, N. C.

*3*8087

conclusion to have the debate on Monday, they started a calculated program to break up the negotiations and they succeeded. They didn't want to be on the program.[57]

Nixon's telethon worried the Kennedy group. They could not estimate its last-minute effects. So a final, election-eve telecast was arranged from Manchester, New Hampshire, featuring the Senator, his sisters, and Governor Hodges.[58]

Nixon's last-hour effort to overcome the possible effects of one dramatic form of television-era campaigning did not appear to appreciably alter the tally boards on election night.

SIDELIGHTS

Both Nixon and Kennedy had reason to reflect on the varied roles television had played in the campaign. Certainly the medium had achieved senior-partner status with the other major influences on the electorate.

In addition to the televised meetings, rallies, debates, and appearances across the nation, there were also a host of television programs that explained what was going on. Taken together, these programs formed a guideline for the majority of Americans, who could not or would not keep constant campaign vigil. These programs enabled the citizenry to monitor the developing story. Television's role of analyzing and displaying current history should not be underestimated.

The industry responds to the public's need to know by preparing many and varied analyses of major political battles. In presidential election years it seems to do its best and most comprehensive work, serving as a public diary.

In 1960, the three major networks all presented programs that tried to "get behind" the news. Sometimes the candidates winced at these presentations, which displayed the critical and often independent efforts of sharp and worldly reporters. Highlighting such programs were sessions of *Meet the Press* (CBS) and *The Campaign and the Candidates* (NBC). Also, special reports were frequently prepared that gave background to vital issues and touchy subjects. Examples included *CBS Reports,* "Money and the Next President of the United States," and *Eyewitness to History,* "The Contest for a Key State" (CBS).

Attempting to rest and to enjoy the warmth of their families after they went to the polling booths to vote for themselves, Kennedy and Nixon could only assume that to the victor went a modern spoil of politics—even more intensive television coverage. The President-Elect would have time for only a short look back at the adventure of the campaign. Soon he would be in full focus again.

THE 1960 EXPERIENCE: RAMIFICATIONS

On June 19, 1963, by a vote of 263 to 126, the House of Representatives suspended the equal-time provision of the Communications Act, Section 315, for the 1964 election campaign. That suspension, which was later bottled up in the Senate in 1964, covered "the 75 day period immediately preceding November 3."[59] Had that bill or a similar compromise version been enacted by the Senate, it would have been legally possible to arrange a second series of debates between the Republican and Democratic presidential nominees. Also, it is probable that the vice-presidential candidates of the two major American parties would have been given the opportunity to debate, either separately or in conjunction with the aspirants to the Presidency.

Presidential debates in 1964 had appeared likely in light of the powerful arguments brought to the attention of the members of the Communications Subcommittee of the Senate's Committee on Commerce by representatives of the broadcasting industry and others;[60] the announced decision of John F. Kennedy that, if he were the Democratic Party candidate in 1964, he would debate his opponent; the public's anticipation that the experience of 1960 would be repeated, one way or another; the political fact that, if President Kennedy subjected himself to debates, his rival would deny himself and his party a tremendous opportunity by refusing to debate; and the widespread acceptance of the 1960 debates as a generally constructive political influence. But in the radically altered situation following Kennedy's assassination, the Senate did not approve the measure that would have allowed similar debates in 1964.

One difference between the debates of 1960 and those proposed for 1964 was that some attention was given, after 1960, to planning in advance. In 1960, proposals and events pressed so closely together that it is fortunate that the affairs went as well as they did.

Students of the 1960 episodes, in thinking about similar and future debates, have more than technical problems to consider. There are certain social and political questions that require satisfactory answers. Two key issues follow.

Minority-Interest Protection

First, there are the rights of the minority parties. Despite the positive value of the debate pattern that was established in 1960, the suspension of the equal-time provision that year did not enhance the position of minority parties. The public interest requires that some means be devised to give these parties proper access to radio and television audiences on a free-time basis. If only the major parties are granted free time by the individual stations and by the networks, then the money problem of politics, already burdensome, will become almost unbearable for some minority organizations.

Perhaps a solution could be worked out based upon privileges proportionate to votes received in the previous general election. For example, if a party received 10 to 15 per cent of the popular vote, it would be allowed a standard amount of time on radio and television. Again, and only to illustrate, if a party received 25 per cent of the popular vote, it might be granted 50 per cent of the time given to the major parties. If a party received more than 30 per cent of the popular vote, it would be considered a major party entitled to equal time with the Democrats and Republicans.

However, such schemes, no matter how skillfully drawn, do not serve all needs. What of the parties that did not exist at the time of the previous general election? One thinks of Theodore Roosevelt's Progressive or "Bull Moose" Party in 1912 and of the Wallace Progressives and the Thurmond Dixiecrats of 1948. If we privilege the major parties without redressing the grievances of the minor parties, we may not only make the situation very difficult for established minor parties, but make it impossible for new groups that represent recent manifestations of public opinion. At a time of national stress, the presence of a responsible third party could affect the outcome of an election if that party's nominees were allowed ample opportunity to reach the public on radio and television.

The theory of democracy does not merely *tolerate* minority opinions, it *encourages* such opinions. A positive minority of one person may offer society better answers to public questions than all the rest of citizenry put together. The practice of democracy requires us to adhere as closely as possible to theory in this respect.

Arguing against changing the equal-time rule, the American Civil Liberties Union wrote in a letter to the members of the House of Representatives, "We are unequivocally opposed to [changing Section 315] because its effect will be to deny a hearing on the air to any minority parties which have legally qualified candidates for the Presidency and Vice-Presidency."[61] In the statement of the ACLU to the Communications Subcommittee of the Senate, Mr. Lawrence Speiser urged it to

> . . . protect the peoples' right to hear, at election time, all shades of political views, and so to enable them to decide what candidate they wish to vote for. We realize that the drive for repeal or suspension of Section 315 makes much of the argument that if such action is taken the public will receive more opinion and information from the two major parties. This might be true, but we suggest that the first amendment was written not only to allow the speech of a favored few but to preserve the right of free speech for all—and the concomitant right of the public to hear all views.

Leonard H. Goldenson, president of the American Broadcasting Company, gave his support to the suspension of Section 315 for 1964, but he restricted his support to presidential and vice-presidential candidates. His opinion was that, below the national level, "there remain substantial considerations and problems which require . . . further study by the Congress before any changes are made."[62]

There is no doubt whatever that the benefits to the public of the Kennedy-Nixon debates have impressed a great many political observers. It is to be hoped that the equally important benefits that society gains from minority-group voices will not be reduced to a trickle by denying these groups access to adequate time on the electronic media.

The Role of the President

Although John F. Kennedy accepted the idea of participation in possible 1964 presidential debates, the role of a President of the United States must be studied more carefully than it has been in this respect. In 1960, both nominees were comparatively free to debate, leaving the nation in the hands of Eisenhower, then its Chief Executive.

The President can debate, but there are difficulties for him and for his opponent. (1) The President cannot allow himself to be drawn into any argument that requires his thoughts on delicate matters involving national security secrets. (2) He may not, in good conscience, debate or easily decry the policies of a nation with whom we are allied. (3) The President, if too successful as a partisan spokesman, may lose effectiveness as the nation's leader. (4) If a crisis faces the nation at the time of debates, the Presidential arguments will carry undue weight, one way or another, with the electorate. (5) If a crisis develops in the course of the debates, the President would literally have the ability to divest the opposition candidate of his role as an equal in a man-to-man confrontation. The opponent would be reduced to words, while the President, for good or for ill, would be seen as a man of action. The election could be over before the electorate was prepared to weigh arguments rationally, without preoccupation with events. (6) The President, as Chief Executive, would command press attention above and beyond that commanded by his rival. He might even take to the air waves during the campaign as President and not as candidate. In all of these respects, his role as President might well conflict with his role as candidate.

Therefore, one concludes that, while the President can debate, the environment must be calm if the challenger is not to be overshadowed by the man in office. All of the possibilities discussed are based on the assumption that neither major-party nominee would be diverted from the highest standards of political ethics for partisan gain. Even with that assumption, there are problems.

The New Republic pondered the problem editorially on November 7, 1960.

> Are a Chief Magistrate and the policies, the secrets, and the prestige of his regime to be made targets of direct, unrehearsed partisan interpellation—perhaps at a dangerous moment of world affairs? Can a President in office afford to gamble on losing ascendancy in a sharp debate within sight of tens of millions? Can the questioners be expected to press a President as relentlessly as they do his opponent? Is a President to be held to a rigid time limit in answering questions involving the heart of national policies? Can the dignity of the office be upheld without conditions unacceptably disadvantageous to the challenger?[63]

66

FOOTNOTES

1. Clinton Rossiter, "The Right Man for the Right Job," *New York Times,* April 3, 1960.

2. "Text of Senator Kennedy's Speech on Presidency at National Press Club Luncheon," *New York Times,* January 15, 1960.

3. Richard M. Nixon, *Six Crises* (New York: Pocket Books, Inc., 1962), p. 389.

4. *Ibid.,* p. 321.

5. Robert K. Carr, Marver H. Bernstein, Donald H. Morrison, and Joseph E. McLean, *American Democracy in Theory and Practice* (New York: Rinehart & Company, 1957), p. 294.

6. Richard M. Nixon, "I Was a Fighter with One Hand Tied," *Life,* Vol. 52, No. 13 (March 30, 1962), p. 72.

7. Richard M. Nixon, *Six Crises,* p. 274.

8. "Nixon Tells how to Win TV Friends," *New York Times,* September 15, 1955.

9. Editorial, "The Nixon Sell," *The Nation,* Vol. 191, No. 5 (August 20, 1960).

10. Russell Baker, "Campaign: Candidates—Nixon's Strategy: Republican Cuts Emphasis on Foreign Affairs," *New York Times,* September 18, 1960.

11. Tom Wicker, "Turning Points for a Man in the Running," *New York Times,* April 1, 1962.

12. "Transcript of Nixon's Statement on His Defeat by Brown in Race for the Governorship of California," *New York Times,* November 8, 1962.

13. Richard H. Rovere, "Measuring the Presidential Candidates," *Harper's Magazine,* Vol. 220, No. 1321 (June 1960), p. 83. See also Meg Greenfield, "The Prose of Richard M. Nixon," *The Reporter,* Vol. 23, No. 5 (September 29, 1960), pp. 15–20; Stewart Alsop, *Nixon and Rockefeller* (Garden City, N.Y.: Doubleday & Company, Inc., 1960), pp. 57–76.

14. Douglas Cater, "The Cool Eye of John F. Kennedy," *The Reporter,* Vol. 21, No. 10 (December 10, 1959), p. 27.

15. *Ibid.,* p. 27.

16. Cabell Phillips, "How to Be a Presidential Candidate," *New York Times Magazine,* July 13, 1958, p. 11.

17. W. H. Lawrence, "Kennedy Calls for Leadership," *New York Times,* September 18, 1960.

18. Richard H. Rovere, "Measuring the Presidential Candidates," p. 83.

19. "Campaign Issues in the Words of the Two Candidates," *New York Times,* October 2, 1960.

20. *U.S. News and World Report,* Vol. 47, No. 24 (June 13, 1960).

21. Richard M. Nixon, *Six Crises,* p. 350. For other material on the issues, see Paul H. Nitze, "The Key Issue: 'We Must Debate It,'" *New York Times,* June 5, 1960; Courtney Sheldon, "Parties, Positions and People," *Christian Science Monitor,* September 21, 1960; Rowland Evans, Jr., "Kennedy, In Talk, Writes a Platform," *New York Herald Tribune,* June 15, 1960.

22. George Gallup, " 'X' Factor in '60 Race—Record 58,000,000 Looking Forward to TV's Great Debate," American Institute of Public Opinion (Princeton, New Jersey), September 17, 1960.

23. For text of the debates and other pertinent information, see Subcommittee of the Subcommittee on Communications, Committee on Commerce, U.S. Senate, *Free-*

dom of Communications, Final Report, Part III (Washington: U.S. Government Printing Office, 1961).

24. Theodore H. White, *The Making of the President, 1960* (New York: Atheneum Publishers, 1961), pp. 283–285.

25. *Ibid.,* pp. 285–286.

26. Earl Mazo, "The Great Debates," in *The Great Debates* (New York: Fund for the Republic, 1962), p. 4.

27. Theodore H. White, *The Making of the President, 1960,* pp. 291–293.

28. "Goodby, Great Debate," *The New Republic,* Vol. 143, No. 14, (September 26, 1960), p. 5; also Richard H. Rovere, "Letter from Chicago," *The New Yorker,* Vol. 36, No. 34 (October 8, 1960), pp. 167–174.

29. "TV Panel Chosen to Quiz Nominees," *New York Times,* September 23, 1960.

30. James Reston, "Kennedy on First by a Fielder's Choice," *New York Times,* September 28, 1960.

31. Russell Baker, "Kennedy and Nixon Clash in TV Debate on Spending, Farms and Social Issues," *New York Times,* September 27, 1960.

32. Editorial, "The First TV Debate," *The New Republic,* Vol. 143, No. 15, (October 3, 1960), p. 6.

33. Alistair Cooke, "The Campaign in Retrospect," *Manchester Guardian Weekly,* Vol. 83, No. 19 (November 10, 1960), p. 5.

34 "TV Debate Switched Few Votes, Nation-Wide Survey Shows," *New York Times,* September 28, 1960.

35. "Debate Audience Yields Wide Range of Reaction," *New York Times,* September 27, 1960.

36. Douglas Cater, "Notes from Backstage," in Sidney Kraus, editor, *The Great Debates* (Bloomington, Ind.: Indiana University Press, 1962), p. 129.

37. Arthur Krock, "The Polite Debate," *New York Times,* October 9, 1960.

38. James Reston, "Vice President Apparently Came Out Ahead in a More Informative Show," *New York Times,* October 8, 1960. For opinions of Fulton Lewis, Jr., see Subcommittee on Communications, Committee on Commerce, U.S. Senate, *Final Report,* Part IV, p. 413.

39. "Two Brooding Men in a Dazzling Duel," *Life,* Vol. 49, No. 15 (October 10, 1960), p. 27.

40. Sidney Kraus, editor, *The Great Debates.* See texts of the debates in this volume.

41. "Debate No. 2," *Time,* Vol. 76, No. 16 (October 17, 1960), p. 23.

42. Russell Baker, "Nixon and Kennedy Clash on TV over Issue of Quemoy's Defense; U-2 'Regrets' and 'Rights' Argued," *New York Times,* October 8, 1960.

43. W. H. Lawrence, "Kennedy Protests Lighting and Cold and Wins on Both," *New York Times,* October 8, 1960.

44. Sidney Kraus, ed., *The Great Debates,* p. 99.

45. Ibid., p. 397.

46. James A. Michener, *Report of the County Chairman* (New York: Bantam Books, 1961), p. 143.

47. James Reston, "The Third Debate," *New York Times,* October 14, 1960.

48. "Survey of TV Viewers Calls the Debate a Draw, Few Voters Said to Find Cause to Shift Votes," *New York Times,* October 15, 1960.

49. W. H. Lawrence, "Nixon is Shocked by Kennedy Notes," *New York Times,* October 14, 1960.

50. Sidney Kraus, ed., *The Great Debates,* pp. 427–430. For observations about the fourth debate, see James Reston, "The Fourth Debate," *New York Times,* October 22, 1960.

51. Eric Sevareid, "Are They Men of Measured Tears?" *Boston Globe,* August 6, 1960.

52. "Fifth Debate Still Up in Air," *Broadcasting,* October 24, 1960.

53. Max Ascoli, "Intermezzo," *The Reporter,* Vol. 23, No. 8 (November 10, 1960), p. 18.

54. Philip M. Stern, "The Debates in Retrospect," *The New Republic,* Vol. 143, No. 22, (November 21, 1960), p. 18.

55. Saul E. Halpert, "A Can of Paint for Two," *The New Republic,* Vol. 143, No. 19, (October 31, 1960), p. 30.

56. Alan Harrington, "Asking for a Job," *The Nation,* Vol. 191, No. 15 (November 5, 1960), p. 342. For other aspects of the debates, see "What Happens after Jan. 20?" *Broadcasting,* Vol. 59, No. 20 (November 14, 1960), pp. 29–31. See also Robert Lewis Shayon, "Pavlov and Politics," *Saturday Review,* Vol. 43, No. 4 (January 23, 1960), p. 28; Richard S. Salant, "The Television Debates: A Revolution That Deserves a Future," and Stanley Kelley, Jr., "Campaign Debates: Some Facts and Issues," *Public Opinion Quarterly,* Vol. 26, No. 3 (Fall 1962), pp. 335–350 and pp. 351–366, respectively.

57. "Remarks of Vice-President Richard M. Nixon, National Telethon, ABC Network, Southfield, Michigan, November 7, 1960," *The Speeches of Vice President Richard M. Nixon, Presidential Campaign of 1960,* Subcommittee on Communications, Committee on Commerce, U.S. Senate (Washington: U.S. Government Printing Office, 1961), pp. 1082–1116.

58. Jacques Lowe, *Portrait, the Emergence of John F. Kennedy* (New York: Bramhall House, 1961), p. 175.

59. C. P. Trussell, "House Would Lift Equal Time in '64," *New York Times,* June 20, 1963.

60. Communications Subcommittee, Committee on Commerce, U.S. Senate, Hearings July 10–12, 1962, *Political Broadcasting* (Washington: U.S. Government Printing Office, 1962).

61. "Squabble Over 'Equal Time' To Be Resolved, Temporarily," *National Observer,* July 8, 1963.

62. Communications Subcommittee, *Political Broadcasting,* pp. 225–226, 128–130; doubts of Senator Jacob K. Javits, pp. 15–24; Norman Thomas, "Great Challenge of the Dissenter," *New York Times Magazine,* November 15, 1959; "New Perils in Airing Politics," *Broadcasting,* Vol. 58, No. 19 (May 9, 1960).

63. "TV Debates in '64," *The New Republic,* Vol. 143, No. 20, (November 7, 1960), p. 6. See also Frank Stanton, "How TV Won the Battle—How It Hopes to Win the War," *Television,* Vol. 18, No. 1 (January 1961), pp. 67–85; Morris J. Gelman, "TV and Politics: '62," *Television,* Vol. 19, No. 10 (October 1962), pp. 64–67, 82–87; Charles A. H. Thomson, "Mass Media Activities and Influence," in *The Presidential Election and Transition 1960–1961* (Washington: The Brookings Institution, 1961), esp. pp. 111–115.

4 / Television and the
New Frontier

ECLIPSE

A cruel fate set the stage for the premature opening of the 1964 presidential campaign. The assassin's bullets that tore into the body of John Fitzgerald Kennedy stripped the nation of its leader and the world of one of the most imposing personalities of the time.

The New York Times of November 22, 1963, carried much about the youthful Chief Executive and about his Administration. At Houston, the opening stop of a two-day Texas tour designed to advocate governmental policies and to mend political fences, he gave his pledge that the space program, one of his "new frontiers," would move steadily ahead. In view of the volatile passions that worked to factionalize the state's Democratic Party, a major Presidential effort was aimed at soothing several of the more difficult situations.

Prior to Kennedy's landing at San Antonio's International Airport, reportorial attention was diverted to the feuding between Ralph Yarborough, the senior U.S. Senator, and Texas Governor John B. Connally. Miffed at being bypassed as the invitations went out for a scheduled reception to be given by the Governor for the President and the First Lady, the Senator displayed the bitterness of the rivalry. Yarborough asked his friends not to take offense. "I want everyone to join hands in harmony for the greatest welcome to the President and Mrs. Kennedy in the history of Texas. Besides, Governor Connally is so terribly under educated governmentally, how could you expect anything else?"[1]

Another *Times* article dealt with the presentation to be made the following month to Dr. J. Robert Oppenheimer at a White House ceremony. Kennedy planned to help restore the good public image of the controversial physicist by honoring him with the Enrico Fermi award. Further news items stressed Administration difficulties with French President Charles de Gaulle; the attempt made by Kennedy and his advisors to urge that Congress pass an unemasculated foreign aid authorization; a declaration brought to the United Nations by the United States and the Soviet Union on the peaceful uses of space; and a proposal by Dr. Frank Stanton, president of the Columbia Broadcasting System, that an early start be made in arranging for television debates between the major parties' presidential nominees in 1964. Stanton proposed to the Democratic and Republican national chairmen format revisions that would give the candidates the final option as to the type and number of their joint appearances. The candidates themselves would decide whether the 1960 experience would be repeated.[2] Kennedy, of course, was already on record as being willing to debate his opponent.

While the President was traveling in Texas, opposition hopefuls were also mending fences. On November 21, Governor Rockefeller met with Governor Scranton in New York City in order to sound out the Pennsylvania leader about the possible leanings of the 64 Pennsylvania delegates who would go to the 1964 Republican national convention. The two men did not even imagine that their rather preliminary skirmishing for position occurred but hours from a completely changed political situation.

They could not foresee that all Democrats and Republicans were soon to join in grief at a national tragedy. Nor could they have been mindful that very shortly they, and all responsible politicians, would have to plod ahead into the political darkness, even though all open and public campaigning would be suspended. The day after their meeting, personal and partisan ambitions would have to be subdued in order to give support to a new President—a man thrust ahead by fate.

For the working press covering the White House beat, Kennedy's Texas tour was just another trip by an adventurous and untiring man who always made good news copy and provided the feature material that was grist for the radio, television, newspaper, and magazine mills.

To be sure, there was added news value to the President's traveling in Texas so soon after Adlai Stevenson had been jostled and maligned by extremists there, but newsmen had more than once reported minor incidents connected with the safety problem of the man in the White House!

Before we consider the impact of those historic rifle shots in Dallas, let us go back and set the scene by describing the Kennedy who existed before man and myth were merged by history. For students of the political campaign of 1964, the story of the Kennedy years at 1600 Pennsylvania Avenue is indispensable, because the character of the 1964 race was in large measure determined by his legacy.

THE VICTOR

On election-day morning of 1960, John and Jacqueline Kennedy were in Boston. A little before 9 A.M., the couple voted at the West End Branch Library. With civic duty attended to, they flew to the family compound of homes at Hyannis, Massachusetts, on Cape Cod.

As soon as the first meaningful returns began to pour in from the nation's voting precincts that evening, the Kennedy clan joined millions of other avid viewers who watched television's tally boards.

A fascinating photograph, taken that night by Jacques Lowe, shows an anxious John Kennedy seated before a television set. Behind him stand Ethel and Robert Kennedy; Pierre Salinger hangs on the back of a couch staring at the television screen, and campaign workers crouch, lounge, and stand near JFK.[3] They are caught tensely watching as Richard Nixon enters the ballroom of the Ambassador Hotel in Los Angeles, his campaign headquarters. Into Robert Kennedy's Cape Cod home comes the image of the opponent and the shouts of his loyal but disturbed supporters—"We want Nixon!" and "You're still the best man!" Then Nixon speaks. It is 3:30 A.M. "I am sure that many are listening here who are supporting Mr.—Senator Kennedy. I know too that he probably is listening to this program."

"And while the—and I—please, please, just a minute—and I—as I look at the board here: while there are still some results still to come in—if the present trend continues, Mr.—Senator Kennedy will be the next President of the United States."

It was not until 12:33 the next afternoon, when the results from Minnesota clinched JFK's victory, that Nixon sent a telegram of concession. "I want to repeat through this wire the congratulations and best wishes I extended to you on television last night. I know that you will have the united support of all Americans as you lead the nation in the cause of peace and freedom in the next four years."[4]

Television brought scenes of the sort that previous generations had only been able to imagine—for example, scenes of Pat Nixon trying to keep back the tears as her husband's defeat began to register. Joy and humility were mixed at the Hyannis Armory when the victor arrived to go before the nation and assure the American people that he recognized the enormity of his responsibility.

INAUGURATION DAY

Inauguration day dawned on a capital city recovering from a bout with foul weather. The outlook was anything but auspicious. A blizzard had blanketed Washington with heavy snow while the temperature descended. By herculean efforts, the center of the city was cleared of snow—the city administration and the armed services had rushed men and equipment to do the job.

Dwight David Eisenhower spent his last morning in the White House in novel ways. Evicted from his old office because the painters were busily preparing it for a new occupant, he wistfully exchanged fish stories with his aides in the Navy mess hall. Last-minute paper work was attended to in the Cabinet room, with Ike sporting a bow tie—the only one left after his valet finished packing his clothing. Even the retiring President's personal chair had to be temporarily surrendered to the moving van. A man so used to being at the center of attention was momentarily in the wings of the public stage. His major job done, Eisenhower was reflective and nostalgic. He prepared for his last public duty, that of attending the rites required to make John Kennedy President in fact, as well as by popular designation.

Later that morning Eisenhower's successor arrived at his new place of business and new home. The two men, attired in formal cutaway dress suits, went together to the ceremonies. Eisenhower escorted the first President-Elect born in the twentieth century. The nation had endorsed the right of a new generation of Americans to lead.

Shortly thereafter, the young thirty-fifth President of the United States was on the inaugural rostrum. Surrounding him were his family; the outgoing President and Vice-President and their personal parties; legislative leaders; members of the outgoing Cabinet and certain members of the new one; religious dignitaries; military chiefs; justices of the Supreme Court; friends; wives of those prominent enough to be given the privilege of sharing the grandstand; and, as always, Secret Service men.

Fringing the grandstand were the honor troop contingents from the armed forces, military bands, echelons of municipal police, FBI and other officers, and reporters.

In the plaza below was the public. Americans predominated, but there were hundreds of foreign nationals as well drawn to the ceremony.

The many thousands in attendance at the ceremony were joined by tens of millions of other Americans (and later by tens of millions of foreign nationals) who listened and watched via the electronic media. Radio carried the sounds of the event and the evaluations made by the reporters. Television was there, and because of this modern miracle, we who could not enjoy the privilege through physical presence were also there. We were there to see the display, the panoply, the leading characters of the affair, and our fellow Americans. Television also saved us from the bitter cold of outdoor Washington that day.

Everyone on the rostrum, except John Kennedy it seemed, was wrapped tightly in coats and mufflers. They almost seemed to be huddling together.

When Cardinal Cushing stood behind the lectern to intone a public prayer, there was a belching of smoke because of a wiring defect. The trouble was soon attended to, but it was fascinating to watch the Cardinal, firemen, Secret Service men, dignitaries, and Presidents squinting to see whether the adage about smoke and fire would prove true.

Earl Warren, Chief Justice of the Supreme Court of the United States, asked John Kennedy to raise his right hand and to swear the solemn oath that, when taken, would deposit the heavy burden of our highest public office upon his shoulders. Court clerk James R. Browning, holding the Bible and seemingly a witness for the nation, stood between the two men. Shortly thereafter, the new President began to read a message that would set the pattern for his whole

Administration. A hush fell on the scene. As the camera switched from the President to groups and to individuals in the audience, we all caught the mood that spread from the platform to the world. The rigors of the past campaign were pushed aside by popular pride in a system of government that could unify so soon after the public rivalry that had given us this leader. Eisenhower and Nixon, no less than others, were ready to support their Constitutional chief. Robert Kennedy was glimpsed, incongruous in a top hat, beaming with satisfaction at his brother's words.

The message was pregnant with significance, and the media of sight and sound helped to etch it on our minds. For the President, the opportunity was not entirely positive. If he failed to make the most of it, a faltering start to his work could be most costly. Happily, he was equal to the occasion and to the mass communications environment.

His approach was straightforward; his demeanor serious; his voice strong; his language significantly eloquent and pithy; and his intention clear! In that short address, John Kennedy managed to inspire and to direct without resorting to pretensions.

> We observe today not a victory of party but a celebration of freedom—symbolizing an end as well as a beginning—signifying renewal as well as change.
>
> Let the word go forth from this time and place, to friend and foe alike, that the torch has been passed to a new generation of Americans —born in this century, tempered by war, disciplined by a hard and bitter peace, proud of our ancient heritage and unwilling to witness or permit the slow undoing of those human rights to which this nation has always been committed, and to which we are committed today at home and around the world.
>
> Let every nation know, whether it wishes us well or ill, that we shall pay any price, bear any burden, meet any hardship, support any friend, oppose any foe to assure the survival and the success of liberty. . . .
>
> To those old allies whose cultural and spiritual origins we share, we pledge the loyalty of old friends. . . .
>
> To those new states whom we welcome to the ranks of the free, we pledge our word that one form of colonial control shall not have passed away merely to be replaced by a far more iron tyranny. . . .
>
> To those peoples in the huts and villages of half the globe struggling to break the bonds of mass misery, we pledge our best efforts to help them to help themselves, for whatever period is required—not because we seek their votes, but because it is right. . . .
>
> So let us begin anew—remembering on both sides that civility is not a sign of weakness, and sincerity is always subject to proof. Let us never negotiate out of fear. But let us never fear to negotiate. . . .
>
> And if a beachhead of cooperation may push back the jungle of suspicion, let both sides join in creating a new endeavor, not a new balance of power, but a new world of law, where the strong are just and the weak secure and the peace preserved.
>
> All this will not be finished in the first one hundred days, . . . nor

even perhaps in our lifetime on this planet. But let us begin. . . .
And so, my fellow Americans: ask not what your country can do
for you—ask what you can do for your country.[5]

SEEKING COOPERATION

From the first, President Kennedy and his advisors recognized the importance of television and the other mass media of communication to the success of
his Administration. In his article "The President's Most Powerful Tool," Professor Elmer E. Cornwell, Jr., observed "The President, in the nature of things,
must deal with the citizenry largely through the media of communication and
the impact of the revolution in communications on the Presidential Office
during the present century has obviously been tremendous."

An even more perceptive Cornwell conclusion is that publicity is not enough.
To be sure, publicity can open the doors to men's minds and start them thinking
along certain paths. But will publicity move them from thought to action? Will
the ideas be translated into laws in Congress, into resolutions in the minds of
judges, into progressive activities from administrators at every level of government? The President can obviously *command* public attention, but can he
convert attention into perceived personal interest among his listeners? That is,
can he really *persuade* them? These problems are central to Presidential maneuvering. At the heart of every core effort, be it on foreign affairs or civil rights
or economics, the President faces the danger of being ahead of the practical
sentiments that lead men to accept change willingly. After all, the ringing
messages of any time are eclipsed by the force of what did or did not happen!
Cornwell (writing after Kennedy's death) repeats the truth that "the legislative
accomplishments of the Kennedy administration seem meager indeed when
measured against the amount of effort and virtuosity expended to obtain
them."[6]

John Kennedy, as President, fascinated the nation, if the amount of attention
given by the mass media is a criterion. But it was his fate to be caught up in
problems, national and foreign, that defied his solutions. The Eisenhower
Administration faced problems no less serious and complex—indeed most were
transferred to Kennedy at the inauguration! A key difference was that Eisenhower, because of his temperament and approach, tended to compromise on
most issues. Kennedy met several issues head-on and dared to try remedies. This
made Kennedy more fascinating, but eminently more controversial.

CERTAIN PRECEDENTS

Clues to Kennedy's opportunities and his shortcomings can be observed in
the way he utilized the press conference. But before we plunge into our
examination of John Kennedy's three-year experience, it is important that we
survey the procedures of his predecessors.

Speaking of President Eisenhower, Clinton Rossiter observed that "he . . .
used arts of persuasion that were once controversial but are now considered

altogether regular. . . ."[7] One of the most regular arts of the modern Chief Executive is the art of utilizing the press facilities provided by the communications industry. Until quite recently, Presidents were apt to misuse the press. Cleveland was ill at ease with newsmen and was especially rigid when he "became convinced that the press continually misrepresented him"; Benjamin Harrison felt that the press continually "persecuted" his family; during the McKinley Administration, "White House relations with the press were left largely to chance"; Taft's relationship and respect for the press left much to be desired, as did Hoover's.[8]

Despite the fact that Presidents Theodore Roosevelt, Wilson, Harding, Coolidge, Franklin Roosevelt, and Truman registered some disenchantment with the press treatment they were accorded, each in his own way provided for better public relations through the press. Theodore Roosevelt always gloried in publicity and worked to aid the press representatives. Carrying on the spirit of the informal press conferences that he had conducted during his tenure as governor of New York, he "provided the White House correspondents with regular quarters" for their work and was generally helpful and cordial. Of course, Roosevelt was given to strong opinions about various members of the press who violated his confidence or who appeared offensive. Mark Sullivan, journalist, social historian, and crony of President Theodore Roosevelt,[9] depicted the zestful leader as a politician who took "especial pains" to know the popular journals and journalists of his day. When he read an article with which he disagreed, the President was likely to write a letter to the responsible editor or author "in which belligerency and graciousness were so mingled as to seem to say, 'You can print this if you want to and we will fight it out before the public; or you can come to see me in fair friendliness and I will give you the facts that will enable you to see the light.' "[10]

Not until Woodrow Wilson's tenure did the beginnings of formalized procedures for press relations enter the picture on the national level. Through his initiative, formal and regular press conferences came into being. For two years following his inauguration, he met with the press twice weekly. Wilson the theorist believed that the power of publicity is important in a democracy—"I feel that a large part of the success of public affairs depends upon the newspaper men . . . because the news is the atmosphere of public affairs."[11] Wilson the professor prepared for the conferences "as carefully as for any lecture." Wilson the sensitive politician was dismayed when he "discovered that the interest of the majority" at those conferences "was in the personal and trivial rather than in principles and policies." When the Lusitania was torpedoed, the President decided to spare himself from one source of agitation—press conferences came to an end in his Administration. Wilson was hurt when the press reported on his family life, and he resented the kind of treatment given the Wilson clan. However, to him goes credit for the institution of the regular press conference and such "camouflage" inventions for airing Administration views as the "official spokesman" and "high authority" devices.[12]

Each President since Theodore Roosevelt, with the exception of Herbert Hoover, has been credited with broadening the press coverage of the Chief Executive's office. Harding, with some success as a newspaper publisher behind him (the Marion, Ohio *Star*), reinstituted the press conference during his tenure in office and was said to have enjoyed the "give and take" at those meetings. Coolidge received the press in keeping with the formal method established by others, but he was not as personally cordial in his relationship with the newsmen. Since the days of Theodore Roosevelt, Presidents had reserved the right to decide whether they would be quoted directly, and Coolidge added to that condition the requirement that all questions were to "be submitted in writing in advance." The silent man from Massachusetts frequently made the reporters ascribe what he said to a "White House spokesman."

Herbert Hoover also continued the press conferences but suffered because of a bad personal relationship with the reporters. Persons close to President Hoover at the White House often showed a flair for inept handling of the press, but Hoover himself was largely responsible for the state of affairs. After the financial upheavals of 1929, the situation between President and press worsened. "Long before the end of his administration he was on worse terms with the [press] corps as a group than any President had been since Theodore Roosevelt initiated White House press conferences."[13]

Some indication of the changes that were in store for the press representatives assigned to cover Franklin D. Roosevelt in the White House can be gleaned from the fact that, while Hoover held a total of only 66 press conferences during his four years at the helm, FDR held 337 during his first term, 374 during the second, 279 during the third, and eight before he died during his fourth term—a grand total of 998 meetings.[14]

Franklin D. Roosevelt, like his cousin Theodore, had a flair for publicity. For all of his thundering at "the fat-cat newspapers—85% of the whole—[that] have been utterly opposed to everything the Administration is seeking," and in spite of the fact that only a minority of newspapers were usually in favor of his policies during most of his years in power, FDR was a favorite of the working press.

The man from Hyde Park used press conferences effectively. James Mac-Gregor Burns, in his well-titled political biography *Roosevelt: The Lion and the Fox,* commented, "No one knew better . . . that the press conference was a two-edged sword; he could use it to gain a better press, but the reporters could also use it to trip him. Much depended on knowing when *not* to answer a question."[15] At his very first Presidential press conference, on May 8, 1933, Roosevelt demonstrated his talent.

> It is very good to see you all. My hope is that these conferences are going to be merely enlarged editions of the kind of very delightful family conferences I have been holding in Albany for the last four years. . . . We are not going to have any more written questions; and,

of course, while I cannot answer seventy-five or a hundred questions because I simply haven't got the time, I see no reason why I should not talk to you ladies and gentlemen off the record in just the way I have been doing in Albany and in the way I used to do in the Navy Department down here. . . . There will be a great many questions, of course, that I won't answer, . . . because they are "if" questions . . . and the others, of course, are the questions which for various reasons I do not want to discuss, or I am not ready to discuss, or I simply do not know anything about.[16]

After setting other ground rules, such as the rule that direct quotation of the President would not be allowed without special authorization from Steve Early, the press secretary, and the rule that confidential or off-the-record information was not to be bandied about outside the press conference hall because nonparticipants could then use the material, Roosevelt declared, "Now, as to news, I don't think there is any."[17] However, FDR was always in the news, from his inauguration until his death.

Taking office at a time when radio was coming of age as a media for mass communication, the President was shrewd enough to take advantage of this facility for reaching the public. His radio "fireside chats" were to influence public opinion strongly as he assumed the "role of a father talking with his great family." His chats were "fresh, intimate, direct, [and] moving" even if, when "read in cold newspaper print the next day," the talks "seemed somewhat stilted and banal."[18] His political opposition became all the more distressed because he radiated charm. An Illinois farmer commented, "Sometimes when I listen to Roosevelt I even get to thinking he's right and all the time I know he's wrong."[19]

Harry S. Truman was "especially interested" in seeing how his first Presidential press conference, on April 17, 1945, would go. "By way of the press," he said, "he [the President] maintains a direct contact with the people." With the exception of a procedural change that established a pattern of one press conference each week instead of two, Truman maintained the rules established during the Roosevelt tenure. All went well during that first conference, and Truman, looking back after his return to private life, reported that he "always got along well with the reporters. They try to do an honest job of reporting the facts. But," he added, voicing a complaint also raised by his predecessor, "many of their bosses—the editors and publishers—have their own special interests, and the news is often slanted to serve those interests, which unfortunately are not always for the benefit of the public as a whole."[20]

When questioned about the value of press conferences on March 15, 1956, the forty-third anniversary of those meetings, President Dwight D. Eisenhower summarized his views on the subject.

As a matter of fact, I think this is a wonderful institution . . . while I have seen all sorts of statements that Presidents have considered it a bore and it is a necessary chore to go through, it does a lot of things for me personally.

For one thing, at least once a week I have to take a half hour to review in my own mind what has happened during that week, so that I don't make errors, just through complete inadvertence and failure to look them [the facts] up.

Moreover, I rather like to get the questions because frequently I think they represent the kind of thinking that is going on, not so much —I don't mean in tone—everybody is always, of course very polite and respectful, but I mean the character of the questions frequently shows just exactly what is the thinking that is going on.

Now, this group of people here are sent here undoubtedly because they represent the better class of reporters available to the papers and the associations that send them here and, consequently, their mass opinions or the general impressions ought to have some value, I think, for any, in any democratic government.[21]

President Eisenhower, although he learned to handle himself well and even enjoy the weekly press conferences, was initially quite anxious about those meetings. During his first eight months in office, he held only 14 conferences, or an average of less than two a month. Newsmen were concerned by what appeared to be his reluctance to carry on "one of the major institutions playing an important role in the conduct of the government"—one representing the "nearest approach to the British Parliamentary system" as a method for questioning high officials.[22] However, as the President gained political maturity and confidence, he developed a warm, friendly style that has come to be identified as his approach to public contact problems.

In several respects, the Eisenhower Administration's press contacts were more complex than those in previous Administrations. For one thing, television, born commercially during the Truman days, was in full flower when Mr. Eisenhower took office. Although photographs, radio, and motion pictures had served to put Presidents on public display before 1953, it was the lot of the Eisenhower Administration to have to learn how to master *all* of the media. For that reason, the status of the President's press secretary changed.

Since the installation of James Campbell Hagerty as aide to President Eisenhower, the press secretarial job has developed into one of the key posts in official Washington. Mr. Hagerty carried on all of the work of his predecessors and, in addition, functioned like a mass media majordomo, not only arranging the contacts between media representatives and his boss, but also acting as a spokesman for the White House. Mr. Hagerty was an ever-present representative of the President and was the microphone for the President's views in the many instances when the Chief Executive could not, or did not want to, speak directly. Inevitably, with the demands upon him as great as they were, Mr. Hagerty became a political personality in his own right. As the liaison man between the President and the press, Mr. Hagerty was known to be torn "between his natural instinct as a reporter and his strict responsibility to his boss." Again, "occasionally . . . he [was] obliged to pick up the pieces after the President [had] made some inept remark at his press conference." Hagerty's *clarifications* were of vital importance to the working press. His *views*, as evidenced by the situation at the time of Mr. Eisenhower's heart attack, were sometimes challenged when offered as straight news. "In many subtle and unintentional ways," observed Cabell Phillips of *The New York Times*, "he has created the impression that he is now primarily dedicated, not to getting out the White House news, but to preserving its political status quo."[23]

The charge was made by many observers of the Washington scene that the Eisenhower Administration, in addition to being more public relations conscious than those that preceded it, paid greater attention to the gimmicks and superficial aspects of public relations. For example, it was pointed out that the President's television appearances were sometimes given the so-called "Madison Avenue" or advertising agency treatment. It is true that in the early days of that Administration, the President was advised to try out so many slick merchandising techniques that he reached the point where "he looked somewhat like an unsteady actor as he threaded his way through prop baskets of letters and [wore] almost stagey make-up." Those "backstage Svengali" ideas were soon dropped in favor of more natural tactics.[24]

Examples of the more original use of television by President Eisenhower and his immediate advisors are not difficult to come across. Just to mention a few of the more interesting problems raised by the new medium, the first telecast of a meeting of the Cabinet, on October 25, 1954, was criticized because the affair, actually arranged as a means for presenting an address on foreign affairs by Secretary of State John Foster Dulles, was plainly "staged." President Eisenhower and the other members of the Cabinet had to sit for almost 30 minutes while Mr. Dulles spoke. In effect, high officials were assembled as a kind of prop audience to lend the effect of an actual conference. Members of the Cabinet had tailored questions to ask the Secretary of State at prearranged times. In addition to the participants' obviously missing cues, which the cameras recorded for the national audience, it was clear that "statesmanship and showmanship do not always mix." When the Attorney General, Mr. Herbert Brownell, asked the Secretary of State "whether foreign parliaments had to approve the terms of the defense plan" that Mr. Dulles discussed, the Secretary of State "explained they did." One prefers to think that the Attorney General of the United States knew the answer to the question before he asked.[25]

Administration by Spotlight

In 1956, Secretary of Defense Charles E. Wilson learned that certain public relations enterprises of a promotional nature can cause more disturbance in the governmental world than in the commercial world. Differences between the Army, the Navy, and the Air Force flared into a public relations tempest that spring and threatened public understanding of questions pertaining to our national security. Each of the armed services appeared bent on winning the publicity battle for its view as to how the nation could be best protected. Under examination at the time by the defense chiefs, the President, the Congress, and the public were such vital military subjects as weapons, money, and missions. After an extraordinary series of propaganda campaigns issued by important persons attached to each of the armed services, the Secretary of Defense had to try to restore public confidence in and understanding of the Administration responsible for the nation's safety. Mr. Wilson applied the press conference technique to this problem and directed the "top officials" of the military establishment to meet the press with him at a conference highlighted by television coverage. Eight civilian and military heads of the Army, Navy, Air Force, and Marine Corps assembled as directed.

Mr. Wilson opened the conference by reading a statement saying, "Any reassignment of the roles and missions that may be required in the future among the services will be based on what is in the best interest of the country and must not be adversely influenced by the promotional activities of partisan service representatives." Later during that conference, Secretary of the Air Force Donald A. Quarles was asked by a reporter whether a public relations document that instructed Air Force public relations personnel to "flood the public with facts and to lay off during an election year because politics are unreasonable and ruthless competitors" was the type of document that the Defense Department could approve. Mr. Quarles's answer was that the "document in question was a pep talk in a sales talk that went beyond any type of sales language that I ever like to indulge in myself. . . ." Still later, Mr. Wilson, in reply to another reporter's question, observed that "the controversy developed apparently in the press . . . and blew up a bigger wind than I like."[26]

The public relations issue behind the conference was not discussed directly at the time, but it deserves attention. Administrators, when faced with crucial problems upon which there have been registered important differences of opinion, are tempted to seek victory for their views by leaving the arena of responsibility and appealing to the public for support hoping that rival opinions will be drowned out by bombardments on the publicity front. Occasionally, under circumstances similar to those described above, overemphasis on publicity can jeopardize end objectives. If publicity becomes the tail that wags the dog, then policies will be influenced by every wind that blows.

TELEVISED PRESS CONFERENCES: JFK'S APPROACH

It was estimated that "65 million people in 21.5 million homes" viewed the first press conference of the creator of the "new frontier."[27]

Kennedy was the first President to appear regularly on *live* broadcasts and telecasts of the sessions. He was the thirty-fifth Chief Executive of the United

States, but the first to come into the office with a television industry technically ready to broaden the coverage of press conferences so dramatically. Before his time, the press conferences were primarily meetings between Presidents and professional journalists. From the start of the Kennedy Administration, these conferences were converted into sessions between the President and the public at large, with the reporters serving as questioners and as an immediate audience.

John Kennedy's predecessors, in the days before live conferences, could ask reporters to attribute some of their statements to so-called "reliable sources" or "high government officials," and they could thus speak off the record whether the reporters liked it or not. Offenders who challenged Presidential wishes found themselves out of favor. After 1961, however, with the camera images and the sounds relayed almost instantly to private radio and television receivers, the opportunity to camouflage remarks was no longer available to the President. At his news conferences, Kennedy more than made up for this loss by being, seemingly, very direct. He was fond of offering the audiences his "judgments" on different problems. Sometimes, reporters wondered whether he had been as clear and blunt as he appeared to be.

Because the White House could no longer rely on editing to delete sensitive information from taped remarks, the President had to be constantly alert to the dangers of unintended opinions and of implications that could so easily be drawn from his words.

The first press conference was held in the State Department auditorium at 6 P.M. on Wednesday, January 25, 1961. Because of the foretastes of the Kennedy news approach that had been made evident through a long campaign, the reporters in attendance knew that an interesting pattern would probably be established that day. Obviously, Presidential press conferences had come a long way from the gatherings around Franklin Roosevelt's desk. Indeed, this conference would be considerably different even from Eisenhower's meetings in the old State Department Indian Treaty Room, with the President standing at floor level before seated reporters and James Hagerty close by. In those days, the television tapes produced were released by the White House only after Hagerty had made certain that the messages and the responses to reportorial questions were those intended.

Perhaps the reporters waiting for Kennedy to appear for his first Presidential press conference also pondered the fact that, although most of those covering the conference were from newspapers and magazines, the session would be as available to the public as to them. Television coverage of such events had begun to force newsmen to concentrate on background and behind-the-scenes material. To be sure, they related what they saw and heard, but since millions of others heard and saw along with them, the news value of this approach was limited. Meanings and related information had to be stressed.

John Kennedy entered from a stage wing and strode to a lectern decorated with the Presidential seal. Behind him ambled Pierre Salinger, his press secretary. Mr. Salinger seated himself in a nearby chair to be ready if his chief wanted his assistance in some way. On subsequent occasions, other officials from the White House and the departments appeared on stage with the President if Kennedy thought that they would be helpful. Except for unusual situations, JFK handled the affairs neatly, and without surface support. But he was well prepared for these confrontations. Salinger, in appraising these meetings later wrote:

> Before each conference—and the conferences were always scheduled beforehand—the press secretaries of the various executive departments met with me and compiled a list of questions they expected the reporters would ask. President Kennedy was provided with a list of these questions together with suggestions for answers; often he requested additional information. The whole process was topped off by a session with his White House advisers at which the possible answers were analyzed and weighed. Although the staff explored every major issue in depth, they could not give the President ready-made responses since there was no way of knowing what questions would be asked nor how they would be phrased. Nevertheless, when he strode out to face the White House press corps, he was primed to think on his feet; his answers came easily from a store of facts, figures and judgments he could marshal with confidence. Most of the time he relished the give and take.[28]

All was businesslike at that first conference. Kennedy opened with announcements. He fully intended to set the pace and to make certain news before the questioning began. He made a statement about the Geneva negotiations for an atomic test ban, said that Mr. John J. McCloy was his principal advisor on these negotiations, and alluded to a list of distinguished experts on the subject who would study the problem and make recommendations. He said that Salinger would have the names of those on that list at the end of the conference.

Referring then to the Congo, the President told the assemblage that the United States was going to substantially increase food, hospital, and seed supplies in order to relieve the distress there.

Then he announced that the crew of an RB-47 bomber, detained by the Russians since July 1, 1960, had been released. The officers were en route home as he spoke.

The announcements completed, he turned to the questions, which poured in hard and fast, covering a variety of subjects relating to foreign and domestic problems. As was true during the campaign, the Kennedy approach was to wade right into each question and to give surprisingly adequate responses on even the more complex issues.

A touch of irony was that the last question asked that day dealt with the issue of Presidential succession. Kennedy suggested that, while he had not gone into the matter in detail, he thought that the Eisenhower type of agreement between the President and the Vice-President was good. "I think it would be a good matter on which we could proceed."[29]

Television displayed a most personable leader, able and forthright. These conferences provided the President with a most adequate display case for his talents. He was quite capable of humor, but his major interests were to register his opinions and to state what he and his Administration would or could do about various foreign and domestic problems.

Before long, the press conferences were eliciting a tremendous mail response, largely because of television coverage. It should not be forgotten, however, that television only partially satiated the vast public curiosity about the President. This young man was a center of national attention virtually every day of his tenure in office. A substantial portion of the citizenry, their appetites whetted by all of the mass media, placed John Kennedy and his family in a hero-worship category formerly reserved for movie stars and the like.

On March 8, 1961, he was asked to comment about the manner in which reporters sought his attention. Scenes of newsmen jumping to their feet and shouting "Mr. President" had distressed many, who felt that the President was being imposed upon and even abused. Kennedy was good-humored in his reply, reassuring the nation and joshing the reporters. "Well," he said to the newsman, "you subject me to some abuse, but not to any lack of respect."[30]

Representatives of the Fourth Estate sometimes complained that, no matter who jumped up, on certain occasions the Administration had decided to recognize a certain favored reporter because the President wanted to answer the question that he knew that reporter would ask. Others suggested that the President had a tendency to return to key and established journalists when recognizing newsmen at a press conference.

There were those who urged the President to "improve" the press conferences by devoting certain sessions to a single subject or by having written questions at certain points. On September 12, 1963, Kennedy replied that these suggestions, if adopted, would not necessarily improve the conferences.

> I think we do have the problem of moving very quickly from subject to subject, and therefore I am sure many of you feel that we are not going into any depth. So I would try to recognize perhaps the correspondent on an issue two or three times in a row and we could perhaps meet that problem. Otherwise it seems to me it serves its purpose, which is to have the President in the bull's eye, and I suppose that is in some ways revealing.[31]

Revealed to the nation was a terribly vigorous, aggressively dynamic, and yet deeply introspective personality. Television suited him well, and he seemed made for it—a true partnership of man and medium.

When he caught the sense of an interesting question, the cameras caught that flash of eyes or that gritting of jaws that told us we should watch and listen carefully. In all candor, JFK was a treat as he fired off the replies of a man well aware of his own worth. When he was fully in action his right palm would rise and start to slowly chop the air; when he was explaining most carefully, his face was often draped in a half-frown and the forefinger of his right hand might point the way through the argument.

As President, he tried to preserve a proper distance between himself and the assembled reporters. Ever mindful of his heavy responsibilities and the great power that he directed, Kennedy consciously endeavored to maintain the dignity of his high office. But there were also many moments when his reserve melted and he engaged in the form of humor he most appreciated—satire.

One persistent headache for the President was the charge that he gave too many "trivial" answers to reporters. Another problem was the charge that he attempted to "manage" the news.

Ted Lewis, writing in *The Nation,* summed up leading complaints as early as February 1961. Lewis suggested that the conferences were constructed so as to force the President to be overly cautious in his choice of words. The question-and-answer portions of the conferences were "rapidly becoming a way of extracting only a great deal of superficial information." As late as Harry Truman's days in the White House, wrote Lewis, the question-and-answer procedure was a "method of ferreting out what [lay] deep in the Chief Executive's mind." Lewis concluded his critical article by suggesting that Kennedy might develop a version of Franklin Roosevelt's "fireside chats." "What better way for the President to convey important information, packaged in simple, direct, language, to the millions over the country whose support he wants as he seeks to end the cold war and lift the economic burdens at home?"[32]

On balance, and despite well-grounded charges against the Kennedy press-conference technique, the sessions served the nation well as national meetings between the people and their Chief Executive. The meetings were held with some regularity, and even if the reporters lamented the changes wrought in their trade by the advent of television, the nation was better informed than before.

Elmer E. Cornwell, Jr., in his perceptive study *Presidential Leadership of Public Opinion,* suggests that the conferences "became productions, far closer to a Hollywood epic than to the informal family gatherings of a scant two decades before."[33] Agreeing with Cornwell's conclusion, one still senses that Kennedy took the press conferences as far as he could into the television era. On 63 separate occasions, he used television as an instrument for mass education. It will take some time before we all recognize the restraint he displayed in the face of considerable temptation to experiment further. While the complaints were justified, we should keep in mind that it had been a mere six years before, on January 19, 1955, that the first conference had been filmed for television.

It was during the Eisenhower Administration, after the development of so-called "fast film" had eliminated the need for glaring and hot lights, that the first tentative steps were taken for regularizing of the filming of the press conferences and for national (delayed) viewing on television. These films were released by the White House after the fall of 1954. However, the public's response, which was first conditioned by high interest in the proceedings, dropped rather quickly to only moderate curiosity. The novelty wore off. It must be stated that, aside from the critical moments of the Eisenhower period, the President's calm, easygoing manner tended to diminish drama and, hence, the number of viewers. The networks became less and less interested in scheduling the sessions in their entirety. Soon, excerpts from the conferences were most commonly seen on news programs, although educational television stations often carried them in full.

More interest could have been stimulated among the public and in the television industry if the trend had been toward *live* programming in the period 1954 to 1960, but James Hagerty felt that live coverage would have been "too dangerous."[34] When one reads the sometimes acid interpretations of the Eisenhower Administration in such books as Clark R. Mollenhoff's *Washington Cover-Up* (Doubleday & Company, Inc., 1962) or the friendlier but caustically composed *The Ordeal of Power* by Emmet John Hughes (Atheneum, 1963), one senses that Hagerty may have been right.

Kennedy not only ushered in a new Administration with his oath of office; he ushered in a new and more daring era.

Walter Lippman recently compared Presidents Kennedy and Johnson as to their relationships with the press. Like a great many other astute observers, Lippman appreciated the Kennedy flair for combining individual brilliance with audience participation in the press conference. "I don't blame him [Johnson] for not trying to do what Kennedy did with the press conference. Kennedy was a virtuoso. It would be like asking Johnson to sing Tosca."[35]

Pro forma, the Kennedy press conferences were flawless! The procedures established at the first meeting were continued and proved highly effective, largely because the routine gave the reporters something to report, weighty or not, right at the start. The President was able to maintain a lively pace in the question-and-answer portions, instinctively matching the degree of seriousness of the question with an appropriate mood for the reply. Frequently, the reporters were treated to his wit, and they obviously enjoyed it.

May Craig, a perceptive and persistent lady of the press corps, was a favorite of the President. On occasion, she would receive a Kennedy response that seemed reserved for those he liked. Miss Craig sometimes needled him, but he took pleasure in that small pain. For example, on January 24, 1962, Miss Craig, given the Presidential nod, began, "Mr. President, you said yesterday that more people ought to drink milk. None of the young marrieds I know of lay off it on account of radioactivity. They lay off it because they can hardly buy enough for the children, and not themselves, on account of price."

She went on to ask why the prices were so high for milk and butter, when the nation had surpluses "that we buy up and give away."

Typically, the President responded in rather amazing detail, ranging from comments about the over-all consumer price level in the preceding year, to the percentage increase in population, to the average hourly income of the dairy farmer. Then he said, "I was attempting to reassure on radio-active, and on the matter of—and also to see if we could stimulate by example. Mr. Salinger drank it this morning—[laughter]—with no adverse effect."[36]

JFK was impressive and fascinating, even to the old hands at Washington journalism. For most of them he was a nearly perfect leader to cover. However, his television image and the adulatory cast of him fashioned by the mass media in general did not reflect the weakness he seemed to display to many astute political observers. Increasingly, as the novelty of the Kennedy role as President gave way to day-by-day and issue-by-issue impressions, he was accused of overcaution on serious national problems. Civil rights is a problem in point. The President pleased few reactionaries or progressives with his political maneuvering. One senses that his major problem stemmed from the fact that more issues were coming to a head in his time than he bargained for. James Tracy Crown and George P. Penty, in their post-Cuba-crisis book *Kennedy in Power* (1961), labeled Kennedy "no ideologist" but a "pragmatic realist." They suggested that he was "an honest broker between extremes" who interwove "cautious moderation" with "rather advanced liberalism." Again, "Kennedy is hardly going to lead any conservative generation, if he can help it. . . . But he does think that the mood of the country is more conservative than he had reckoned during the campaign."[37]

A serious weakness of televised press conferences of the Kennedy type is that they tend to gloss over weakness and play up strengths. His major strength was his forceful personality, and television is well suited to display personality. But when the reporters found that their role was largely one of audience participation in a show, they also learned, to their consternation, that there was little that they could do about it. The shows were directed by the major character; Pierre Salinger was an aide, and not a majordomo as James Hagerty had been with President Eisenhower.

John Kennedy was as outstanding in the press conference situation as he had been during the debates with Nixon, but his statements in both situations tended to enhance his charisma without always prompting significant support for his policies. He had more clear successes—and failures—when he appeared on television to address the nation at moments of national decision or crisis.

URGENT AND SPECIAL TELEVISION APPEARANCES

Mississippi: A Failure

Fall 1962 was a very special time for the University of Mississippi, for Constitutional order in the United States, for the tenth of our population who are Negroes and the nine-tenths who are not, and for world opinion.

James Meredith, a 29-year-old Negro veteran of the United States Air Force and a native of Mississippi, had, by virtue of a federal court order, broken the color barrier and enrolled as a student at the University of Mississippi. The problem for the U.S. government was how to keep him safe in the face of a largely hostile student body, a generally reluctant faculty and administration, and a defiant state government.

Governor Ross Barnett, a strident segregationist, seemed to be negotiating with the Attorney General of the United States, Robert Kennedy, in order to ease the situation. Actually, in his telephone conversations with Robert Kennedy, Barnett took a position of apparent compromise that he did not uphold in practice. The "Ole Miss" campus rang with chants such as "Give us the nigger!" and "Keep Mississippi white." There were, no doubt, more reasonable people on the campus, but they were quiet. Popular sentiment, fanned by a long and undemocratic tradition, was creating mobs.

In Washington, Robert Kennedy and his chief aides, Burke Marshall and Nicholas Katzenbach, were determined to see that the federal courts were obeyed. The situation was one of many specific consequences of the Supreme Court's *Brown v. Topeka* desegregation decision of May 17, 1954.

Finally, with adequate reports of events available to Washington, the President advised his brother to go ahead and do what the Attorney General and his staff thought necessary to protect Meredith. Meredith was already in the protective custody of federal marshals and spent the fateful weekend preceding his scheduled enrollment in New Orleans. When a border patrol plane took him to Oxford, the campus town was pregnant with agitation. Three hundred and twenty marshals were on the scene, ready for trouble and wearing helmets and special protective vests with pockets for tear-gas canisters.

The plan had been to register Meredith on Sunday, but on Mississippi state police advice (Sunday registration would offend deeply religious people, they said), Meredith and his convoy headed for Baxter Hall, where Meredith would stay the night, immediately protected in his two-room suite by eight marshals.

Shortly after 7 P.M., what has become known as the "Battle of Oxford" began. Through that long night, the awful momentum of segregationist fervor carried students and others from sentiment to action.

President Kennedy had approved an order on Saturday, September 29, that demanded an end to resistance and federalized the Mississippi National Guard, depriving Barnett of the opportunity to use those men to defy their national government. The state police and the local police stood aside as the marshals fought the mob to protect their charge and defend themselves. By 9 P.M., former Major General Edwin A. Walker had appeared on the campus to help lead the insurrection. The man who had directed federal troops five years previously at Little Rock was heard to shout that he was now on the right side. He was all that was needed to produce complete chaos.

Federal power barely carried the day. For Paul Guihard, a 31-year-old Agence France Presse reporter, it was his last story. About 9 P.M., his body was found on the grass between a women's dormitory and the Fine Arts Center. He had been shot between the shoulder blades.

In determining the effectiveness of John Kennedy's televised speech that night, it must be stated that his "honest broker" approach of the past, on civil rights, was obviously insufficient. The text of his speech was inappropriate in the context of the events. He appealed to reason and urged the force of history upon those who were running amuck. How could they listen when they were otherwise occupied? The nation could not reconcile the news pictures from the scene with the President's speech, which obviously said too little far too late.

> The orders of the court in the case of *Meredith versus Fair* are beginning to be carried out. . . .
>
> This has been accomplished thus far without the use of the National Guard or other troops. . . .
>
> All students, members of the faculty, and public officials in both Mississippi and the nation will be able, it is hoped, to return to their normal activities with full confidence in the integrity of American law. . . .
>
> Americans are free, . . . to disagree with the law but not to disobey it. For in a government of laws and not of men, no man, however prominent or powerful, and no mob, however unruly or boisterous, is entitled to defy a court of law. . . .
>
> This Nation is proud of the many instances in which Governors, educators, and everyday citizens from the South have shown to the world the gains that can be made by persuasion and good will in a society ruled by law. . . .
>
> I close . . . with this appeal to the students of the University, the people who are most concerned.
>
> You have a great tradition to uphold, a tradition of honor and courage won in the field of battle and on the gridiron as well as the University campus.
>
> . . . let us preserve both the law and the peace and then healing those wounds that are within we can turn to the greater crises that are without and stand united as one people in our pledge to man's freedom. Thank you and good night.

Later, in May 1963 at one of his news conferences, the President was asked for his thoughts on how to improve race relations. A bad situation at Birmingham, Alabama, was then in the forefront of the news, and Mr. Kennedy recalled his efforts at the time of the Oxford, Mississippi, uprising. Responding to a query as to whether a "fireside chat" on civil rights might improve race relations, he answered that he thought such an endeavor might be useful. Then he said, "I've attempted to make clear my strong view that there is an important moral issue involved of equality for all our citizens and that until you give it to them you are going to have difficulties as we have had this week in Birmingham." He went on, "The time to give it to them is before the disasters come and not afterwards. But I made a speech the night of Mississippi—at Oxford—to the citizens of Mississippi and others. That did not seem to do much good, but this doesn't mean we should not keep on trying."[38]

The Cuba Crisis: Appropriate

Curiously enough, an example of a more appropriate use of television for an address to the nation came hard on the heels of the Oxford situation. On October 22, 1962, after a long week of Administration anxiety caused by intelligence uncovering a Soviet missile buildup in Cuba, the President alerted the nation to the danger. Secrecy had shrouded the problem until he spoke. Earlier that day it was announced that the President would broadcast at 7 P.M., and enough information was allowed to "leak" so that it became known that the subject was Cuba.

From John Kennedy's vantage point, the crisis began to brew as soon as Special Assistant McGeorge Bundy came into his bedroom at 9 A.M., Tuesday, October 16, 1962. The President had just finished his breakfast and was going through the morning papers. Bundy brought urgent news that had just come from the Central Intelligence Agency. The night before, the CIA experts had examined aerial photographs that proved, beyond doubt, that nuclear missile emplacements were being mounted by the Soviets in the Cuban coastal regions. These missile emplacements, when completed, would put the United States within close range of Soviet aggressive power. Jet bombers (Ilyushins) and medium-range missiles were also discovered. Sites, planes, and missiles were there, and ground crews were feverishly making all ready. In short order, this nation would be in the bull's eye, and the Communists would have the material for nuclear blackmail located less than 100 miles from the Florida peninsula. The heartland of this country would be in the clutch of Soviet button-pushers.

By order of the President, a tight security curtain was thrown around the whole affair, and for a week the top defense and political chieftans studied, evaluated, and proposed.

While their urgent deliberations were in progress, the President maintained a public pose of "business as usual" in order to shield the public from premature concern and panic and in order to give himself and his advisors time to consult and plan. Even advocates of the open society who oppose every form of government secrecy would have to agree that there are times when those who have responsibility must exercise the discretionary power that goes with it. Unhappily, for democracies as well as for other forms of government, the tell-all policy cannot be absolute when stark realities must be dealt with by the few for the safety of the many.

The next day, in order to preserve the "cover," the President left the meetings and kept to his previously planned schedule of political campaigning in Connecticut. Never was he out of direct touch with the White House. After returning to the capital that night, he held brief discussions with Robert Kennedy and Secretary of State Dean Rusk. Next morning he met with the Soviet emissary, Foreign Minister Andrei Gromyko, and kept discussion about Cuba to a minimum. He gave the Russians no indication that our government knew about the missile buildup. It was a pleasant meeting. Both men were photographed smiling.

More routine work followed. Papers were signed. Issued from the President's office on the day of the fateful speech was "Memorandum of Disapproval of Bill to Amend the Tariff Classification of Lightweight Bicycles."

The speech was delivered on Monday, October 22; on the preceding Friday, the President and the White House correspondents had flown to Cleveland to begin three days of scheduled campaigning from there to the West Coast. Before he left Kennedy told Theodore Sorensen to start a draft of the speech. Saturday the President curtailed his tour because of a "cold." Later that day the news hawks began to sense that something was up. They suspected that the "cold" that caused the Vice-President to fly back to Washington from a short trip to Hawaii was remarkably coincidental. And then, what about those large troop movements in Florida?

That week end, the State Department and the Defense Department were hectic in key offices. John Kennedy's speech was rephrased and further re-phrased. By Sunday, vital figures were in high gear. Congressional leaders were beginning to make plans for last-minute, special, secret consultations; national allies were being alerted to the problem; Adlai Stevenson was receiving instructions about his upcoming role at the United Nations; the defense establishment was completing its arrangements; additional flights over Cuba were ordered to provide confirmatory information; and the National Security Council was reaching final conclusions after extensive deliberations. When John Kennedy paused at 4 P.M. on the day of the speech to the nation to greet the new Prime Minister of Uganda, all was settled save for his 5 P.M. conference with Congressional leaders.

At 7 P.M., the President of the United States let the American public in on the Russians' plot. It is believed that, for a greater part of the preceding week Russian intelligence was unaware that this government was alert to their scheme.

The President was clear and effective.

Good evening, my fellow citizens: This government, as promised, has maintained the closest surveillance of the Soviet military buildup on the island of Cuba. Within the past week, unmistakable evidence has established the fact that a series of offensive missile sites is now in preparation on that imprisoned island. The purpose of these bases can be none other than to provide a nuclear strike capability against the Western Hemisphere. . . .

The 1930's taught us a clear lesson: aggressive conduct, if allowed to go unchecked and unchallenged, ultimately leads to war. We are also true to our word. Our unswerving objective, therefore, must be to prevent the use of these missiles against this or any other country, and to secure their withdrawal or elimination from the Western Hemisphere. . . .

I have directed that the following initial steps be taken immediately: . . . a strict quarantine on all offensive military equipment under shipment to Cuba . . . increased close surveillance of Cuba and its military buildup. . . . Any nuclear missile launched from Cuba against any nation in the Western Hemisphere . . . [would be] an attack by the Soviet Union on the United States. . . . I have reinforced our base at Guantánamo. . . . [I am] calling for an immediate meeting of the . . . Organization of American States. . . . We are asking to-night that an emergency meeting of the Security Council be con-voked. . . . I call upon Chairman Khrushchev to halt and eliminate this clandestine, reckless, and provocative threat to world peace. . . .

. . . let no one doubt that this is a difficult and dangerous effort on which we have set out. No one can foresee precisely what course it will take or what costs or casualties will be incurred. . . .

. . . one path we shall never choose . . . [is] the path of surrender or submission.[39]

The highest goal of politics is to lead a people wisely. This observer believes that the Administration did its best in that critical period and used the mass communications media appropriately.

At the start of 1962, on January 8, *The New York Times* in an editorial looked ahead to John Kennedy's second year in the White House. At the end of a rather harsh evaluation of the President's lack of "fighting spirit" and a complaint about his "mood of careful political calculation," there appears a line relative to the then upcoming State of the Union address. "If he summons this nation . . . to do the impossible, in wisdom and in justice, he will find a following."[40]

MILITARY BRIEFING FROM THE DEFENSE DEPARTMENT: CERTAIN QUESTIONS

For months after the Administration advised that the Cuba-based Soviet missile threat had been removed, Senator Kenneth Keating (Republican-New York, defeated in 1964 by Robert Kennedy) insisted that medium-range sites were still in existence there and that the danger had not abated.

Secretary of Defense Robert McNamara made it known that he thought that Keating was carping over a dead issue. As the official with access to all of the relevant secret information, the Secretary suggested that his evaluation was incontestable. Nevertheless, the Keating charges attracted more and more publicity in a nation already nervous because of the great confrontation with Soviet leadership and power.

At the heart of the debate was the argument over the *facts*. Keating indicated that information made available to him made him confident in his assertions. On the other hand, the Defense Department and the White House issued regular statements assuring the American people that there was no cause for concern. The crisis of 1962 had been relegated to the pages of history, in the judgment of Defense Department officials.

The Keating allegations, abetted by the opinions of other critics, began to snowball. By February of 1963, the torrent of doubt reached such proportions that the Administration decided to meet the challenge head-on.

Behind the scenes was the secret information held by the defense establishment. Very little of that information was released because the government felt that the enemy would profit if this country's military and intelligence chiefs disclosed what they had learned. A basic assumption one must make is that the decision to keep security wraps over that knowledge was based not on politics, but solely upon military considerations. Otherwise, we must conclude that information kept from the people was withheld improperly. For a free people, secrecy is onerous unless the justification for maintaining secret information is based upon proper standards of official privilege or upon unimpeachable national security objectives.

Because of the pressures, a last-minute decision was made by the defense chiefs and by the President to refute the charges. The most efficient refutation, they concluded, would be to go before the nation on television and display a detailed analysis of nearly 100 photographs, selected from thousands taken by U.S. reconnaissance aircraft since July 1, 1962.

Pressed into service was John Hughes, a subordinate of the Secretary of Defense. On February 6, 1963, at about 10 A.M., Mr. Hughes was alerted and told to prepare himself for a telecast (to be carried by radio as well) that would commence at 5 P.M. that day. This special assistant to Lt. General Joseph F. Carroll, chief of the Defense Intelligence Agency, was advised that an almost complete removal of security restrictions would permit him to describe to the nation, in respect to those selected photographs, substantially what he had previously described in private to high government officials.

The day before that hastily arranged telecast, spies aiming at the destruction of this society would have considered that information worthy of their greatest efforts; the next day, it was available for common gossip. Despite the gray area that separates absolutes, one is struck by the scope of the decision to give out information that had been so guarded before.

Mr. McNamara appeared with Mr. Hughes and delivered a terse introductory statement. After Hughes completed his work, the Secretary briefly answered press questions. His responses, however, were the epitome of circumspection, and he quickly brought the proceedings to a conclusion.

Standing with a long pointer before blowups of the photographs and charts originally prepared for the inner circle of defense planners, Hughes gave a long and primarily extemporaneous recitation. Picture after picture and chart after chart were analyzed. One photograph after another flew by as Hughes, the intelligence officer, proved that the danger was past. He showed a dismantled site; then he pointed to a missile complex in various stages of erection and dismantling; then to a chart giving statistics of one sort or another. The television presentation, as a package, was designed to allay suspicions that Robert McNamara and associates had misled the American people.

On the whole, the program was effective, despite the opinions of politicians and others who continued to be skeptical over what was *proved* by the telecast.

The persuasive quality of television was clearly recognized by Secretary McNamara when he decided, one assumes with the President's approval, to use the medium to divulge military information to counter Senator Keating's charges.

By the maneuver McNamara's political power potential was made quite evident. Leaders of our defense establishment must find political critics hard to take at times. They are duty-bound to suffer political criticism, without striking back, unless they conclude that national security requires some limited entry into the open political arena.

It is obvious that the Defense chiefs decided that a silent Keating was even more valuable than certain secrets held by them. All advocates of freedom hope that the television program under discussion produced greater national security than existed just before it was produced. If the Communists got vital information the American public did not need, then domestic politics overrode national security. If Secretary McNamara was right in his action to restore public confidence, he did not offer us any good explanation of why other means than the release of the photographs would not have proven equally useful.

In recent history many nations have learned that it is easier for the military to intrude upon political processes than it is for politicians to influence the military echelons. Television, in its short history, is already involved in this very consequential problem.[41]

TELEVISION ON THE SCENE

A major value of television's coverage of the news is that the viewing public is taken to the scene of events. Television's cameramen and reporters can, when they are at their best, adroitly provide viewers with pictures and perspectives often lost to immediate participants. Television coverage can raise a local event to national significance.

For many situations, television coverage, by enlarging the number of persons involved, implicates those who watch from afar as they have never been implicated before. It is one thing to read about an event; it is quite another to be a close observer. Conversely, participants in events have, in many cases, responded to the presence of television by acting differently than they would have otherwise.

In 1962, people of the nation responded to news presentations of our arms buildup for the Cuban missile crisis, and to the direct Presidential address on that subject, as participants only once removed. We thrilled to the first live

94

trans-Atlantic television via Telstar; we were spectators vitally influenced by the commentators' interpretations of the Administration-industry confrontation over threatened price increases for steel; we held our breaths when Colonel John H. Glenn was launched into his historic earth-orbiting flight; we saw the plight of James Meredith in the scenes from "Ole Miss"; we debated the school-prayer decision of the United States Supreme Court, vastly aided and impressed by television's analyses; and we surveyed the national mid-term elections of 1962.

In 1963, the nation saw and heard the President on the subject of the longshoremen's strike and received background from news and other programs; we saw JFK welcome President Betancourt of Venezuela to the White House; we observed scenes of demonstrations and violence in Birmingham, Alabama, and Jackson, Mississippi; we followed the historic civil rights march on Washington; we participated in those four days of national mourning that began with the tragic event in Dallas; and we saw the new President at Andrews Air Force Base, preparing to do his duty with our help and a prayer.

FACTORS OF CONSEQUENCE

A Cult of Personality

Sister Mary Paul Paye, RSM, was blunt in writing about "The Kennedy Cult" in the August 11, 1962, issue of *The Nation*.

> The gentleman smiles, the youngster sidles up to a pony on the lawn, the lovely lady bows. Cameras click, tape-machines whirl, and the American public is exposed again to that dangerous phenomenon: the personality cult of the President. I protest—vehemently, vigorously, apolitically and almost alone.
> Three threats are inherent in this constant projection of the personal image of the President: the suppression or the obscuring of significant news; the amassing by the President of personal power; and—most insidious of all—the irrational worldwide identification of him with the country as a whole. We all—mass media and mass audience—could well pause to assess the ramifications of what less sophisticated societies termed hero worship, a phenomenon that, in our own electronic age, has become more complex and more potent.[42]

These observations about the "welter of feature material" that the mass media found in the President, his family, and his entourage are well worth study. In the Kennedy Administration, more than in any other before, communications technology; the personality of the President; vast popular curiosity about the personal lives of celebrities; the drives of news agencies to meet the insatiable demand for stories; and the tense world situation merged to throw television somewhat off balance. The medium was so young that it tended to follow events rather than trying to evaluate what it should be doing and where it was going.

Introspection on Occasion: Interviews with Pundits

On occasion, television provided a sense of the inner John F. Kennedy, as separate from the President. When the Chief Executive consented to be interviewed by news critics and analysts, he tried to explain and to interpret his beliefs. Four or five of these lengthy interviews, which were filmed for later television presentation, survive as testimony to the hopes and ambitions of the man.

When deep in conversation with Walter Cronkite, for example, his replies penetrated into inner meanings and were frequently philosophical. Responding to a Cronkite question (CBS, September 2, 1963) about the reservations many leaders, including former President Dwight D. Eisenhower, had about the atomic test-ban treaty, Kennedy revealed his personal views clearly. Then, commenting about the Viet Nam problem, he said, "We are prepared to continue to assist them, but I don't think that the war can be won unless the people support the effort and, in my opinion, in the last 2 months, the government has gotten out of touch with the people."[43] That statement caused diplomatic repercussions around the world. It was an opinion that he could not express so forcibly in a press conference, but one that, in the calm and dispassionate environment of that moment, he was prepared to cast on the waters of public opinion.

A television special entitled "After Two Years—a Conversation with the President" was filmed on December 16, 1962. Interviewing the President were William H. Lawrence (ABC), George E. Herman (CBS), and Sander Vanocur (NBC). The three network newsmen were all veterans, sage enough in politics and government to get *behind* the story. Vanocur, at one point in the hour-long discussion, asked Kennedy to comment about his earlier remark that he was "reading more and enjoying it less." In his reply the President said, ". . . the press has the responsibility not to distort things for political purposes, not to just take some news in order to prove a political point. It seems to me their obligation is to be as tough as they can on the administration but do it in a way which is directed towards getting as close to the truth as they can get and not merely because of some political motivation."[44]

That interview was filmed in the President's office at the White House and telecast the next day, December 17, 1962, by the three networks. NBC scheduled its program for presentation two hours later than the other networks.

A controversy developed between Pierre Salinger and the Columbia Broadcasting System because of White House insistence that the filmed discussion last an hour and twenty minutes to allow White House deletion from the television program of what Salinger termed "slow periods" and "less interesting" sections. Two minutes of what was deleted contained a spoonerism by the President. A compromise was reached, whereby Salinger made the networks responsible for what was cut out and left in; a committee composed of one representative from each of the three networks made the editing decisions. Central to the problem was not CBS's worry about the particular program, but the whole issue as to whether, at future times, editing could change the complexion of a Presidential appearance.[45]

Of Tours and Pageants

Presidents make news, and when that process is eminently visual in character, the television industry has learned the importance of being there to record it. If politics is so much the art of influencing people, then the television record of Presidential jaunts, at home and abroad, is made up of news and politics.

Politicians must make news in order to survive professionally, and the television industry needs news. Consequently, there is something like a two-way umbilical cord connecting politicians and the television industry. Neither the politicians nor the industry can sever the cord without cutting off a major source of their own nourishment. We may soon be able to refer to this "polivision" problem with more understanding, as our understanding of it matures through experience.

So much of Woodrow Wilson's diplomatic triumph in Europe in the months immediately following the First World War remained untranslatable into political currency at home, because he could not impress the people with a triumph that they could only read about and not see.

Since television's arrival on the political scene, modern Presidents have been able to deal in the inflated currency of publicity to a greater and greater degree. What the film industry began with its dramatic but limited newsreels, the television industry has advanced. Eisenhower was the first to reap the fruits of this development. News program materials for the daily summaries and specials took Eisenhower a long way from Wilson. His so-called "peace trip" of December 1959 is a good illustration. He traveled a triumphal path from Washington to Rome, Ankara, Karachi, Kabul, New Delhi, Tehran, Athens, Tunis, Paris, Madrid, and Casablanca (December 3–22, 1959).

At each stop there were the massive crowds, the welcoming foreign leaders with their kind words about our President and our country, and the pagentry that was so carefully arranged and so splendid. The international effect was matched by a domestic swing of public opinion to pride in our leader. Panoply and politics melded together.[46]

On the other hand, the abortive summit meeting at Paris in 1960 cast a pall over the Eisenhower image that he was not able to dispel in his last months in office. The full effect of Khrushchev's harangue at his special press conference in Paris was dramatically brought home. Flanked by his Defense Minister and his Foreign Minister, Khrushchev's denunciations of the United States over the U-2 affair were lethal public opinion weapons.

"Mr. K.," during his 1959 tour of the United States, frequently managed to bend our television coverage to his will. He neatly restricted the reporters' interpretive efforts, on most occasions, by creating "hard news" that the industry had to cover. The leading actor was almost impossible to upstage.[47]

The same was true when he journeyed to United Nations headquarters in New York on another occasion. He dominated the coverage of the meeting by banging his shoe on the desk during Prime Minister Macmillan's address to the delegates. On that trip he desired even more attention than the press was scheduling; so he went to the second-story balcony of his Park Avenue suite and started talking to the few reporters who were below in the street. Soon he was arguing matters of international consequence with a mass of reporters and others. Quickly, the word went to all news headquarters in the city that "Mr. K." was creating an event. Television crews hastily assembled their equipment and rushed to the scene. It was dramatic, it was news, and for television in particular, it was Khrushchev's schedule for programming.

Television coverage of the Kennedy trips to Europe in 1961 and 1963 and of Vice-President Johnson's travels in Southeast Asia in May of 1961 was adequate to overwhelming. The speeches, receptions, and balls were filmed and rushed back by jet aircraft to the United States. Within hours, regular and special news programs brought us to the scene. That the Chief Executive of the United States deserved the coverage is beyond dispute. That the industry had no choice is also beyond dispute. When a modern President decides to make news, television follows. Kennedy's nuclear test-ban treaty speech of October 7, 1963, and his speech of September 20, 1963, before the United Nations General Assembly were clearly historic. So was his tour of England, Ireland, Italy, and Germany in 1963.

Historians may dispute whether John Kennedy should have delivered some of the phrases he did to a huge gathering of Berliners and other Germans (Rudolph Wilde Platz, June 26, 1963), but analysts of television's role in politics have less leeway. The President made the moment; television only recorded and broadcast it. At any rate, his triumphal tour of Germany was not detracted from, in German eyes, when he proclaimed, "Two thousand years ago the proudest boast was 'civis Romanus sum.' Today, in the world of freedom, the proudest boast is 'Ich bin ein Berliner.' "[48] It was pure Kennedy, and the crowd loved him. This observer, on a recent trip to England, was made aware of the fact that many Britishers thought, at the time, that Kennedy gilded the lily. The public square where he spoke is in front of West Berlin's City Hall. That square is now John F. Kennedy Platz.

MANAGED NEWS

Television News by Arrangement

One of the major complaints against the Kennedy Administration was that the President and his coworkers, especially those in the Department of Defense, tried to *manage* the news from time to time.

THE PRELIMINARY SKIRMISH

An interesting sidelight pertaining to domestic affairs has to do with the integration of the University of Alabama, at Tuscaloosa, in the spring of 1963. It will be recalled that the university was the scene of Governor George Wallace's famous "stand at the schoolhouse door."

Television brought us news coverage from a place with a history of strife over the question of whether all citizens of Alabama were eligible to attend the state university. Miss Autherine J. Lucy had secured admission in 1956 through the power of a federal court order, but her stay on the campus was very brief. A march of 1,000 students and others to the university president's home, protesting her presence on the campus, was one contributing factor. They shouted many slogans, but most popular was "Keep 'Bama white." Two days after that first march, a riot forced Miss Lucy to flee the campus. When she accused university officials of being somewhat responsible for the riot, she was expelled. The events of 1956 were vividly brought to national attention by television and the other mass media.

INTEGRATION IN 1963

Seven years later, when three Negroes—Vivian J. Malone, Sandy English, and James Hood—filed suit in federal court for an injunction to force the University of Alabama to admit them under the force of the order of 1956 that had been secured for Miss Lucy, the curtain opened for a second act.

National television networks supplied their local affiliates with much live and filmed material of the unfolding spectacle. In regard to this and the many other instances of public strife over civil rights, it is fair to say that the educational power of television is so enormous that no one can estimate it. We know that television's ability to increase familiarity with fact has affected the processes through which subtle societal changes occur. We do not know, with any precision, how those subtle changes will or will not influence future history.

However, we do know that television's presence is a matter of considerable importance to the active participants in a situation. They may play up to it by acting differently than they otherwise would, or they may scurry to seek cover from overexposure before the nonlocal audiences. But when television coverage is good, there are often no places left to hide!

During the University of Alabama crisis of 1963, one of the three television networks gathered rather unique filmed materials that it fashioned into a feature presentation. The purpose was to give the viewing public a sense of what the key figures in the crisis went through as they faced their problems from hour to hour and day to day.

This program, "Crisis: Behind a Presidential Commitment," was one hour in length and was displayed in prime time on a Monday evening. One newspaper critic, Jack Gould, called it a "melodramatic peep show."

The intrepid television crews, as a result of arrangements made with Robert Kennedy and George Wallace, were allowed to look over shoulders and record most interesting meetings and discussions. They were on location in the office of the Attorney General of the United States. These scenes, largely concerned with conferences between Robert Kennedy and his chief aides, were shot when the leaders of the Justice Department were planning how to thwart George Wallace and enforce integration. Naturally, the material produced was carefully edited before it was approved for public viewing on the television special that purported to show how leaders made decisions. In the case of Robert Kennedy, the program tried to depict his inner sanctum when he and his advisors were under great stress. Unusual filmings of federal officials in action in Alabama were also produced.

The enterprising network prepared well for its special. It also persuaded George Wallace to allow cameras to record some conversations that he held in his office with top state officers, as he and they planned to counter federal moves. The edited versions, especially the sound tracks, offered the national television audiences a rather unimpressive and unconvincing account of how officials operate under stress. Wallace's rendition of the virtues of public responsibility to his inner circle of friends and advisors was obviously prepared for public consumption. One could sense that, after the cameras stopped, they got down to the real business at hand.

Cameramen were also permitted to mount a camera and sound-recording equipment in Assistant Attorney General Nicholas Katzenbach's car to capture him in conversation with harried coworkers. We saw him in conference with military and other officers at "field" headquarters. Many other settings were provided that gave supposedly "inside" views far different from the more open and public scenes usually available to television's news hawks. The result of these arrangements was presented after the crisis, as a background-to-recent-news feature. It was highly antiseptic in character. In this observer's opinion, Wallace came off better than the federals in this particular program—a strange situation, since Wallace was the "heavy" in the actual event.

All of the "inside" insights were in addition to coverage of campus events of a public nature. Advocates of freedom have every cause to be concerned by the manner in which "news" was arranged.

POSTSCRIPT

The confrontation between federal responsibility and George Wallace was interesting to see but almost anticlimactic. Wallace made his stand and then stepped aside. He was well prepared for his moment in the television sun. A lectern was in place in front of the famous door. Wallace was ready, with his microphone around his shirt collar. The public address systems were humming! We saw it all!

When the token integration had been accomplished, the President decided to go before the nation with an important statement about civil rights from what Theodore Roosevelt had called a "bully pulpit." John Kennedy delivered one of the greatest speeches of his career,[49] yet his eloquence appeared strangely lost in the context of the events that preceded it. A lesson seemed to be implied! Great speeches are delivered when men wonder about what they are to do. Offer the same resolutions after men have acted, and you will fail to make the strongest possible impression.

News the Weapon

In a 1962 speech to the Air Force Association, Arthur Sylvester, Assistant Secretary of Defense for Public Affairs, made comments that raised a controversy of immense proportions. His address, made behind closed doors, was soon widely reported. When attacked by his many critics, he denied that his remarks had been so strong. However, cautious observers have adequate grounds for defending both his right to his views and the opinion that the "leaks" about them were substantially accurate.

Sylvester is quoted by reporter Ted Lewis as saying, ". . . today in the cold war, the whole problem of information, how it is used and when it is used, when it is released, becomes a very vital weapon." Also, ". . . determination of releasing, withholding, in this sphere must lie not down the line, or with me, but has to be geared into what the man who goes before the people every four years to submit his stewardship, no matter who he may be, must be in line with what he and his top advisors are doing. . . ."[50] Shades of "Big Brother"!

All students of mass communications are well aware of the fact that security needs sometimes dictate official news policies. However, the Kennedy Administration was accused of a consistent policy of managing the news with goals not universally tied to national security objectives.

For the television industry, as well as for all other segments of the press in this society, the implications of officialdom having the power to decide between security and politics raises problems that will be with us for a long time to come. It is necessary that advocates of freedom, working in television and the other media, be well versed in this problem.[51] News is a weapon for the progress or regression of democratic institutions, and the news policy of the Kennedy Administration deserves careful scrutiny in this regard.

FOOTNOTES

1. Tom Wicker, "Kennedy Pledges Space Advances; Opens Texas Tour," *New York Times,* November 22, 1963.

2. Jack Gould, "More TV Debates in '64 Race Urged," *New York Times*, November 22, 1963.

3. Jacques Lowe, *Portrait, the Emergence of John F. Kennedy* (New York: Bramhall House, 1961), pp. 186–187.

4. *Ibid.*, p. 186, p. 193.

5. *Public Papers of the Presidents of the United States, John F. Kennedy, 1961* (Washington: U.S. Government Printing Office, 1962), pp. 1–5.

6. Elmer E. Cornwell, Jr., "The President's Most Powerful Tool," *Saturday Review*, January 2, 1965, p. 16.

7. Clinton Rossiter, *The American Presidency*, (New York: The New American Library, 1956), p. 83.

8. James E. Pollard, *The Presidents and the Press* (New York: The Macmillan Company, 1947), pp. 502–503, 548, 552, 602–603, 742–770.

9. "Exit an Old Roman," *Time*, Vol. 60, No. 8 (August 25, 1952), pp. 37–38.

10. Mark Sullivan, *Our Times*, Vol. 3 (New York: Charles Scribner's Sons, 1930), p. 80.

11. James Reston, "Press and President," *New York Times*, March 14, 1956.

12. Leo C. Rosten, *The Washington Correspondents* (New York: Harcourt, Brace and Company, 1937), pp. 24–25.

13. James E. Pollard, *The Presidents and The Press*, pp. 702, 716–717, 769.

14. Cabell Phillips, "Q. & A. on the Press Conference," *New York Times*, February 13, 1955.

15. James MacGregor Burns, *Roosevelt: The Lion and the Fox* (New York: Harcourt, Brace and Company, 1956), p. 189.

16. Samuel I. Rosenman, *The Public Papers and Addresses of Franklin D. Roosevelt*, Vol. 2 (New York: Random House, 1938), p. 30.

17. *Ibid.*, p. 31.

18. J. M. Burns, *The Lion and The Fox*, p. 205.

19. Paul F. Lazarsfeld and Frank N. Stanton, *Radio Research* (New York: Duell, Sloan and Pearce, 1941), p. 267.

20. Harry S. Truman, *Memoirs, Year of Decisions*, Vol. I (New York: Doubleday and Company, Inc., 1955), p. 47.

21. "The Transcript of Eisenhower News Conference on Foreign and Domestic Issues," *New York Times*, March 15, 1956.

22. W. H. Lawrence, "Eisenhower's Press Parleys Rival Hoover's in Scarcity," *New York Times*, September 27, 1953.

23. Cabell Phillips, "Speaker of the White House," *New York Times*, August 12, 1956. Also see Merriman Smith, "White House Front Man," *New York Times*, October 4, 1953.

24. Merriman Smith, "Evolution of Eisenhower as Speaker," *New York Times*, August 7, 1955.

25. Jack Gould, "Television in Review—First Presentation of Cabinet Meeting Marred by Professional Touch," *New York Times*, October 26, 1954. See also Jack Gould, "TV: Matter of Technique—Viewer Distracted from Secretary Dulles' Message by President's Presence," *New York Times*, May 20, 1955.

26. "Transcript of New Conference Held by Wilson and His Military and Civilian Aides," *New York Times*, May 22, 1956.

27. Remarks of Pierre Salinger introducing A. H. Lerman and H. W. Chase, editors, *Kennedy and the Press* (New York: Thomas Y. Crowell Company, 1965), p. x.

28. *Ibid.,* p. ix.

29. "The President's News Conference of January 25, 1961," *Public Papers of the Presidents, 1961,* pp. 8–17.

30. "News Conference of March 8, 1961," *Kennedy and the Press,* p. 41.

31. *Kennedy and the Press,* p. 494.

32. Ted Lewis, "TV Press Conference," *The Nation,* Vol. 192, No. 6 (February 11, 1961), pp. 112–113.

33. Elmer E. Cornwell, Jr., *Presidential Leadership of Public Opinion* (Bloomington: Indiana University Press, 1965), p. 190.

34. *Ibid.,* p. 188.

35. John K. Jessup, "Two Most Eminent and Strikingly Different Columnists," *Life,* Vol. 58, No. 18 (May 7, 1965), p. 41.

36. *Public Papers of the Presidents, 1962,* p. 63.

37. James Tracy Crown and George P. Penty, *Kennedy in Power* (New York: Ballantine Books, 1961) pp. 17, 19.

38. *Public Papers of the Presidents, 1962,* pp. 726–728. For background, see "Mississippi," *Newsweek,* Vol. 60, No. 16 (October 15, 1962), pp. 23–29; *New York Times,* October 1, 1962, especially pp. 1, 22–24; address by Dr. James W. Silver, Professor of History at the University of Mississippi and President of the Southern Historical Society at the Society's annual meeting. Dr. Silver analyzed the closed, monolithic situation in his state, *New York Times,* November 8, 1963. For the President's 1963 comments, see *Public Papers of the Presidents, 1963,* p. 378.

39. *Public Papers of the Presidents, 1962,* pp. 806–809. For background, see Richard Oulahan, "Step by Step in a Historic Week," *Life,* Vol. 53, No. 18 (November 2, 1962), pp. 42B–49; Robert D. Crane, "The Cuban Crisis: A Strategic Analysis of American and Soviet Policy," *Orbis,* Vol. 6, No. 4 (March 11, 1963), pp. 3–21; Fletcher Knebel, "Washington in Crisis: 154 Hours on the Brink of War," *Look,* Vol. 6, No. 26 (December 18, 1962), pp. 43–54.

40. "Mr. Kennedy's Second Year," editorial, *New York Times,* January 8, 1962.

41. *Boston Globe,* February 7, 1963; see also Bernard Rubin, "Secrecy, Security, and Traditions of Freedom of Information," in Otto Lerbinger and Albert J. Sullivan, editors, *Information, Influence, and Communication* (New York: Basic Books, 1965), pp. 136–175.

42. Sister Mary Paul Paye, "The Kennedy Cult," *The Nation,* Vol. 195, No. 3 (August 11, 1962), pp. 49–51.

43. *Public Papers of the Presidents, 1963,* pp. 650–653.

44. *Public Papers of the Presidents, 1962,* pp. 888–905.

45. Leslie Carpenter, "CBS Protested Kennedy Edits," *Boston Sunday Herald,* December 23, 1962. Also, for relevant material, see, Worth Bingham and Ward S. Just, "The President and the Press," *The Reporter,* Vol. 26, No. 8 (April 12, 1962), pp. 18–23.

46. Special section on "Eisenhower's Peace Trip," *Boston Sunday Globe,* January 17, 1960; articles on the trip in *New York Times,* December 3–22, 1959.

47. James Reston, "Khrushchev's Odyssey," *New York Times,* September 24, 1959; "U.S. Cartoonists' Opinions on Khrushchev's Visit," *Editor and Publisher* (September 26, 1959), p. 84; "The U.S. Asks: What Hit Us?" *Life,* Vol. 47, No. 14 (October 5, 1959), pp. 35–42.

48. *Public Papers of the Presidents, 1963,* p. 524.

49. Michael Dorman, *We Shall Overcome* (New York: Dell Publishing Company, 1964) for one account of the Alabama story. For citation relative to the

program, "Crisis: Behind a Presidential Commitment," see Jack Gould, *New York Times,* October 23, 1963.

50. Ted Lewis, "Sylvester Blows Up over Being Called 'Sour Trumpet,' " *Boston Sunday Herald,* February 3, 1963.

51. For background, see *Report of the 1962 Sigma Delta Chi Advancement of Freedom of Information Committee,* November 1, 1962; Arthur Krock, " 'Managed News' Growth Feared," *Boston Herald,* week of November 12–16, 1962; "How Much Censorship? How Much Distortion?" *Newsweek,* Vol. 60, No. 20 (November 12, 1962); Kenneth Crawford, "News Management," *Newsweek,* Vol. 61, No. 10 (March 11, 1963); Committee on Government Operations, *Safeguarding Official Information in the Interests of the Defense of the United States* (Washington: U.S. Government Printing Office, 1962); John E. Moss, "The Perils of Secrecy," Appendix, *Congressional Record,* Vol. 108, No. 26 (February 22, 1962), pp. A 1352–A 1353; Jack Raymond, "Pentagon Imposes Restraint on News Coverage," *New York Times,* November 1, 1962; Edward Crankshaw, "Case History of an Unfree Press," *New York Times Magazine,* December 2, 1962; Stanislav Koutnik, "Cooking the Cuban News—That Historic Week as Seen in Czechoslovakia," *The New Republic,* Vol. 147, No. 26, December 29, 1962.

5 / Those Four Days

AIR FORCE ONE

The air traffic at Andrews Air Force Base in Maryland was heavy on the evening of November 22, 1963—heavier than usual, under the circumstances. Air Force One, the Presidential airplane, cut its engines about 6 P.M. and was bathed by a circle of spotlights.

That afternoon Air Force One had been a stage for history when U.S. District Judge Sarah T. Hughes had given the oath of office to Lyndon B. Johnson in the President's suite, a combination conference and sitting room. Twenty-seven people had crowded into the room to witness the solemn ceremony. Mrs. Johnson had stood at her husband's side along with Mrs. Kennedy. The oath-taking had lasted two minutes, and at its conclusion the new President had said, "Now, let's get airborne." In the rear compartment during that flight from Dallas to Washington was the casket containing the body of John F. Kennedy. Mrs. Kennedy kept vigil beside it, attended by four staff members who had been close friends of the late President.

After the coffin had been removed from the airplane, President Johnson and his wife emerged and walked to a nearby spot on the field where a bank of microphones and cameras had been hastily assembled. Fighting his emotions, Lyndon Johnson read his first public statement as President.

> This is a sad time for all people. We have suffered a loss that cannot be weighed. For me it is a deep personal tragedy. I know the world shares the sorrow that Mrs. Kennedy and her family bear. I will do my best. That is all I can do. I ask for your help—and God's.

THOSE FOUR DAYS AND TELEVISION

The wave of shock caused by the assassination spread quickly over the nation. From the time of the first terse and baffling announcements that came over radio and television, the need to know what had happened predominated over most other concerns. At first, the news was that the President had been wounded. For some time after John Kennedy's death, the sheer crush of events that pressed on all persons close to the scene of disaster precluded any attempt to decide about the form and content of the announcement. After the first cryptic bulletins, the public endured what seemed an almost interminable period of uncertainty. Then all too soon, we learned the worst.

Shock and disbelief over John Kennedy's death were accompanied by deep and profound public uncertainty. Everyone's mind contained a jumble of questions! Who had shot the President? Was it a plot designed to overthrow the government? Where was the Vice-President? Was he safe and able to direct the government? What would happen now?

During that crisis, the television industry found itself ready to perform the great role thrust upon it. Never in its short history had the medium been so implicated in the success or failure of democracy. The industry rose to the occasion and to its duty.

One fact should be recognized. When the leaders and reporters of the electronic media heard the dreadful news, they were almost as unprepared as the rest of the population. Their fine work was a reflection of the impressive and substantial resources that they had built up to deal with such emergencies. Instinctively they set about their tasks, mindful that television was immediately in a powerful position to help restore stability to a nation and a world rocked by disaster.

As soon as the top managers of the three major networks received the first bulletins from Dallas, they decided to abandon all normal and scheduled programming and concentrate only on the unfolding story. As it worked out, they later revised their decision to suspend normal schedules until after the funeral.

There was a monumental logistics problem during those four days, but with astounding speed, the networks met the challenge. The result was the longest continuous reporting of a single story in the history of television. NBC covered the events for 71 hours; CBS for 69; and ABC for 60.

Administrative problems were compounded by the standing arrangement whereby coverage of Washington news was pooled among the three networks, with each network taking a turn once every three months. It was CBS's turn that month. The pooling was largely a matter of equipment and personnel assignment; NBC had 23 cameras in the pool at that time, CBS had 16, and ABC had 13. In addition, for the Washington operations, each network rushed other cameras into service for its own coverage (NBC, 21; CBS, 11; ABC, 5). Add to the logistics problem the enormous problem of alerting total network organizations to each shift in news, and one begins to appreciate the magnitude of the television operation. The networks' staff units in Washington were considerably enlarged—for example, NBC's staff doubled. Units in Dallas were augmented and aided in every possible way as the story there continued to unfold.

When NBC president Robert Kintner got a hunch about further violence in Dallas, he ordered William R. McAndrew, executive vice-president in charge of news, to beef up the staff on duty there. NBC newsman Tom Pettit was called urgently from the Los Angeles office to fly to the assistance of an already large staff group in Dallas. Pettit arrived just in time to witness and report the second startling news event in three days. Who can forget the scene in the basement of the Dallas city jail, when Jack Ruby intercepted Lee Harvey Oswald as the President's suspected assassin was being escorted to a police van for transfer to the county jail? Pettit was there and had just shouted out to NBC control, "Take me, take me!"[1] Chaos broke loose in the room, and an incredible scene unfolded before the vast television audience. Witnessing a murder, all wondered whether the dreadful experience that had begun with the horror at the Presidential motorcade would ever end.

Also, many wondered why the television cameras had been allowed so close to the prisoner. The TV cameramen—and Jack Ruby—might have been more restricted in their movements that day if the Dallas police had been more attentive and wise. In the words of the American Civil Liberties Union:

> Minimum security considerations would dictate that the transfer of this prisoner at least out [sic] not, in effect, have taken on the quality of a theatrical production for the benefit of the television cameras. These concessions to the demand for publicity, however, resulted in Oswald being deprived not only of his day in court, but of his life as well.[2]

From the moment when United Press International's Teletype machines began to clack out the first messages on the shooting of the President, logistics constituted but one problem for the networks. Shortly after 12:34 A.M., the results of Merriman Smith's frantic efforts to reach UPI's Dallas Bureau were seen in the message, "UPI A7N DA—Precede Kennedy—Dallas, Nov. 22 (UPI —Three shots were fired at President Kennedy's motorcade today in downtown Dallas. JT1234PCS."[3]

Set in motion was the most intensive coverage ever given to one big story and its ramifications. Television crews went to Parkland Memorial Hospital in Dallas to film the comings and goings from street vantage points; government officials in Washington were interviewed for first-shock reactions; the White House was covered for any possible developments; impromptu reportage, largely commentary, poured out as stunned reporters went on the air to relate everything that they could responsibly surmise; private citizens across the nation were interviewed for man-in-the-street reactions; and films were screened that showed the principals in the developing story dashing here and there. Later that day, the scenes of the ambulance and its escort entering White House grounds became public domain. Word came from Dallas that Oswald had been arraigned for the murder of Patrolman Tippit, and reporters badgered police officials for a story. If they got something of apparent consequence, those tidbits were relayed to the spellbound television audience.

One conclusion about television's role emerged most clearly. If given a choice between radio and television, most Americans chose television. This is not to play down radio coverage, but to suggest that citizens will not ignore the added dimension that television offers! Especially at a time when the government itself seemed threatened, the populace tended to turn on their television sets. A great many people left television vigils reluctantly, and when they did so, they snapped on their radios.

There is a marriage between television and radio at times of crisis. We tend to turn to both partners when our curiosity cannot be satisfied by either alone. Since so much of what came to us via the electronic media was confusing and repetitious, it became necessary to utilize both prime news outlets and to seek comfort from whatever we could see as well as from whatever we could hear.

On the second of those four horrible and memorable days, the television and radio industries managed to tie together some loose ends of the staggering story and to produce more meaningful work. As the government planned for the funeral, for receiving foreign dignitaries, and for special meetings of Congress, the network managers shifted operations according to a very much improvised and emerging pattern. Material tied to foreign reactions began to appear.

Later, we saw the awesome ceremonies in the White House near the bier of the slain President; short films of the arrivals and departures of American and foreign dignitaries who came to attend the last rites and to confer with President Johnson; photographs of the new President in conference; and the removal of President Kennedy's furniture into the vans waiting in the street outside the White House.

On Sunday, John Kennedy left the White House for the last time in a solemn state ceremony. We saw the mournful, dignified, and starkly impressive processional to the Capitol; the placing of the flag-draped coffin in the magnificent rotunda; the eulogies by Senator Mansfield, Speaker of the House McCormack, and Chief Justice Earl Warren before an assemblage composed of the late President's family and friends, officers of governments, and an honor guard; and the prayers of the late President's wife and daughter at the coffin. These scenes were all, through television's eyes, a public mosaic. "Nothing etched itself so sharply on the minds of all those who watched, in that rotunda and on television, as the moment when Jacqueline Kennedy and her daughter went to the bier and knelt beside it. The young widow kissed the flag and Caroline reached under it to touch her father's coffin."[4]

Through a long afternoon and night, television focused on that rotunda to record the pilgrimage of thousands of private citizens who came to pay their last respects. If ever it can be said that television coverage was appropriate and not intrusive in any way, those scenes should be pointed out as supporting examples!

On Monday, November 25, there was the processional from the Capitol to Arlington National Cemetery. The funeral march, the requiem service at St. Matthew's Cathedral, the long cortege to the grave site, and the funeral ceremonies were all brought before our eyes by the television cameras.

THE INFLUENCE OF TELEVISION

Television often fails to live up to what is considered to be its potential, in the thinking of reasonable critics. It is contended that opportunities for educational and cultural progress through more adroit utilization of the medium are often bypassed in favor of far less salubrious entertainment objectives. Many serious advocates of television even question whether the bulk of the more unimpressive *entertainment* programs are adequately and deliberately planned. Objective partisans of television are not blind to the obvious limitations of the medium.

Despite all the valid points that can be made against poor programs, be they cultural, political, or frivolous in character, the television industry frequently frustrates uncomplimentary critics by growing roses in the wasteland.

The news departments of the three major networks have grown steadily in stature in the past years. In the assassination crisis, those departments, aided and augmented by the news staffs of affiliated stations, not only reported events and sidelights of events, but fulfilled an even more important mission! By separating fact from fancy, to the extent possible, the news departments managed to keep the story within limits. The public needed to know that the ship of state, although dealt a severe blow, was not going to founder and sink.

Looking back on those four days, one can see that the worst effects of the national calamity were *subdued*, if that is the word, by television. Imagine the same circumstances that were at the heart of the Kennedy disaster occurring in an age without television. There would inevitably have been more mystery and prolonged fear. Statements by leaders, designed to comfort the public, would have sounded more dramatic or more vague. When we saw the hospital where the President was taken and saw the traffic around it, our agitation was somehow given a specific setting. Being familiarized with the particular places and faces in the drama helped us to settle down to the more important unknowns. We were able to see the terrible event in terms of its Dallas and Washington environments.

Because we saw accurate pictures of the scenes of disaster and ceremony and reconsecration, we could begin to define the perspectives involved. Of course, had there been a widespread plot to overthrow the government, then there would, undoubtedly, have been an attempt to capture control of the television industry at the same time. One lesson we have all learned is that we rely upon television for information in moments of crisis. If the instruments for communicating news had fallen into nondemocratic hands, even for the shortest period, then objective reporting would have been replaced by rumormongering and distortion. People tend to believe what they hear and see. If what they hear or see is untrue and concocted by evil minds, a crisis can be made far more grave.

For communications-industry leaders and for the leaders of government, the four days following the assassination of John F. Kennedy, thirty-fifth President of the United States, raised many issues that went beyond that particular crisis. We are all advised to study them in detail, in order to learn if the democracy is reasonably protected.[5]

FOOTNOTES

1. Eleanor Roberts, "NBC's Hunch: The Oswald Slaying," *Boston Traveler,* November 27, 1963.

2. "Text of the American Civil Liberties Union Statement on Dallas Police," *New York Times,* December 6, 1963.

3. United Press International and *American Heritage* magazine, *Four Days* (New York: American Heritage Publishing Co., Inc., 1964), p. 22.

4. Ibid., p. 83.

5. Materials relevant to the crisis abound. For the reader's further study the following sources, utilized in the preparation of this chapter, are recommended: *President Kennedy, Report* (Washington: U.S. Government Printing Office, 1964); Urs Schwarz, *John F. Kennedy* (London: Paul Hamlyn, 1964); *New York Times,* issues November 22–December 2, 1963; *Boston Globe,* issues November 23–25, 1963; *Sunday Herald Tribune,* November 24, 1963; "John F. Kennedy Memorial Edition," *Life* (1963); "The Talk of the Town," *The New Yorker* (November 30, 1963), pp. 49–53; Max Ascoli, "The 22nd of November," *The Reporter,* Vol. 29, No. 10 (December 5, 1963), p. 19; "Text of American Civil Liberties Union Statement on Dallas Police," *New York Times,* December 6, 1963; "And Then It Was November 22 Again," *Newsweek* (November 30, 1964), pp. 25–28; Erwin N. Griswold, "When Newsmen Become Newsmakers," *Saturday Review* (October 24, 1964), pp. 21–23; Harold Faber, editor, *The Road to the White House* (New York: McGraw-Hill Book Company, 1965), especially pp. 1–10.

6 / Let Us Reason Together

WHICH LYNDON JOHNSON?

When John Kennedy selected Lyndon Johnson to be his running mate in 1960, the choice was not popular with the inner circle of Kennedy advisors, and many liberals high in the power structure of the Democratic Party objected strongly.

Johnson, they argued, was primarily a sectional politician, and even in the South and the Southwest, he did not have the strong support needed to carry the ticket to victory in November. He was weak on the civil rights question, they objected, and he was badly prepared and politically vulnerable on many vital issues such as labor problems and foreign affairs.

There is some reason to believe that, when Kennedy telephoned Johnson to offer him the nomination for Vice-President, the Massachusetts Senator did not expect Johnson to accept. Kennedy would then have been free to pick someone closer to him ideologically. Adlai Stevenson, Hubert Humphrey, and Stuart Symington, among others, seemed to be strong contenders for the honor.

However, the call was made, and Johnson did accept. Perhaps Kennedy's decision to make the offer was in some measure reflective of the strong position within the Democratic Party of Sam Rayburn, the long-time Speaker of the House of Representatives and Johnson's mentor.[1] Or the power of the liberal wing of the Democratic Party might have been of less concern to Kennedy than the power of the conservative echelons. It is clear that Johnson, in 1960, was considered a Southerner by the majority of the national electorate. Generally, it was assumed that Johnson was a man with a conservative bent.

Were the categorizations fair or accurate? Long before Kennedy achieved substantial national recognition, Johnson was hard at work on the Washington scene. His first involvement in organized politics came when he was appointed Texas state administrator for the National Youth Administration in 1935. After two years in that post, he was appointed secretary to a Texas Congressman. In 1937, Johnson won a seat in the House of Representatives, emerging victorious from a nine-candidate race. Interestingly, Johnson campaigned as a dedicated supporter of Franklin D. Roosevelt at a time when FDR's so-called "court-packing" plans for the Supreme Court had caused many rank-and-file Democrats to desert their chief. The other candidates were critical of FDR, and they lost. When President Roosevelt heard about this youthful party loyalist who was fighting so hard for him in Texas, he invited Johnson to visit him on his boat (the President was fishing off the Texas coast at the time) and subsequently instructed his intimates, "Take care of this boy."[2]

Right from the start of his political career, Johnson earned the reputation of being a loyal party man and a talented political tactician. In 1948, he became the junior U.S. Senator from Texas. By 1952, a reputation for loyalty and for Congressional diplomacy had been confirmed by his record during eleven years in the House and four years in the Senate.

As is well known, the U.S. Senate is a rather unique club. When one of its members impresses his colleagues and is rewarded by his own party's representation, that club certifies his good standing. For the first two years of the Eisenhower Administration, LBJ served as minority leader in the Senate and, for the next six years, he was the Democratic majority leader. With tact, political skill, social grace, and his inherent flair for dealing with other people of consequence, he worked his way to the point that astute observers of the federal scene often rated him as the second most important person in Washington.

As Senate majority leader, Johnson took the view that the success of Eisenhower's major programs was necessary for national health and that his own support of such programs would be in the best tradition of loyal opposition. Johnson is given large credit for putting the 1957 civil rights law through Congress.

If we ponder the meaning of Johnson's efforts on that 1957 legislation, it becomes clear why the Vice-Presidential nominee of 1960 and the new President of 1963 radiated such a cloudy public image to the national electorate. Johnson's strong stand in 1957, which did much to offset Southern opposition, contradicted his earlier record on the thorny race issue. In 1937 he had voted against an antilynching bill, and voted against other versions in 1940 and in 1950. He had opposed anti-poll-tax bills in 1942, 1943, 1945, 1947, and 1950. In 1946 and in 1950, he had voted against proposals for the creation of a federal Fair Employment Practices Commission.

According to Jack Bell, who wrote *The Johnson Treatment* (1965), Johnson sent his constituents a form letter on March 19, 1957, that said, "I do not know where you could have gotten the idea that I am supporting 'the so-called bill for civil rights legislation now before Congress.' Certainly I made no statement to that effect nor have I intimated to anyone that I plan such support." The Senator went on to announce that he was "very much opposed" to that bill and did not "believe that it would advance any legitimate cause."[3]

Largely under Johnson's prodding, the Senate passed the civil rights bill on

August 7, 1957.[4] The erstwhile opponent to civil rights legislation became one of only five Southern Democrats to break with tradition and support the bill. Lyndon B. Johnson and Ralph Yarborough of Texas, Estes Kefauver and Albert Gore of Tennessee, and George Smathers of Florida joined in support of what Richard B. Russell of Georgia had labeled "an instrument of tyranny and persecution."[5]

It is futile to try to put political and ideological tags on Lyndon Johnson because he took this or that position in the past. To get at the inner man adequately, it is necessary to observe how he was shaped by the events of his life. Just as Senator John Kennedy put in a rather lackluster performance regarding the McCarthy problem early in his career, so Senator Lyndon Johnson grew with time and opportunity in his approach to the civil rights issue. The ideal politician, who is consistent throughout a long career, hardly exists. Politics, after all, is the art of compromise.

At the start of his political adventure Johnson showed some courage in supporting FDR despite the "court-packing" issue, but he must have been as aware of the advantages to be gained as he was of the dangers involved in such a stand. Conditions change, and men change accordingly. Johnson, the young Congressman and then the novice Senate leader, developed as his constituency enlarged. First sent to Washington as a product of Texas politics of the time, he epitomized its virtues and its defects. Later, he altered his views drastically, and that change demonstrates, in part, how sharply the political climate can cause reactions. He came to Washington a Southerner; in the capital, he became a national man.

Harsh critics attacking Johnson's character have called him a "wheeler dealer," but friends see him as a great persuader. Speaking on his own behalf, the President likes to have the public accept him as a man who follows the advice of the Biblical prophet Isaiah, who said, "Come now, let us reason together."

There is every reason for the political analyst to come to the conclusion that Lyndon Johnson was vastly underestimated as of his first day in the White House. To a degree, such underestimation ran parallel to the opinions most people held about Harry Truman before political chance and destiny moved the man from Missouri to the top post in the government.

In 1958, Johnson wrote that he was "a free man, an American, a United States Senator, and a Democrat, in that order." Also, "I am . . . a liberal, a conservative, a Texan, a taxpayer, a rancher, a businessman, a consumer, a parent, a voter, and not as young as I used to be nor as old as I expect to be— and I am all these things in no fixed order."[6] He is also, as can be attested to from many sources, a deeply sensitive person of great personal charm who is, above all, a professional politician. One of his associates has said that, after a full work day of politics, the President enjoys a long rest period—of politics!

A good estimation of the new President was given by an editorial writer who, immediately after Johnson took office, observed:

> . . . Lyndon Johnson enters the White House a man basically different from his predecessor. While Mr. Kennedy accented the new and the novel in national life, Mr. Johnson accented the traditional; while Mr. Kennedy represented the urban industrial and international-minded Northeast, Mr. Johnson represented the rural, agricultural and regional interests of the Southwest; while Mr. Kennedy placed his confidence in organization and clear-cut direction from the top, Mr. Johnson believed in the negotiated settlement, the compromise, in settling for the best you could get when the chips were down.[7]

Which Lyndon Johnson entered upon Presidential duties? When the heavy mantle fell on his shoulders, all the old Johnsons came into office, along with a new Johnson, only evident in glimpses before!

Curiously, Johnson came into the Presidency better known *about* than known by the national electorate. To a great many people, he was the man dealt in by Kennedy at the last moment—or the publicized emissary who had been sent to Berlin or to the Dominican Republic or to Southeast Asia by the late President. Unfortunately, he was also well known to a multitude, who knew little or nothing about his governmental career, as the man who had casually invited one Bashir Ahmad, a Pakistani camel driver, to drop in on him "back home," when he was stumping Ahmad's native heath. The camel driver came, and the country took in the whole affair with delight.

On the positive side, it is fair to say that, when Johnson was orbiting in that limbo we reserve for Vice-Presidents, three years of varied activities failed to shake the impression that he was the fellow, remembered from television and the press, who had made a serious stab for the nomination in 1960 after Humphrey had fallen by the wayside in West Virginia's primary and Stevenson had managed to capture more convention sentiments than delegates' ballots.

But Johnson entered office with a major handicap—the overwhelming national upset over the slain leader. In three short years, in this mass media age, Kennedy had become the epitome of the times. We all had watched as he tried to turn the tides of history; to bring new hopes to a weary world; to give new meanings to historic and cherished American dreams. Kennedy, as President, had had style and grace and "vigah."

Against the backdrop of Kennedy's image and a national unpreparedness to accept his loss, there appeared at center stage an older man with a time-lined countenance. He was labeled a sectionalist and was viewed by many as a man who had worked his way to the top only by compromises and by political maneuvering at the 1960 national convention.

Working in Johnson's favor was the instinctive rallying together of a people who wanted to be assured and secured to some adequate tethering post. Despite doubts and worries, the heart of a nation went out to the man who had to assume the great duties of the Presidency.

TAKING HOLD: FIRST DAYS IN OFFICE

As soon as he reached Washington as President on November 22, 1963, Lyndon Johnson began to take hold. There was no time for contemplation when Cabinet meetings had to be arranged, when Congressional leaders had to be met, when former Presidents were calling to offer help and advice, and when a mountain of detail had to be scaled. Among other duties Johnson attended to during that first full day in office was a telephone call to Keith Funston, president of the New York Stock Exchange, to reassure him and thus to steady the trading situation. Problems of foreign affairs and domestic affairs took turn with the need to make sure that the Kennedy "team" would stay on to tide him over his most difficult period.

During the four days preceding the funeral, Johnson stayed as discreetly in the background as possible. However, television showed him as he went from one place to another and as he walked to church for the final service. He was seen frequently but only in snatches. Photographs of him meeting with Dean Rusk or McGeorge Bundy or Anastas Mikoyan or Charles de Gaulle filled the pages of the press and comforted the television audience as signs of continuity in government.

Television, a Major Factor

The President realized that he must go before the nation as soon as possible to give an account of his plans and to give the people a clear prospect of their new leader. Within two days, advisors were working on a draft of his first major speech to Congress, which would be screened on television. The idea of addressing the legislature so quickly was a good one, because in speaking to the solons and beyond them, to the citizenry, he would be in a setting symbolizing the institutions of government and the lasting qualties of our heritage.

To accommodate the man from Texas, the speech had to be inspiring and yet not readily comparable to a similar Kennedy effort. His style of oral communication was radically different from Kennedy's. That Texas drawl, the more languid use of prose, the greater stress on homely phrases, and the earthier and folksier expressions were all matters to be dealt with. Several drafts were prepared—Theodore Sorenson, Kennedy's chief speechwriter, set to work on one; Professor John K. Galbraith of Harvard worked on another; and Horace Busby, a Texas newsman and Johnson friend, went to work on a third. The final version was largely put together by Sorenson, as amended by the President and translated into "Johnsonese" by Abe Fortas, who was a long-time Johnson confidant and whose knowledge of Washington went back to New Deal days.

Fortas not only gave the speech a Johnson imprint, but also instilled into the message something that the new Chief Executive admired—a Rooseveltian flavor. From his earliest days in politics, Johnson had considered himself a follower of FDR. The first formal message had to offer something honed on that political grindstone.

Five days after the assassination, Johnson stepped to the rostrum of the House of Representatives and spoke to a joint session of Congress. Also present were members of the Supreme Court and members of the Cabinet.

Certain key excerpts from that historic speech will suffice to show how well the exigencies of the moment and the long-range needs of the people were treated. The President's sincere resolve was beyond question. Not only his words, but his look and the reception spontaneously given him by his immediate and national audiences impressed the observers of that address.

> All I have I would have given gladly not to be standing here today.
> The greatest leader of our time has been struck down by the foulest deed of our time. . . .
> No words are sad enough to express our sense of loss. No words are strong enough to express our determination to continue the forward thrust of America that he began.
> The dream of conquering the vastness of space—the dream of partnership across the Atlantic and across the Pacific as well—the dream of a Peace Corps in less developed nations—the dream of education for all our children—the dream of jobs for all who seek them and need them—the dream of care for our elderly—the dream of an all-out attack on mental illness—and, above all, the dream of equal rights for all Americans whatever their race or color. . . .
> This nation will keep its commitments from South Vietnam to West Berlin. . . .
> These are the United States—a united people with a united purpose. Our American unity does not depend upon unanimity. We have differences but now, as in the past, we can derive from these differences strength, not weakness; wisdom, not despair. . . .
> The time has come for Americans of all races and creeds and political beliefs to understand and to respect one another. So, let us put an end to the teaching and the preaching of hate and evil and violence. Let us turn away from the fanatics, from the far left and the far right, from the apostles of bitterness and bigotry, from those defiant of law, and those who pour venom into our nation's bloodstream.[8]

The address was fitting and reassuring. We saw and heard a man of *stature*. It was good to see the new Johnson, or perhaps see the old Johnson for the first time. Out of despair had come hope and a sense of urgent mission.

Congress responded favorably, as did the press, in the main. The American people breathed easier; foreign leaders sensed that we had not lost hold as a government; and the New York Stock Exchange registered a recovery. Television had demonstrated its talent to turn the whole world into an audience, and Johnson had passed his first test before this audience.

THE PRESIDENT IN ACTION

Lyndon Johnson surprised a great many people who were ignorant of the details of his long legislative career and were, therefore, excessively impressed with his ability to rise to the occasion. With intense reportorial concentration on the new leader, the people were to learn a good deal more about his personality, interests, family, and habits—in short order. Intense coverage for a number of weeks, especially television coverage, can make a former stranger most familiar.

In contrast to Kennedy's Eastern urbanity, Johnson offered a heady type of Western folksiness and a generally gregarious approach. One of the greatest differences between the two men was the difference between their temperaments. Johnson tends to throw himself into the mood of each occasion. He gets very gay, or very sad, or very sensitive. The Johnson who is gravely intoning a serious message on foreign policy in the morning is likely to be the life of the party that night. In contrast to his more introverted predecessor, Johnson is happiest when surrounded by friends who show delight in sharing his enthusiasms. JFK was a more generally consistent social creature than is his successor. Johnson is consistent only if you fully appreciate the variety of his activities in a recognizable pattern. At the start of his Administration, newsmen were intrigued by the sheer bravado of the President. He was likely to do the unexpected.

On the subject of press relationships, Johnson was leery of trying to follow in Kennedy's footsteps. Recognizing the success that Kennedy had achieved at the stand-up, one-man-show type of press conference, Johnson shied away from inviting contrast by staging such affairs. His reluctance was firmly grounded; he was beginning to be well known, but the image of another leader still cast long shadows. He had said, before he took office as President, "We expect perfection from our President, and when there's some imperfection, as there must be with every individual, we are pretty rough on him."[9]

Press Conferences

In his first six months in office, LBJ set indoor and outdoor records for variety in his relationships with newsmen. He addressed the reporters from a bale of hay at his ranch in Texas; in the theater of the White House; in the White House rose garden; and in the Cabinet Room. On one occasion, he led the reporters on a merry seven-lap tour of the White House grounds. On May 6, 1964, the President had a combination news conference and lawn party for reporters and their families. On many other occasions, he would announce spur-of-the-moment conferences and offer his views to the reporters quick enough to race to his side. *U.S. News & World Report* kept score on those first six months. Johnson, from November 23, 1963, to April 30, 1964, apparently surpassed Kennedy in volume, if Johnson's record is measured against the record for the comparable six-month period of one year before. LBJ delivered 189 speeches (JFK—105) and held 16 news conferences (JFK—9). On news conference technique, he "indicated a preference for the smaller, folksier, *untelevised* meeting with everybody relaxed."[10]

Naturally, the television industry was at first taken aback by the new developments, but it quickly responded by treating the President as a portable event. Later, many television newsmen wearied of the Johnson treatment because it was so hard to get set up for his "quickie" deliberations.

Not until February 1, 1964, did the President attempt something along the lines of the old Kennedy press conferences. He gave only about two hours notice, but the television people were allowed to film the meeting for delayed broadcast. Where was the session held? In the cramped quarters of the White House movie-projection room, which had an estimated capacity of 100 persons. The impromptu call, combined with the location Johnson arranged, caused much unfavorable comment from the newsmen. They suggested, among other things, that the President was fearful of engaging in a full-blown, adequately scheduled press conference.[11]

That sagacious and witty observer of Washington doings, James Reston, later commented about Johnson's first live televised press meeting, which took place on February 29, 1964. "President Johnson achieved his major objective in his first live televised news conference: he survived. He approached this ordeal like a man going to the gallows." And, "he got through today's assignment in good order: no runs, no hits, no errors and several issues left stranded. Lyndon Johnson is a talker rather than a performer. The more natural he is, the more impressive he is, and the smaller the room the better. So he was out of his natural element today." Having described Johnson's needs, Reston went on to describe the room (the International Conference Room in the new State Department Building) as "one of those big, square, half-acre, windowless I.B.M. rooms where the air, the sound and everything else comes out of a pipe."[12]

By the end of March 1964, the criticism about scheduling took its effect, and two live television sessions, announced in advance, were held in more adequate arenas. On April 16, a preannounced press conference was held in the same auditorium that Kennedy had used. Johnson did well, but one suspects that he was glad that the public no longer felt the need to make comparisons.

One impression of that first Kennedy-style press conference was offered by newsman Dickson Preston, writing for the Scripps-Howard newspapers. He sensed a nervous Johnson and nervous aides (his public relations men George Reedy, Jack Valenti, and Malcolm Kilduff). Preston gave credit to the President for choosing "as tough a 'first night' audience as possible. Scores of newspaper editors, in town for their annual convention, were sitting in. They helped swell the press conference to its official total of 512, not counting millions watching on TV." Preston continued:

> But as the moments went by, Reedy, Valenti and Kilduff visibly relaxed. Their man was doing well. If his television technique was not Kennedy's, it was certainly adequate.
>
> The President started off by tossing the assembled reporters a full budget of news announcements before they could even get in their first question.
>
> This ran on for 10 minutes, and by the time Johnson finished both the newsmen and their editors had well stocked notebooks. . . .
>
> Johnson handled the questions which did come with an aplomb equally reminiscent of his predecessor.
>
> He put himself into the Presidential race—if anyone had serious doubts about that—with a deft remark which brought a burst of laughter.
>
> Reminded by a questioner that a poll of editors shows most of them believe he'll be elected President this [1964] fall, Johnson grinned and replied: "I hope that they will feel in November as they do in April."[13]

Since his early period in office, Mr. Johnson has become more favorably disposed toward formal, televised press conferences, but he still prefers the off-the-cuff approach. Increasing, and especially noticeable as his first full term in office moves on, is the President's need to talk to audiences not composed of newsmen. With mounting difficulties facing his Administration and with a much more critical press concentrating on the White House, Johnson accepts many more speaking engagements before college audiences, social organizations, political groups, civic welfare associations, and the like than his predecessor did. One may conclude that the President's nature requires him to consult his constituency often.

A major difficulty one senses about President Johnson's speeches is that he has become too familiar to the television audiences, and thus, as of this writing, has lost much of his effectiveness. The audiences cannot separate a critical address from one that merely *sounds* critical, because he is on their screens so often. He obviously needs good editorial advice on the subject of television. However, it is well known that he does not relish such advice.

THE EXTENT OF PRESIDENTIAL DOMINATION OF TELEVISION

Walter Cronkite hit the nail on the head when he wrote, "Television news requires more cooperation from its subjects than any other reporting medium, and this creates a demand for a new kind of talent among news personnel. In other types of journalism, it is possible to compile a rather round report without the cooperation of the central individual."[14]

The television newsmen who cover President Johnson receive very little help from the subject as they try to prepare "round" reports. The eminence of his position, his personal characteristics, and the dearth of "hard" news in much of the background comment he supplies are all factors that work against the development of programs that clarify as well as display the President. But be it Johnson or another figure in the office of the modern Presidency, the ability of a Chief Executive to lead the television industry around is significant. Primarily, this is due to two related facts. First, the television audiences accept *news* much more readily than they accept *views*. Second, whatever the President does, even if it is as minor as picking up a beagle by the ears, constitutes *news*.

The national public is well aware of how consequential Presidential activities can be. While the citizenry recognizes that much soul-searching lies behind his more important moves, it is aware that a President will rarely confide in the television audience as he does in the counselors of his inner circle. Even newspaper journalists complain that they are prevented from getting the "inside" stories because so many public officials rely on the handout system of bulletins about their work.

To a limited extent, the ability of the President to dictate to the television industry is tied to a need of its own representatives. Television news program directors are always searching for good picture stories. If, for example, the President would don a space suit, enter a rocket, go into space, and walk outside the capsule, that would truly be television's meat!

Usually, however, the President is captured between official acts or when he is making a speech or welcoming a foreign visitor or doing something else equally routine. The speeches, once heard and seen, beggar all but the most astute commentary, even if the President has said little worth enshrining. Far too frequently, among television directors, what the President does or says eclipses any widespread interest in picking apart his words. As evidence, I offer his televised address to the United Nations, of December 17, 1963. The address was extremely pedestrian in content.[15] His purpose was merely to be seen before that international body and not to ruffle feathers. But television, on the theory that *any* major appearance of the President is intrinsically important, dutifully presented the speech as a *major* international event.

However, television newsmen are aware that, at any moment, the President *could* say or do something of earthshaking consequence. Therefore, whether he helps them to serve their audiences fully or not, he is a prime figure for their attention whenever he wants to be. This is not to imply that he can captivate the television audiences, but that he can capture television equipment, crews, reporters, and time. Unlike a Broadway show, his run is a guaranteed four years, the fates permitting!

Also giving the President the upper hand in dealing with newsmen is the fact that there are deep-rooted questions of law as to how far television can intrude in order to secure more meaningful products for its audiences. Certainly, if the President does not want television crews on the White House grounds or on his ranch or at a government facility he happens to be visiting, he can have them excluded. Both he and the television industry know that he can accomplish such exclusion without loss of popular favor, by giving what seems to be a good reason tied to national security or the need for privacy. Explanations can be terse and restricted to a few people, so that the public remains totally unaware that such action has been taken.

On the question of the relationships between television and government, the United States Supreme Court, in reviewing the circumstances of the televised Texas trial of Billie Sol Estes (decision of June 7, 1965), severely limited and crucially questioned television coverage of such proceedings. A portion of the concurring opinion, subscribed to by Chief Justice Warren, Justice Goldberg, and Justice Douglas, is pertinent to our immediate discussion and to the wider problem of political television.

> In summary: television is one of the great inventions of all time and can perform a large and useful role in society. But the television camera, like other technological innovations, is not entitled to pervade the lives of everyone in disregard of constitutionally protected rights. The television industry, like other institutions, has a proper area of activities and limitations beyond which it cannot go with its cameras. That area does not extend into an American courtroom. On entering that hallowed sanctuary, where the lives, liberty, and property of people are in jeopardy, television representatives have only the rights of the general public, namely, to be present, to observe the proceedings, and thereafter if they choose, to report them.[16]

Granting that the Presidency and not the person of the President is a "hallowed" institution, the responsibilities and the power of the Chief Executive preclude any argument as to whether television can force its way into his official life. A wise industry and a wise President will try to achieve proper balance in their relationships. Nevertheless, a President can choose to be unpopular, and to the extent he is capable, to be unpublicized.

Even if television newsmen face difficulties in getting the stories that they would most desire from or about the President, they hardly dare to stand aside when he calls for attention. Whatever the President does is news, because he is the chief Constitutional officer of this government's executive branch. Giving a medal to a hero, shaking hands with a delegation of Boy Scouts, honoring an American "Mother of the Year," or displaying his pride in the roses in the White House gardens, he is the target for cameras and the subject for those on the Washington beat—because, at any moment, he could shift the discussion from roses to Russia. The reporter who ignores the President's routine activities is always in danger of missing out on the "big story" that may suddenly develop.

Of course, the attention given to the President does not give him any ability to control what happens when he casts his opinions out. While the President can make news, he cannot force the industry or the public to accept his interpretation of its importance. Richard E. Neustadt, in his study *Presidential Power,* supports this conclusion. "Without a real-life happening to hoist it into view, a piece of presidential news, much like a man's own voice, is likely to be lost amidst the noises and distractions of the day." However, Neustadt sees both sides of the coin and also remarks, "A President is not in firm control of most events, but there are some that he can manufacture."[17]

Of Politics and Government

Thirty days of mourning for John F. Kennedy, decreed by President Johnson and scrupulously observed in public by all politicians of stature, ended on December 22, 1963. The national mood, an almost universal display of good sense, and an overpowering desire for national unity at a crucial hour in this nation's history all combined to enforce the moratorium on politics for politics' sake.

Long after the end of those thirty days, the emphasis on unity made it extremely difficult for the Republican forces and for those in the Democratic Party who differed with the President to oppose him publicly. Only the occasional rantings of extremist groups threatened to disrupt this unity; the great majority of sober-minded citizens wanted to give the new President every chance to make good.

Indications of a return to a more normal state of affairs were evident as early as January 1, 1964, when Barry Goldwater announced his candidacy and Nelson Rockefeller resumed his drive to win the New Hampshire presidential primary. However, Johnson retained a favored position for many months. Although criticism of the President and of his policies grew livelier with the passage of time, most national politicians were cautious about expressing opinions that might be taken badly by an overly sensitive public.

Examination of press coverage into the spring of 1964 adequately demonstrates how fully Johnson's plans and activities occupied the center stage. As the presidential primaries rolled on, they tended to put a brake on his news domination. But, since news from 1600 Pennsylvania Avenue is always of vital interest, the spirited enterprises of the President did much to dampen the efforts of others to capture the publicity that should have been within their reach so close to election time.

Television, by following events closely, did much to enhance Johnson's status as the leading contender. When the cameras could not gain access to an event— for example, the news conference held in Johnson's office on December 7, 1963 —the news programs of the networks and of the local affiliates stressed evaluations and were replete with screened photographs. Commenting on the conference, they showed short films of the President sitting in his office and making the mile-long walk that morning from his home to the White House, escorted by Secret Service agents and followed by his car and a motorcade of Washington policemen.

Again, when a crisis brewed in Panama in January 1964, attention turned to the President. For more than a month his efforts, combined with the reportage from Panama and the Canal Zone, made headlines and filled telecasts. The telecasting of his "State of the Union" message to Congress that month also put him at the apex of mass media publicity. A great deal of collateral programming dealt with his arguments on budget problems, tax cuts, poverty programs, civil rights, and foreign policy. The President himself did not necessarily have to appear on television for his policies to gain publicity.

On January 29, the President was, in a sense, a part of the television program devoted to the launching of a pioneer Saturn rocket. He was photographed in his office, watching the launch on his own television set. During February, his first formal news conference and the myriad of attention-gathering problems he introduced made big news.[18] Commenting on his first hundred days in office, *The Christian Science Monitor,* on March 2, editorialized that he had earned "very good grades." Referring specifically to Johnson's first live television news conference, that newspaper said:

> We would give him a somewhat lower mark for his first performance in the difficult central role. . . . In reply to reporters' questions, he provided little specific information, on which the many might base their collective judgment. . . .
> Above all, we felt, the President was conscious of the weight of his words being sent around the world. Rather than say the wrong thing, he would err on the side of caution. The result was an impression that some questions were not so much being confronted as explained away.[19]

Visits to the United States by world leaders such as German Chancellor Ludwig Erhard and British Prime Minister Sir Alec Douglas-Home acted as additional spurs to the news media in those early months of the Johnson Administration. Films of the President and Chancellor Erhard at the Texas ranch were featured on television.

Three distinguished television newsmen interviewed Johnson in his office on March 16, 1964. Responding in a relaxed manner to the penetrating questions of Eric Sevareid (CBS), William H. Lawrence (ABC), and David Brinkley (NBC), he came across to television audiences as a man of considerable depth. That one-hour program was aired on all three networks. The President had the opportunity to expound on many questions, including one related to the rumored disaffection between him and Attorney General Robert Kennedy. Reports had it that Kennedy was campaigning for the nomination for Vice-President. After labeling the rumors as "newspaper talk," Johnson said before a national television audience "I would be less than frank if I said that I thought that it was wise at this stage of the game for either the President or the Vice-President [sic] to be carrying on a campaign for the office." Then, ". . . I take his [Robert Kennedy's] word that he had done nothing to encourage those efforts. . . ."

Most of that interview dealt with domestic matters. Considering the President's well-known sensitivity on the subject of Bobby Baker, many viewers wondered whether the newsmen would dare to bring it up. They did! Johnson skirted the issue, denying that Baker was a protégé of his and adding, "I think every man is entitled to a fair trial and I would like to see what conclusion is reached [by the Senate's investigating committee] and what the evidence shows with which I am not familiar before I make a judgment." It was a prime television moment, and it revealed more facets of a President than are usually seen.[20]

News films broadcast on April 9 showed the President making an emotional plea to businessmen, urging that they increase their interest in civil rights and look beyond legislation to the situations in their home communities. More coverage on April 16 was provided by, in Johnson's words, "a regular scheduled, televised, notified-well-in-advance press conference. I did not drive myself over here," he said (there had been much news comment publicizing claims of reckless driving by the President in Texas), "but I did have to come from an informal meeting with some tourists at the gate."[21] That confrontation with tourists also provided interesting camera material for news programs.

During April 1964, public interest was high on the question of whether there would be a national railroad strike. The dispute had dragged on for five years. An eleventh-hour postponement, which Johnson managed on April 9, and the subsequent strike-averting settlement announced on April 23 showed the President to be a forceful persuader indeed. He chose the White House Fish Room to make a dramatic announcement of the settlement before assembled newsmen and television cameras. Reading from letters two inches high on a TV "prompter," a haggard-looking Chief Executive summed up the results of the long period of secret negotiations that he had superintended. "Both management and the brotherhoods have tonight acted in the public interest. They responded as Americans to the request of their President, and they have done what is best for our country."[22]

Examples such as those cited could be produced almost ad infinitum. An editorial entitled "Slow Down Lyndon" in *The Boston Globe* of April 25, 1964, summarized the situation. Here are excerpts.

> . . . the man is just everywhere. If he does not suddenly appear, wearing a miner's hat, through a hole in the floor of one's living room. . . , he had found a new mode of entrance in the "boob tube." Even the sponsors of TV commercials must fear his interruption.
> Consider his activities for just the past week. To begin it, this man

who wasn't supposed to be a specialist in foreign affairs announces, jointly with Britain and the Soviet Union, a cutback in nuclear production. That should have been enough to hold any President for a month or two.

But no. He has to go and confound all the experts by settling the rail dispute. . . .

He has to walk out on innumerable occasions to the front gate of the White House to shake hands, through the palings, with visitors. . . .

He flies to New York to open the World's Fair, and let neither the weather nor the demonstrators dismay him.

He flies out to Chicago, and there, just by coincidence, he is greeted by little Cathy May Baker, who had urged him to settle the rail dispute so her grandmother could visit. He hoists her to his shoulder for a ride, and lands on page one all over the country. . . .[23]

Interested Parties

Johnson's obvious ability to dominate the media during the first months of his tenure as President impressed but at the same time disheartened the presidential hopefuls of the Republican Party, who were forced, by circumstances, to wait. There were two leading Republican contenders before the first presidential primary election took place in New Hampshire in March 1964—Senator Barry Goldwater of Arizona and Governor Nelson Rockefeller of New York. These two had announced their candidacies. Other personalities given considerable media attention were three men more or less available if the leaders in the party race wore each other down during the campaign. Most available was Richard M. Nixon, the man who had lost by such a close margin four years previously, but who had not announced his formal candidacy for 1964.

Flanking the front runners was Henry Cabot Lodge of Massachusetts, former U.S. Senator (he had lost his seat to JFK) and U.S. Ambassador to the United Nations during the Eisenhower Administration. In 1964, Lodge was serving as Ambassador to South Vietnam; he had been appointed to this post by President Kennedy. Although Lodge was widely respected in Washington, he had little support from the Republican Party regulars across the nation who controlled the organizational apparatus. They looked upon Lodge with some disdain because he did not have a home state behind him that he could likely carry in the general election; because, throughout his career, he had been too much the suave, diplomatic, patrician politician and not the more readily understandable loyal party type they favored; because he was compromised, the regulars complained, by the fact that he was a Kennedy appointee; because he could not speak out, politically, while on duty in Saigon; and because he had run as Nixon's mate in the 1960 campaign, without much effect. In fact, there was considerable anti-Lodge sentiment in the Republican rank and file because of his aloof, aristocratic bearing during the previous national campaign. Many

Republican partisans had concluded that Lodge was a weak campaigner; in particular, they considered unfortunate his 1960 statement promising the electorate that, if he and Nixon won, there would shortly be a Negro serving in the Cabinet.

Against all of his handicaps, Lodge had certain assets that few politicians were able or willing to estimate in early March 1964. First, while he was not conceded the ability to carry Massachusetts, a Democratic stronghold and Kennedy country, he was held in high regard in New England and was accepted as a talented and dignified person across the nation. Also, although he was unable to take political exercise while abroad, his overseas post gave him sanctuary from the political reporters who could badger all of the other announced or unannounced contenders.

A dark horse in 1964 was the young, comparatively inexperienced governor of Pennsylvania, William W. Scranton. If the Republican Party had to turn to a new face at the last hour, there were those who touted Scranton because he was superintending a successful state administration after a long tenure by a Democratic governor. He was handsome, eager, a good talker, and independently wealthy. All these were qualities appreciated by realistic, political kingmakers. However, Scranton was not well known nationally, and they recognized that it would take an enormous amount of publicity to overcome that handicap in the months before the convention and the general election.

Beginning with the preparations for the New Hampshire primary, the mass media turned increasingly to figures other than President Johnson. Nevertheless, the President had managed to take a substantial lead over all rivals in the publicity race. Still, the psychological mood induced in the citizenry by Kennedy's death was beginning to change—in part, because Johnson was so adroit in turning national attention to his own affairs and away from the legacy of Kennedy.

FOOTNOTES

1. Harold Faber, ed., *The Road to the White House,* pp. 129–130.
2. *Ibid.,* p. 128.
3. Jack Bell, *The Johnson Treatment* (New York: Harper & Row, 1965), p. 160.
4. William S. White, "Senate Approves Rights Bill, 78–18, with Jury Clause," *New York Times,* August 8, 1957.
5. "Excerpts from Speech on Civil Rights by Senator Russell," *New York Times,* July 3, 1957.
6. Harold Faber, ed., *The Road to the White House,* p. 132.
7. Section 4, "The News of the Week in Review," *New York Times,* November 24, 1963.
8. "Transcript of Johnson's Address to the Joint Session of Congress on U.S. Policies," *New York Times,* November 28, 1963.

9. "The Philosophy of President Lyndon B. Johnson," *U.S. News & World Report,* Vol. 55, No. 23 (December 2, 1963), p. 41; see also "Enter: The 10-Gallon Era," *Life,* Vol. 56, No. 2 (January 10, 1964), pp. 20–27.

10. "The Changes LBJ Has Brought in 6 Months," *U.S. News & World Report,* Vol. 56, No. 20 (May 18, 1964), pp. 46–54. Chart referred to is on p. 49, quotation is taken from p. 53, and the italicizing in the quote is this author's.

11. Elmer E. Cornwell, Jr., *Presidential Leadership of Public Opinion,* pp. 201–202.

12. James Reston, "President's TV Ordeal," *New York Times,* March 1, 1964. For a survey of one of the more unusual Johnson news conferences, that May 6, 1964, gala on the White House lawn for the news corps and their families, see "LBJ News Conference—Family Style," *U.S. News & World Report,* Vol. 56, No. 20 (May 18, 1964), p. 19. For an estimation of problems faced by Johnson with an even more critical press, see Douglas Kiker, "Johnson Honeymoon with Press Ending?" *Boston Sunday Globe,* February 9, 1964. For a British view of how Johnson attempted to "tailor" the public's view of him, see Patrick O'Donovan, "Johnson Tailors His Image," *Manchester Guardian,* August 2, 1964.

13. Dickson Preston, "Johnson Plays TV Role with Kennedy Gambits," *New York World-Telegram and Sun,* April 17, 1964.

14. Walter Cronkite, "Television and the News," in *The Eighth Art* (New York: Holt, Rinehart and Winston, 1962), p. 231.

15. *A Time for Action: A Selection from the Speeches and Writings of Lyndon B. Johnson, 1953–1964* (New York: Atheneum Publishers, 1964), pp. 156–163.

16. "Excerpts from Supreme Court's Opinions on Television Coverage of Estes Trial," *New York Times,* June 8, 1965, p. 30.

17. Richard E. Neustadt, *Presidential Power* (New York: The New American Library of World Literature, Inc., 1964), p. 101.

18. "Transcript of President's News Conference" and "Johnson Takes a Walk in the Truman Manner," *New York Times,* December 8, 1963; "The News of the Week in Review," *New York Times,* January 12, 1964, and January 19, 1964; Max Frankel, "Johnson Cautions Country to Avoid Air of Emergency," *New York Times,* February 2, 1964; Nan Robertson, "Our New First Lady," *Saturday Evening Post* (February 8, 1964), pp. 20–24; Lyndon B. Johnson, "The Politics of the Space Age," *Saturday Evening Post* (February 29, 1964), pp. 22–23; Tom Wicker, "Johnson Seeks Policy on Press," *New York Times,* February 9, 1964; Douglas Cater, "The Politics of Poverty," *The Reporter,* Vol. 30, No. 4 (February 13, 1964), pp. 16–20.

19. Editorial, "Very Good Grades," *Christian Science Monitor,* March 2, 1964.

20. "Transcript of Johnson's Assessment in TV Interview of His First 100 Days in Office," *New York Times,* March 16, 1964.

21. "Transcript of President's News Conference on Foreign and Domestic Matters," *New York Times,* April 17, 1964.

22. "Johnson Wins 15-Day Rail Truce; Averts a Nationwide Walkout with Plan for New Mediation," *New York Times,* April 10, 1964; "The Railroad Settlement: Triumph of Skilled Mediators and an Adamant President," *New York Times,* April 27, 1964; "5-Year Rail Dispute Ends," *New York Times,* April 23, 1964; "The Presidency," *Time,* Vol. 83, No. 16 (April 17, 1964), pp. 33–34.

23. Editorial, "Slow Down Lyndon," *Boston Globe,* April 25, 1964; see also, "The Presidency," *Time,* Vol. 83, No. 18 (May 1, 1964), pp. 17–21; Paul Lazarsfeld, *Mass Media and Personal Influence* (Washington: United States Information Agency, n.d.); and Ithiel de Sola Pool, *The Effect of Communication on Voting Behavior* (Washington: United States Information Agency, n.d.). The last two are reprints of lectures originally broadcast by Voice of America.

7 / Behind the Screens

It has become absolutely necessary for politicians to investigate the relationships between obvious qualities of television and its less apparent aspects, and the implications of television's incursions into political affairs are of prime importance to those who work within the industry.

Therefore, let us interrupt the chronological account of the 1964 campaign for the Presidency to concentrate on certain of its ramifications vital to the electorate, to office seekers, and to the managers of the television industry.

CONGRESSIONAL VIEWS: SPRING 1964

Television's influence on politics was very much on the minds of major-office seekers as the campaign of 1964 entered its fully active stage. Much speculation in the press and by radio and television commentators revolved around the subject. Therefore, it seemed appropriate to this writer that a poll of experienced politicians be taken when the campaign was in full swing.

Of course, it is very difficult to secure responses while the people one wants to question are busily protecting their public positions or trying to depose incumbents. A private poll of a pressured group at a peak of political struggle has obvious, built-in problems. Foremost is the fact that few politicians will take time out to form a critical judgment of a difficult problem when the thrusts and parries of opponents have to be countered. By the very nature of our mass media environment, a private poll that offers the respondents no hope of publicity in support of their immediate struggles and no likelihood of mass media attention later has little appeal for many of those questioned. Still, the prospect of securing vital information from key politicians under campaign stress was too tantalizing to abandon.

In mid-June of 1964, members of Congress were sent a questionnaire. Forty-one members of the House of Representatives and 14 Senators responded to that inquiry. In addition, one Congressman (Robert Taft, Jr.) declined to give his opinions because of "prior connections with the broadcasting industry";[1] two replies were made by staff members of Congressmen because their bosses were absent or unable to reply in sufficient time; and three Senators notified the author that they declined, as a policy matter, to answer such requests. With the exceptions noted, those who replied gave the questionnaire the benefit of their critical thinking.

Here are the questions that were asked of the legislators.

1. What is your opinion regarding the influences of television on American political campaigning?

2. What have been your own experiences which reflect the significance of television?

3. What do you recommend by way of maintaining or improving the present television-political situation? Do you propose any legislation or any procedural changes, vis-a-vis: length of campaigns in a mass communications environment; use of mass media facilities by opposing candidates; costs of campaigning today; need for fairness in regard to access to communication facilities; protection of major or minor party interests?[2]

Most of those who replied treated the three questions as an introduction to one general problem and highlighted the aspects that they considered vital. Three Representatives stressed television as a *detrimental influence.* Harlan Hagen (18th District, California) noted that "the use of the medium is so expensive that it gives great advantage to the candidate with the most money. In addition, I do not regard it as a valuable medium for in-depth discussion of political issues." Also, "television is primarily a personality medium. The candidate with the most attractive personality or the best ghost writers, in the case of spot announcements, would achieve the most success." He felt that the audience potentials for candidates below the presidential and "perhaps" the gubernatorial levels were "extremely limited."[3]

First commenting on the fact that he had made very limited use of television because "at least seven other districts, including four Cleveland districts," were "within the range of the television station" available to him, Frank T. Bow (16th District, Ohio) also was worried that "the handsome face" or the "glib manner" could influence many viewers, who would disregard the "sincere, able and sound" candidate who lacked a "TV personality."[4] Another Ohio Congressman, Oliver T. Bolton, sent materials that he had previously released to the press; these releases highlighted his concern that the methods used by the industry in broadcasting the California Republican primary of 1964 might lead to a more "thorny" issue. He wanted the radio and television networks to agree, on their own, to avoid any declaration of a winner in a national election until all the polls throughout the nation were closed.[5]

Representatives Donald Edwards (9th District, California) and James Roosevelt (26th District, California) said they wondered whether television campaigning was worthwhile. Edwards said that he would do very little of it because of the expenditures required and because the local station in his district (in San

Jose) operated in a region dominated by the big San Francisco network stations; "presumably," he pointed out, "most of the voters watch the big stations."[6] Roosevelt, serving a district that is a "relatively small part of the Los Angeles urban area," felt the impact of the same pressures. He suggested that statewide and national elections were best suited to television campaigning. He also worried about "certain exclusive privileges" afforded to the major parties at the expense of minority parties.[7]

Senator Hubert H. Humphrey of Minnesota (now the Vice-President) joined those who concentrated on the issues of costs and of local versus national television opportunities. He expressed the opinion that "television is becoming a prime factor in determining the undecided vote." He pointed to the Salinger-Cranston rivalry in California.

> . . . I note that Salinger lost 42 California counties and yet won by such an overwhelming majority in Los Angeles County as to overcome the deficit in rural areas. It might be interesting to try to correlate the kind and amount of television campaigning in Los Angeles County of the two respective candidates and try to measure the effectiveness of each. At least there is some evidence to indicate that there is a difference in the behavior of the electorate under saturation television campaigning as opposed to rural areas where television is of less importance. . . .
>
> Costs of radio and television, particularly of television, are getting so extraordinary, and members of Congress who run in a metropolitan area have to pay for reaching the entire metropolitan area rather than just their district, that some study should be made of limiting the amount of television that may be used by political parties and candidates, either in terms of time or terms of amount.[8]

Ernest Gruening (Senate, Alaska) wrote that he found television of more help than "any other medium" in his campaign for re-election.[9] John G. Tower (Senate, Texas) suggested that television had replaced the "courtyard rally" and that much was decided by virtue of the "attractiveness" of a candidate and by how effective his speechwriters happened to be. He was impressed by the way in which a candidate could use television to "become familiar to a far larger number of potential voters, much more quickly, than formerly."[10] Milward L. Simpson (Senate, Wyoming) also cited what he termed the "Ipana smile" impact upon voters and lamented television's exaggerations of nonintellectual and nonphilosophical qualities. Simpson said he was "very thankful for my successes in front of the cameras." He hoped for some type of fairness doctrine for presidential candidates but urged the waiving of the equal-time requirements for aspirants to the highest office.[11]

The factors of personality, of costs for television time, of network versus local station opportunities, and of fairness to minority-party contenders were alluded to repeatedly by those who responded to the poll. Other factors that appeared in these letters will now be considered, but it should be borne in mind

that there was widespread apprehension on those key problems just mentioned.
Looking ahead to possible reforms of election processes in the television era,
Gerald R. Ford (5th District, Michigan) observed, "Six to eight weeks of
campaigning [are] fully adequate as far as mass communications are concerned.
I would not object to a limited campaign of four weeks."[12]

Clement J. Zablocki (4th District, Wisconsin) wrote:

> . . . the amount of correspondence which I receive following a TV
> appearance, by far exceeds the response . . . from any other contact
> with the people, such as speeches, newsletters, radio programs or
> newspaper stories. . . . The people who write following a TV appear-
> ance have grasped the issue better than those responding to some other
> media.[13]

According to Fred B. Rooney (15th District, Pennsylvania), television has
provided the greatest technological advance in the history of politics. He
declared that it had "revolutionized" American campaigning. Along with that
"revolution" was one that, he said, "has come about from a general increase in
interest among amateurs or non-professional politicians."[14]

Abraham J. Multer (13th District, New York) commented that direct and
traditional campaigning by candidates on television was not the only way in
which the medium affected the outcome of elections.

> A different, a more subtle, and in most cases unintentional type of
> campaigning occurs, . . . throughout the year due to television news
> coverage and special programs designed to examine people, places and
> events in the news. . . .
> The more a public figure is in the news, attracting the public's
> attention, the more his actions are reported to the people through the
> medium of television, the more indelibly impressed are the viewers
> with the name, the face, and especially the value of that figure.[15]

These Congressional opinions, written during the heat of the 1964 national
campaign, point up the practical implications of television enterprise to men
who must compete with political rivals while adjusting their tactics to this
"revolutionary" new instrument for mass communications.[16]

MONEY AND PARTISAN OBJECTIVES

Access to television is gained by only two routes, as far as political campaign
managers are concerned. Time for programs is purchasable; but the costs have
escalated steadily during the past decade. The only other way to obtain television time is to secure some form of donation. Sometimes that donation process
involves the added benefit of "news" coverage. A *sustaining time,* or public
service, program (or series) may feature candidates and their competitors.
Under this arrangement, a debate between rivals may be sponsored by an

individual station or by the entire television industry for the benefit of the public.

However, in a practical sense, the candidate must purchase program time directly if he wants to be certain of appearing under the most advantageous circumstances. Of course, politicians and their advisors expending substantial sums of money have produced some rather dreadful programs; one dab of makeup and a blue shirt, and they think that a new charmer has filled the home screens from edge to edge. But for all of the technical mistakes and failures, the politician feels safer when he has bought the time and can control what is in the program. News programs and other public service offerings may bring him before the public, but he is rarely satisfied that he is captured as he sees himself and would have others see him. Furthermore, a joint appearance with his opponent on a public service program leaves the candidate worrying that the voters have heard too many of his rival's arguments.

For party rallies, most candidate speeches, special presentations of a campaign from one political viewpoint, dramatic conversations between a candidate and a group of supporters, and most other partisan presentations, money must be available.

In 1964, E. William Henry, the former chairman of the Federal Communications Commission, estimated, "Roughly 30 to 40 per cent of the candidates' expenditures are for radio and television." He added, "The problem is especially acute in a statewide or national race. But that's the way to get across to people now, and the candidates just have to pay the price."[17]

A few illustrations will point up the problem. When Governor George Wallace of Alabama was trying to win support for his so-called presidential campaign of 1964, his campaign organization paid $100,000 for a ten-day television effort preceding the Maryland primary. That money was to purchase time over stations in Washington; Baltimore; and Salisbury, Maryland. The $100,000 figure, which was given by an advertising representative in Maryland, was not confirmable but was considered low.[18]

On April 2, 1964, the American Broadcasting Company presented a public affairs program entitled "The Price of Politics." In the course of that program, very interesting calculations were given. Howard K. Smith noted, "Law permits the spending of 25,000 dollars by a candidate for the U.S. Senate. In fact, it costs as much as $2,000,000 in some states. . . . Where does the money go? Well, it costs: $120,000 for an hour of network television time, exclusive of production costs."[19] Dean Burch, Republican National Committee Chairman in 1964, related the troubles he encountered in trying to reach the public directly on behalf of Barry Goldwater. His experience led him to estimate a much higher base figure for an hour of network time.

A 30-minute telecast on a network costs in the neighborhood of $125,000, cash in advance, exclusive of production charges or reimbursements to the program which has been bumped. A one-minute spot announcement can cost $36,000. Even with cash in hand, obtaining desirable time is difficult, for the TV executives are usually anxious to protect their most popular shows from the incursions of a mere candidate for the presidency of the United States.

Burch is bitter in his article "Presidential Campaigns Are a Sham," written after the catastrophic defeat of Goldwater, and we sense that he wonders whether vast amounts of money simply went down the drain. He can be excused for some acidity in the light of these comments. "The greatest problem . . . is simply attracting the attention of the public to a political broadcast. The rating services reported that on the evening of October 29, for example, some 14 million Americans watched *Peyton Place* while on a rival network, Goldwater drew his peak audience of the campaign—7.3 million."[20]

How much has been expended for television by the major parties in recent campaign years? From the FCC's analysis, *Survey of Political Broadcasting: Primary and General Election Campaigns of 1962* (May 1963), we learn:

> Total television and radio station charges for political broadcasts were approximately $20 million (about $8 million in the primary campaigns and about $12 million in the general election.) Radio accounted for about $7½ million and television for $12½ million. . . . Candidates and their supporters spent about three times as much for spot announcements as they did for program time on television and radio combined . . . [and] on television it [the ratio] was 3 to 2.
>
> Democratic candidates and their supporters spent about $12 million for time and announcements on television and radio stations, whereas Republicans spent about 7½ million. The balance of the money (less than $700,000) was spent for candidates of other parties.[21]

In midsummer of 1965, the FCC conclusions about 1964 became available, along with comparisons of 1964 and the two presidential races directly preceding.[22]

Some method must be found to regulate campaign expenditures so that one candidate cannot virtually monopolize the electronic media during a political contest. Also, with the emphasis so strong on the cost factor in politics, the tendency of political parties to look for wealthy candidates closes opportunities to many talented, able individuals who have modest incomes but good ideas. It is possible that, in the near future, the situation will get so out of hand that Congress will have to enact legislation to ensure more equal opportunities for candidates who lack massive financial backing.

The trend toward pool coverage of campaign events by the networks will probably continue, perhaps to the point where much time that the partisans now pay for will be available under network sponsorship. Of course, the television industry will have to face increased governmental regulation if it becomes more pool-oriented and, therefore, more monopolistic.

From the 1962 figures cited, it is clear that the minority parties are largely out of the ball game when it comes to the ability to pay for television time.

TOTAL CHARGES[1] FOR POLITICAL BROADCASTS: 1964

	Total Charges	TELEVISION			AM RADIO		
		Total	3 Networks	Stations	Total	4 Networks	Stations
Primary and General Election—Total	$34,610,714	$23,776,935	$4,063,640	$19,713,295	$10,833,779	$121,705	$10,712,074
Republican	15,916,905	11,373,208	2,168,245	9,204,963	4,543,697	91,203	4,452,494
Democratic	17,841,125	11,911,916	1,895,395	10,016,521	5,929,209	30,502	5,898,707
Other	852,684	491,811		491,811	360,873		360,873
Primary Election—Total	10,006,725	6,280,530	256,629	6,023,901	3,726,195	2,340	3,723,855
Republican	2,884,330	1,942,098	256,629	1,685,469	942,232	2,340	939,892
Democratic	6,828,499	4,196,822		4,196,822	2,631,677		2,631,677
Other	293,896	141,610		141,610	152,286		152,286
General Election—Total	24,603,989	17,496,405	3,807,011	13,689,394	7,107,584	119,365	6,988,219
Republican	13,032,575	9,431,110	1,911,616	7,519,494	3,601,465	88,863	3,512,602
Democratic	11,012,626	7,715,094	1,895,395	5,819,699	3,297,532	30,502	3,267,030
Other	558,788	350,201		350,201	208,587		208,587

[1] Before commissions and after discounts.

TOTAL CHARGES[1] FOR POLITICAL BROADCASTS—GENERAL ELECTION 1956, 1960, AND 1964

	1964	1960	1956
Total Charges	$24,603,989	$14,195,278	$9,818,342
Republican	13,032,575	7,558,809	5,381,891
Democratic	11,012,626	6,204,986	4,120,712
Other	558,788	431,483	315,739
Television—Total	17,496,405	10,052,322	6,635,946
Network—Total	3,807,011	2,927,235	2,930,514
Republican	1,911,616	1,820,360	1,733,073
Democratic	1,895,395	1,106,875	1,197,441
Other			
Stations—Total	13,689,394	7,125,087	3,705,432
Republican	7,519,494	3,610,933	2,004,090
Democratic	5,819,699	3,307,987	1,549,347
Other	350,201	206,167	151,995
Radio—Total	7,107,584	4,142,956	3,182,396
Network—Total	119,365	78,867	320,940
Republican	88,863	44,546	144,645
Democratic	30,502	34,321	176,295
Other			
Stations—Total	6,988,219	4,064,089	2,861,456
Republican	3,512,602	2,082,970	1,500,083
Democratic	3,267,030	1,755,803	1,197,629
Other	208,587	225,316	163,744

[1] Before commissions and after discounts.

Note: 1960 and 1964 figures are from FCC **Survey of Politicial Broadcasting.** 1956 figures are from 85 Cong., 1 Sess., "1956 General Election Campaigns," Exhibit 24.

Increasingly, all parties, both major and minor, are climbing a mountain of costs with no summit in sight.[23]

THE NETWORKS ORGANIZE TO REPORT THE CAMPAIGN

Imagine for a moment that you are one of the key directors of a national television network and that you are meeting with your news and public affairs advisors to plot a program schedule for a forthcoming presidential campaign. Perhaps the first matter for discussion would be the plan for coverage of all of the state primaries, with special concentration on those that shape up as being crucial. Also, the major- and minor-party conventions would have to be reported upon. Important decisions would have to be made as to the amount of commitment that you could afford for live televising, for films for delayed use, for general commentator work, and for feature reporting. A pattern of television specials would have to be worked out but left flexible enough to allow time for coverage of special circumstances that might arise later in the campaign. To finish a major portion of the sketching-out procedure, proposals for election-night reporting of returns would have to be carefully weighed. Inevitably, this planning session would be, in part, based upon conversations between agents of your own and the other networks.

Having drawn a broad, superficial, and inherently changeable picture of key elements, a careful study of reserve resources would follow to ensure network capacity to handle the million and one unexpected but inevitable problems.

The comptroller of the network organization would be tracing an outline of the discussion and providing very rough financial figures. On occasion, he would veto a proposal by pointing out the severe drain involved. From time to time, the logistics authorities would interrupt the discussion to query another staff member about the magnitude of a request or to offer salient observations on what would be possible or impossible to accomplish.

Noting that you had set some good thinking in motion, you would likely adjourn the meeting after a short speech in which you expressed serious reservations about individual proposals and stated emphatically that your staff people had better "start climbing down from cloud nine and get practical." Your advisors would be ordered to go back to their departments and start their subordinates charting acceptable courses.

Later meetings would be held with numerous network officials and talented reporters to get their base requirements for the myriad of activities to be undertaken. Each candidate would have to be followed closely, once the campaign began; important background programs featuring public sentiments, voting history, ethnic problems, and so on would have to be set into the proposed schedule. A reserve fund would have to be earmarked for the "extras" that the staff would need. Commercial sponsorship would have to be obtained to support as much of the total enterprise as possible. Network affiliates would need guidance and would have to be utilized wisely. Seemingly, after months of organizing for the coming campaign, it would appear that the magnitude of the plan surpassed anything ever done before—even four years before!

To the credit of the networks and their local affiliates, it is evident that such planning is done meticulously. This care is fortunate, because the television industry not only reports a campaign; in a real sense, for tens of millions of Americans, the television view *is* the campaign.

In order to get a factual picture of the heavy obligations that have been assumed by the industry, consider the actual network programming for the 1964 presidential contest. A good picture is obtained if we survey elements of the schedule of the Columbia Broadcasting System up to the conclusion of the Republican convention.

As early as November 21, 1963, CBS president Frank Stanton offered free time for "an extended series of joint appearances of the major parties' Presidential and Vice-Presidential candidates."[24] January 23, 1964, saw the announcement that 21 special broadcasts "covering the personalities, the issues and the backgrounds of the 1964 political campaigns" would be presented from March 10 until November 4. Richard S. Salant, the chief of CBS News, said that all but one of those programs would be in prime time.[25] Stanton, on May 5, addressed the Tenth General Conference of CBS Network Affiliates to fill them in on the details.[26] An outline of the work that the network had planned in great detail for the Republican national convention was made public on June 19, and a similar release on planning for the Democratic convention was issued in August.[27]

Here is the sequence of other key schedule announcements released in June and July of 1964. A study of headlines and excerpts from CBS releases will demonstrate how much was done.

June 17   "CBS News Election Unit Chief to Address California Editors"

June 22   "Key Republican Leaders—Miller, Rhodes, Morton—Will 'Face the Nation' on Three Live Pre-Convention Broadcasts from San Francisco on Sundays, June 28, July 5, and July 12"

June 23   "City-Wide Radio Paging System in Both San Francisco and Atlantic City Will Quickly Contact CBS News Personnel Covering National Conventions"

June 24   "First Studio-Quality Portable Wireless Television Camera To Be Used by CBS News at Republican National Convention"

June 25   "On Wednesday, July 8 . . . , CBS News will present the first of two hour-long special broadcasts . . . devoted to the recent history of the conventions of both parties."

June 29   "The appearances of Senator Barry Goldwater of Arizona, Governor Nelson Rockefeller of New York, Governor George Romney of Michigan and other top Republican leaders before the Platform Committee of the . . . Convention in San Francisco will be carried live in a series of daily broadcasts beginning July 7."

July 1   "Chief Goldwater Spokesman on Republican Platform Committee To Be Questioned on 'Face the Nation' . . ."

July 7   "24 Hours of Actual Convention Coverage Spread over Four-Day Period"

July 8   "Three Convention Reports on CBS Television Network Today Will Include Scranton's Arrival and Press Conference"

July 10   "Goldwater Appearance before Republican Platform Committee Climaxes Big Pre-Convention Week Coverage . . ."

July 13   "CBS News Convention Eve Special Includes Coverage of Eisenhower Arrival, Report on Rights Protest"

July 15   "CBS News Protests Restrictions on Newsmen Covering Republican National Convention"

July 15   "Disputes not only among delegates to the Republican National Convention but also between convention personnel and members of the news media covering the event, as well as picketing and sit down demonstrations outside the Cow Palace, as the third session ended after midnight, marked the Tuesday CBS News gavel-to-gavel-and-beyond coverage of the GOP meeting."

July 16   "Networks, Convention Officials Reach Accord"

July 16   "Goldwater Nomination at Republican Convention Caps Third Day of CBS News Coverage at Cow Palace"

July 17   "Republican Convention Coverage on the CBS Television Network Totaled 33 Hours, 47 Minutes"[28]

This highlighting of a segment of the CBS effort could easily be duplicated by a rendition of NBC or ABC activities. Operating on a smaller scale was the National Educational Television (NET) organization. With a very modest budget, NET concentrated on *background* programming to offer viewers penetrating studies of important problems raised by and during American elections. One valuable product of NET, in 1964, was the series *Of People and Politics.* In the course of 21 half-hour programs, the NET cameras and commentators traveled across the United States to follow campaign progress, to appraise the importance of developments, and to look into "the matters of voter apathy, minority blocs, public opinion polls, the presidency, and campaign financing. Richard D. Heffner served as series host on programs that featured evaluations by good observers such as Richard Scammon, director of the U.S. Bureau of Census; Earl Mazo of *The New York Times;* Arthur Schlesinger, Jr.; Malcolm Moos, educator; John Bailey, Chairman of the Democratic National Committee; William Miller, Chairman of the Republican National Committee and later candidate for the Vice-Presidency; James A. Farley; James MacGregor Burns; Harold Stassen; The Reverend Martin Luther King, Jr.; Hodding Carter; Senators Abraham Ribicoff, John Sparkman, Birch Bayh, and Maurine Neuberger; and pollsters George Gallup, Louis Harris, and Elmo Roper.[29]

Other NET programs of the type just described also offered the citizenry important views and information. Hampered by small budgets, the NET producers had to learn how to complement and sometimes to extend the scope of the commercial network presentations.

FAIRNESS

Well into the campaign, in late September 1964, the FCC ruled by a 4-to-3 vote that President Johnson's news conferences held during the campaign were not bona fide news events or news interviews and, therefore, were not exempt from the equal-time restrictions. That decision was prompted by inquiries to the FCC made by Dr. Frank Stanton of CBS and Vincent Wasilewski, executive vice-president of the National Association of Broadcasters.

Stanton commented, upon hearing of the ruling, that he was not surprised, although he was disappointed. "Our fear that the presidential press conferences were not exempt from the equal time requirements has been one of the reasons we have pressed so vigorously for the suspension of Section 315." Wasilewski declared that the ruling demonstrated "once again the absurdity of the equal-opportunity section of the Communications Act."[30]

The issue of fairness, as it applied to television industry works and objectives, was very much a part of the 1964 campaign. Ramifications abounded, stimulated by the industry, by the candidates, and by the government. A few illustrations follow.

Barry Goldwater and many of his supporters felt that some CBS news analysis programs of the campaign tended to be attacks on the Senator's character and career. The CBS organization, they contended, was following some sort of policy to defame Goldwater by "smearing" him.[31] In effect, CBS was accused of editorializing against Goldwater and in favor of Johnson.

Such howls may not be dismissed out of hand because, when television reporters relate various scenes, they do say more than a candidate likes if they report on a development that does not enhance him. Rarely do backers of a candidate accuse reporters of favoring the man they would have elected. Theoretically, it is always possible to connect news reporting with news editorializing. Would anyone support the thesis that there exists what has been called "straight news"? When a reporter gives his honest impressions of what has happened, he never expects all who hear his words to agree with his interpretations of the event.

Today a substantial number of television stations do take stands on matters of public interest and broadcast these positions in presentations clearly labeled as editorials. However, these editorials do leave the public with a continuing fear that other editorial comments may be made without such clear labeling. Especially in the context of an election campaign, when emotions run high, there is a tendency to accuse broadcasters of hidden editorializing whether the charges are justified or not.

Broadcasters must, in theory, adhere to the "fairness doctrine" set down by the FCC, but the preachment is easier than the practice.

Sociologists Kurt and Gladys Lang studied the network coverage of the 1952 Democratic convention by recording and comparing television viewers' running comments. A monitoring group followed each of the three networks, and the Langs concluded that each group received "an entirely different impression of the convention." To quote from *Television Magazine* (July 1960):

> Network A [none were identified] stressed the "action" of the convention, relying on pictures of floor activity during the high points and filling the lulls with special features. Little interpretation was supplied.
> Network B followed events through a commentator "watching the same screen as you are," who repeatedly expressed his bewilderment, avoided lengthy commentary and stressed the human interest angle.
> Network C covered the convention as a news service, attempting to identify the various political maneuvers and make sense of what was going on.[32]

Why did each network operate differently? Partially, this contrast must have been due to the differing capabilities of the three network staffs. Second, certain policy decisions were probably made by each network administration to take advantage of the particular strengths of each organization. Last, the reporters for each network reflected their home organization's idea of what really constituted good news coverage!

Is it possible for viewers to decide that one or another network was *editorializing* and that, therefore, its product was slanted? Of course, the networks (or their affiliates) are always open to charges, justified or not, that they are unfairly bending the news. The industry must try to be fair; but it must also counterattack when it believes that the attacks on it are without pertinent foundation. It must never allow its critics to bully it away from its basic news job—and that is to make an honest attempt to tell the public what is happening. If one or another candidate is, let us say, playing the part of a demagogue, it is not the obligation of newsmen to pretend not to notice; on the contrary, it is their duty to report his antics squarely. Square and honest reporting is, of course, very difficult, but the difficulties should only propel reporters to greater efforts.

John Paul Sullivan, professor of law at The George Washington University, has commented, "The fairness doctrine imposes upon the media of mass communication an affirmative obligation to present all responsible viewpoints with respect to controversial questions actually selected for presentation." He then adds, underlining the vital importance of honest reporting to the electorate, "At a time in history when wise judgments are of critical importance, anything which would short-circuit the process of judgment is anathema. Since judgment in a philosophic sense is at the pinnacle of knowledge, it can be only as valid as the information and knowledge available to the one making it."[33]

Fair Enough?

To return to the FCC ruling whereby the agency decided that its equal-time regulations *did* apply to President Johnson's news conferences during the 1964 presidential campaign, that decision had hardly been delivered before it was challenged. The President, on October 18, addressed the nation for some 15 minutes on the change in Soviet leadership and the Chinese nuclear explosion; Dean Burch, the Republican National Committee Chairman, promptly demanded equal time for Goldwater.

The FCC rejected the Burch demand, as did the three national networks. However, NBC gave Dean Burch 15 minutes in which to answer on October 19. In his talk, Burch said that Johnson had "demonstrated his contempt for the right of every citizen to have meaningful information." He also made another charge off the air, contending that the Democrats had first attempted to buy time for Johnson's appearance and, when that had proved impractical, had preempted the time. He appealed for contributions from all "who believe in fair play" and said it would cost $500,000 to buy equal time for Goldwater on all three networks.[34]

In their turn, the Democrats attacked the Burch speech and complained that NBC had been much too gracious in giving Burch free time. A Democratic spokesman said, "They went on national television to raise funds under the masquerade of equal time for the President's speech." John Bailey, the Democratic National Chairman, sent NBC a message asking "whether NBC believes the Democratic Party is now entitled to time to respond." NBC did not! William R. McAndrew, NBC executive vice-president for news, replied that ". . . our offer of time to a spokesman of the Republican Party was an appropriate one in the exercise of news judgment but . . . further treatment of the matters involved can now most suitably be covered in regular news programs."[35]

After the Johnson address of October 18, the Republicans took the issue to court. On October 27, on a tie vote in the Washington Court of Appeals, they lost. The court upheld the (6-to-1) decision of the FCC,[36] which rejected Dean Burch's demand for equal time.

Even if all else about equal time and fairness is open to speculation, it is a simple matter of record that in 1964, Congress bottled up the proposal to waive the equal-time restrictions on major-party Presidential and Vice-Presidential candidates. It is widely believed that the President, during an August 18 breakfast at the White House with Democratic Congressional leaders, communicated to them his lack of enthusiasm for participating in debates with the Republican nominee. Irrefutable are the facts that Section 315 was not waived as it had been in 1960[37] and that the President showed no visible sign of disappointment at this development.

FOOTNOTES

1. Letter to author from Congressman Robert Taft, Jr., dated August 17, 1964.
2. Bernard Rubin, from questionnaire letter sent to members of Congress, June 1964.
3. Letter to author from Congressman Harlan Hagen, dated July 6, 1964.

4. Letter to author from Congressman Frank T. Bow, dated June 25, 1964.

5. See "Bolton Calls on Broadcasting Networks to Withhold Declaring November's Presidential Winner Until All Polls Are Closed," release dated June 8, 1964; from the office of Congressman Oliver T. Bolton.

6. Letter to author from Congressman Donald Edwards, dated June 24, 1964.

7. Letter to author from Congressman James Roosevelt, dated July 31, 1964.

8. Letter to author from Senator Hubert H. Humphrey, dated June 24, 1964.

9. Letter to author from Senator Ernest Gruening, dated June 15, 1964.

10. Letter to author from Senator John G. Tower, dated June 22, 1964.

11. Letter to author from Senator Milward L. Simpson, dated June 22, 1964.

12. Letter to author from Congressman Gerald R. Ford, dated July 2, 1964.

13. Letter to author from Congressman Clement J. Zablocki, dated June 30, 1964.

14. Letter to author from Congressman Fred B. Rooney, dated June 24, 1964.

15. Letter to the author from Congressman Abraham J. Multer, dated July 9, 1964.

16. The author thanks the other members of the Congress who aided him. Most perceptive information was provided by letters from Oren Harris (Arkansas), June 25, 1964; Thomas P. O'Neill, Jr., (Massachusetts), July 9, 1964; Henry B. Gonzalez (Texas), June 30, 1964; Jim Wright (Texas), June 30, 1964; Claude Pepper (Florida), June 26, 1964; Paul G. Rogers (Florida), June 26, 1964; Roland V. Libonati (Illinois), June 24, 1964; John W. Wydler (New York), June 23, 1964; John Kyl (Iowa), June 23, 1964; Allen J. Ellender (Senate, Louisiana), June 19, 1964; Charles E. Bennett (Florida), June 22, 1964; Frank E. Moss (Senate, Utah), June 19, 1964; Clinton P. Anderson (Senate, New Mexico), June 16, 1964; Leverett Saltonstall (Senate, Massachusetts), June 15, 1964; E. C. Gathings (Arkansas), June 23, 1964; John M. Murphy (New York), July 1, 1964; Spark M. Matsunaga (Hawaii), June 29, 1964; Samuel N. Friedel (Maryland), June 30, 1964; Howard W. Robison (New York), June 25, 1964; Bob Sikes (Florida), June 26, 1964; Clifford G. McIntire (Maine), June 25, 1964; George McGovern (Senate, South Dakota), June 25, 1964; Joseph S. Clark (Senate, Pennsylvania), July 1, 1964; John W. McCormack (Massachusetts), June 29, 1964; Bernard F. Grabowski (Connecticut), July 22, 1964; Frank Horton (New York), July 9, 1964; Philip J. Philbin (Massachusetts), July 14, 1964; William Henry Harrison (Wyoming), June 23, 1964; David N. Henderson (North Carolina), June 23, 1964; James C. Corman (California), June 30. 1964; D. R. Matthews (Florida), June 24, 1964; George P. Miller (California). June 25, 1965; Herman T. Schneebeli (Pennsylvania), June 24, 1964. Also Edward M. Kennedy (Senate, Massachusetts) arranged for the author to receive the *Congressional Record*.

17. "Interview with E. William Henry," *U.S. News & World Report* (July 6, 1964), p. 52. Also, for an estimate of the "Amount of Radio and Television Time Used by Presidential and Vice-Presidential Nominees, 1960," see chart in Edward C. Dreyer's "Political Party Use of Broadcasting in 1960," *Journal of Broadcasting,* Vol. 8, No. 3 (Summer 1964), p. 213. He says that the Democratic and Republican nominees used a total of 3,077 hours of television paid time and 266 hours of television sustaining time.

18. "Wallace Making a Costly Effort," *New York Times,* May 3, 1964.

19. American Broadcasting Company, television series *ABC News Reports,* program of April 2, 1964, "The Price of Politics." The author thanks ABC president Elmer W. Lower for sending a transcript.

20. Dean Burch, "Presidential Campaigns Are a Sham," *The Saturday Evening Post* (March 27, 1965), pp. 12, 14.

21. Federal Communications Commission, *Survey of Political Broadcasting*, 1963. See pp. i–iii; See also exhaustive detailed cost summaries in this volume.

22. Tables made available to this researcher, in July 1965, by the Federal Communications Commission, through the courtesy of Dr. H. H. Goldin, Assistant Chief for Policy Planning. These tables are part of the FCC's *Survey of Political Broadcasting*, 1965. See especially Table 1 and Table 3.

23. For illustrations, see Don Ross, "Stevenson To Join Ike in Public Campaign-Fund Plea," *New York Herald Tribune*, June 26, 1964; editorial, "A Better Way to Finance Campaigns," *New York Herald Tribune*, June 25, 1964; Edward Cowan, "Mail Fund Drive To Aid Campaigns," *New York Times*, June 9, 1964; editorial, "Only for Millionaires?" *Boston Globe*, June 1, 1964; Frank Church, "Campaign Money—How Much? From Whom?" *New York Times Magazine*, August 26, 1962; Report of the Committee on Interstate and Foreign Commerce, *Television Network Program Procurement* (Washington: U.S. Government Printing Office, 1963).

24. Columbia Broadcasting System, press release of November 21, 1963, "CBS Offers Major Candidates Free Prime Time for Extended Series of Joint Appearances."

25. CBS Television Network, press release of January 23, 1964, "Twenty-One Special Broadcasts Covering Political Campaigns To Be Presented on the CBS Television Network This Year."

26. Columbia Broadcasting System, press release of May 5, 1964, "Tenth General Conference of CBS Television Network Affiliates, Remarks of Frank Stanton, President . . ."

27. CBS Television Network, press information, "Democratic Convention '64," August 1964; "Republican Convention, '64," June 1964.

28. The author wishes to thank the CBS organization for its consideration in sending him the daily press releases during the election period.

29. The author thanks Nazaret Cherkezian for his kindness in sending a complete description of the series *Of People and Politics*. Mr. Cherkezian is the Director of Public Information for National Educational Television.

30. "Equal Time Applicable to L.B.J. News Sessions," *Broadcasting* (October 5, 1964), p. 45.

31. Quincy, "Capital Bulletin," *National Review Bulletin*, August 4, 1964.

32. "Television and Politics," *Television Magazine*, Vol. 17, No. 7 (July 1960), pp. 47–49, 91–93, especially p. 91.

33. John Paul Sullivan, "Editorials and Controversy: The Broadcasters' Dilemma," *The George Washington Law Review*, Vol. 32, No. 4 (April 1964), pp. 719–768, especially pp. 747–748. See also, John E. McMillin, "New Voices in a Democracy," *Television Quarterly*, Vol. 3, No. 3 (Summer 1964), pp. 26–52.

34. "Goldwater Loses Equal-Time Move," *New York Times*, October 20, 1964.

35. Anthony Lewis, "Democrats Denied Equal Time after Assailing G.O.P. Speech," *New York Times*, October 21, 1964.

36. Anthony Lewis, "Equal-Time Appeal Lost by Goldwater," *New York Times*, October 28, 1964. For other aspects of the problem, see Robert W. Sarnoff, "Television Journalism: The Shackled Giant," *Vital Speeches of the Day* (January 1, 1965); "Campaign Coverage '64," *The Quill*, Vol. 52, No. 8 (August 1964), pp. 12–18.

37. "Section 315 Debated, but No Action," *Broadcasting* (August 17, 1964), p. 62; "No Relief from Equal Time in This Campaign," *Broadcasting* (August 24, 1964), pp. 70–73; "Section 315 Hits Political Fan," *Broadcasting* (October 26, 1964), pp. 54–56.

8 / To the Boardwalk and the Golden Gate

PRESIDENTIAL PRIMARIES

When a man who aspires to be President of the United States decides to offer himself to the voters in one or more of the states' presidential primaries, he knows that the opportunities are fewer than the risks. A substantial victory in a key primary could give his candidacy a push great enough to carry him to his party's nomination; but a glaring defeat in any of these elections could finish him off as a serious contender.

These state primaries, which allow voters to express opinions about whom they favor for the top executive post in the nation, are uniquely American in concept. Foreign observers may well wonder why candidates allow themselves to be measured by gauges of public opinion that are of limited value and that can be downright dangerous.

In part, the status of such primaries is due to our native preoccupation with public opinion. Few men dare to defy *vox populi*. The primaries tempt politicians with the lure of victories that can separate their efforts from those of other campaigners. Once he has won such a victory, a candidate can make the great length of the presidential campaign work to his advantage by impressing the public with the fact that he leads in the race for office.

Achieving a clearly recognized lead also gives a candidate important opportunities to attract publicity. Today, a politician who considers himself presidential timber is doomed unless he can secure coverage from the greatest of the contemporary publicity machines—television. Since massive injections of publicity are necessary, the temptations offered by the primaries increase in proportion to the candidate's need to emerge from the pack of hopefuls.

In the recent past, some leading contenders have, with good results, pointedly avoided primary elections, and others have shown great promise in these primaries only to watch the plums of politics slip from their hands. Senator Kefauver would be a good example of the latter situation, and Adlai Stevenson of the former; in 1952, Stevenson managed to secure the nomination of his party while standing aloof from such public opinion polls. On the other hand, when Senator John F. Kennedy defeated Senator Hubert Humphrey in the West

Virginia primary of 1960, that victory helped to clear the way for Kennedy's nomination in Los Angeles.

Aside from the special-purpose drive of Governor George Wallace of Alabama, the major 1964 interest in primary battles centered on the Republican contests. There was no popular doubt that President Johnson would be able to secure the Democratic nomination.

George Wallace, in the state primaries of Wisconsin, Indiana, and Maryland, capitalized on the racial crisis to exploit what was labeled the "white backlash." He aimed his campaigning at the destruction of the civil rights bill then before the Congress. In Wisconsin, he did surprisingly well and received 33.8 per cent of the vote in the Democratic primary; in Indiana, Governor Welsh managed to grasp 65 per cent of the votes to hold Johnson control there, but Wallace got 29.8 per cent; in Maryland, a record Democratic turnout gave Wallace 214,837 votes to Johnson-supported Senator Brewster's 267,104. The television networks and their local affiliates brought the story of the Wallace adventure to the national audience.

On the Republican primary campaign front, the significant battles took place in New Hampshire (Lodge, Goldwater, Rockefeller, Nixon, Margaret Chase Smith, Stassen); Illinois (Goldwater, Smith, Lodge, Nixon, Wallace, Rockefeller, Scranton, Romney); Oregon (Rockefeller, Lodge, Goldwater, Nixon, Smith, Scranton); and California (Rockefeller, Goldwater). Many voters in those primaries cast ballots for nonactive candidates and, as in the cases of Lodge, Nixon, Scranton, and Romney, for unannounced candidates. The decisive outcomes came in New Hampshire (where Goldwater fell to a poor second behind Lodge, and Rockefeller finished a close third in a nip-and-tuck race); Illinois (where Goldwater won, but received a bad image in securing only 512,840 votes to the 209,521 votes racked up by his only announced opponent, Margaret Chase Smith); Oregon, the only state where the names of all six prominent Republicans were entered by the secretary of state (Rockefeller won 33 per cent of the vote, Lodge 27.7 per cent, Goldwater 17.6 per cent, Nixon 16.8 per cent, Smith 2.9 per cent, and Scranton 2 per cent); and California, which turned out to be the scene of a head-on Goldwater-Rockefeller bout (Goldwater 51.4 per cent and Rockefeller 48.6 per cent).

Intense public interest in the Republican primaries was fanned by television efforts. Nothing is so compatible with television enterprise as an affair that provides a spectacle, good opportunities for commentary of all sorts, man-in-the-street interviews, presentations of public figures at bay, and a neat and tidy hour when there is a definite result that begets vast amounts of additional commentary.

Let us turn to the first of these presidential primaries, the one in New Hampshire, to get an idea of what was involved in all of them.

NEW HAMPSHIRE

New Hampshire's Republican presidential primary of March 1964 gave the nation the first real clue that the national contest was likely to be fraught with illusory situations. To begin with, the two major adversaries campaigned vigorously in the Granite State, but a third man—one who did not even set foot there during the entire course of the preprimary period—won the contest. Rockefeller crisscrossed the state during 28 days of soliciting votes from registered Republicans, and Goldwater spent a total of 23 days urging their support of his candidacy. Lodge boosters carried on even though their candidate, in distant Saigon, remained silent on domestic politics. When the Hampshiremen of Republican persuasion finished trekking to the polls, through up to 14 inches of snow, the results were Lodge 33,007 (35.7 per cent); Goldwater 20,692 (22.4 per cent); Rockefeller 19,504 (21.1 per cent); and Nixon 15,587 (16.9 per cent).

Two write-in campaigns, sponsored by supporters of the overtly inactive candidates Lodge and Nixon, snared 52.6 per cent of the ballots. Other choices in the preferential primary (Margaret Chase Smith, Harold E. Stassen, and one Norman Le Page, a perennial candidate in New Hampshire) received less than 4 per cent of the votes.

This major battle was for only 14 delegates to the Republican national convention and was held in a state whose population of about 607,000 is roughly equivalent to that of the city of Boston. Nevertheless, the television networks and both American and foreign reporters from the other mass media treated the New Hampshire primary as a matter of great consequence because, on that snow-swept terrain, first views of the big race of 1964 would come into focus. It was a foregone conclusion that Johnson would take to the field as the Democratic standard-bearer, and everyone wanted hints of who was likely to oppose him as the Republican choice.

Television's Roles: Background to New Hampshire, 1964

New Hampshire is small and lightly populated. National victory for Democrats or Republicans is easily possible whether this state is won or lost in the general election. Nevertheless, in an age when mass communications are so important, the actual voting on primary day was less significant than the fact that the contest there was the first Presidential primary of 1964 and that the voters across the nation would be much impressed by its results.

The press in general and television in particular were hard at work right after Christmas 1963, trailing the major political solicitors around on their swings through the state and assembling all sorts of reports about voter thinking. The forum was small, but the audience was not at all restricted to New Hampshire.

The first testing of men and of policies overshadowed all that had gone before and would set a pace for the campaign. For Barry Goldwater, appeals to Granite State Republicans, with a long history of conservative thinking about politics, could lead him to greater rewards than approximately 100,000 registered Republican voters normally have in their power to give. On the other hand, a defeat in such territory would be hard to explain. His opponents were well aware that, if Goldwater were to lose there, he could be handled more easily in other areas of the country where political sentiments, historically, have been more progressive. At any rate, the issues raised in New Hampshire were of intense interest in all 50 states. As Theodore H. White says in his *The Making of the President, 1964,* "For the first time, Americans were required, publicly, to decide their posture on war and peace in an age of nuclear terror."[1]

A good picture of how the television networks exerted themselves to record and transmit the New Hampshire political scenes is given by John Fenton, correspondent for *The New York Times,* whose report was headlined "Electronic Plague Hits New Hampshire." CBS and NBC, he noted, had task forces numbering 150 apiece in the state by primary night. ABC had 175 people there. In addition, hundreds of part-time workers were engaged. "For every television reporter, there is a cameraman, a technician and a soundman. . . . The New England Telephone Co., with at least $250,000 in capital outlay for equipment, has erected seven new towers to handle television and radio broadcasts. The state's one television channel capacity will be increased to 12 on primary night to meet the industry's demands." Also in use was expensive equipment borrowed from other Bell Telephone systems. "Between 800 and 900 telephone workers will be on the job Tuesday [primary day] serving television and typewriter press alike." According to Fenton, the networks spent about $5 for each of the 100,000 registered Republican voters in the effort to get the returns in first.

> One housewife in a supermarket complained the other day "You go to reach for a box of washing machine soap and there is a microphone sticking out of the shelf and someone asking if you agree with Happy Rockefeller that sudso washes best. . . ."
> . . . whole regiments of electronic press representatives have been maneuvering and skirmishing across the countryside. More than once, Senator Barry Goldwater of Arizona and Governor Nelson A. Rockefeller of New York have pleaded with cameramen and microphone-armed reporters to stand back, please, so they could shake hands with registered voters.[2]

Barry Goldwater

Before New Hampshire's primary, a great many Americans remembered Barry Goldwater as the man who stood with his wife on the platform at the Republican convention in 1960 and bid his followers to support Richard Nixon.

Mrs. Goldwater was caught by the cameras with tears in her eyes as her husband made a good show of demonstrating his sportsmanship. It seemed beside the point at that moment that Goldwater had never had a real chance of capturing a majority of delegates to that 1960 convention! One could sense Goldwater's awareness as he stood on the rostrum that, should Nixon lose, that stage would be a setting for launching his own campaign for the 1964 nomination. Asking that his name be withdrawn, Goldwater appended a short, partisan speech for the edification of the assemblage.

> Now, you conservatives and all Republicans, I would like you to listen to this. While Dick [Nixon] and I may disagree on some points, there are not many. I would not want any negative action of mine to enhance the possibility of victory going to those who by their very words have lost faith in America. I know that conservatism here and in November will show the strong sense of responsibility which is a central characteristic of the conservative temper. We must remember that Republicans have not been losing elections because of more Democrat voters. Now, get this. We have been losing elections because conservatives too often fail to vote.[3]

From that moment and for four long years, a mystique developed around Goldwater. Instrumental to that mystique were the past defeats of Republican presidential candidates Wendell L. Willkie and Thomas E. Dewey. Both had, according to this new prophet, failed to offer the electorate a clear choice. Then when Nixon lost by a hair in 1960, the Goldwater bandwagon really started to move. Goldwater would, his trumpeter Phyllis Schlafly asserted, offer *A Choice Not an Echo*. In her book on Goldwater Schlafly inveighed against the "kingmakers" of the liberal wing of the Republican Party who, she said, controlled the mass media. There was, she concluded, "a very simple solution to what to do about the whole 'looney' mess in Washington today—elect Barry Goldwater, the man with the courage to give us simple solutions" about foreign affairs, world Communism, peace and disarmament, labor, and business.[4]

As the Goldwater arguments began to take hold on a Republican Party torn apart by defeats, the news media paid closer attention to the Senator from Arizona. What did he represent? Who were his ardent supporters? How successful was he in his attempt to win organizational Republican Party support in state after state? Why did he appeal to certain right-wing fringe and extremist groups? The networks devoted many specials to Goldwater and to his emergent movement. Intense coverage was rained upon Goldwater speeches, actions in the Senate, and meetings with Republican leaders. Collateral programming was prepared on voter sentiments, upon the fringe groups themselves, and upon reactions to Goldwater by other key Republican leaders.

Before November 22, 1963, Goldwater was seen as the man other Republican hopefuls would have to stop. Astute observers of national affairs saw a strong possibility that Goldwater would be the candidate who would oppose Kennedy. If the "new frontier" was one alternative, Goldwater's brand of conservatism was surely another.

When Kennedy died, the Goldwater movement went into temporary eclipse; popular sentiment forced Goldwater and his supporters into a bad position. Had they not, so the theme went, been so opposed to Kennedy that they were in some measure responsible for what had happened? Were they not too extreme as conservatives? Of course, the immediate identification of the opposition with a part in the tragedy was unfair and unjustified. Nevertheless, it was a psychological fact that such allegations were easily accepted by non-Goldwater people!

For a while it appeared that Goldwater was finished as an active candidate for 1964. However, in an age of mass communications, the absolute psychological facts of a specific time often do not endure for long. As early as January 1964, Goldwater regained lost ground and made up for losses by emphasizing his underdog status and the struggle ahead for conservatives.

Despite the efforts that went into explanations of Goldwaterism by writers and speakers and organizers friendly to him, the ideological movement he headed was more easily labeled than understood. Comparatively few Americans have given a careful reading to the tracts that appeared as authored by him or those that were designed to support or attack his views. Books such as his *The Conscience of a Conservative*, Edwin McDowell's *Barry Goldwater: Portrait of an American*, and John A. Stormer's *None Dare Call It Treason* did little to raise arguments above the level of polemics. So-called "critical" efforts such as Arthur Frommer's compilation of quotations, *Goldwater, from A to Z*, tended to be as aggressively anti-Goldwater as Fred J. Cook's *Barry Goldwater: Extremist of the Right*.[5]

Television viewers interested in current events were exposed to renditions of Goldwater conservatism as provided by various admirers and detractors. Despite such presentations, before the New Hampshire primary of 1964, the majority of Americans speculated in vague manner as to what he was up to and what kind of man he was. New Hampshire provided a real opportunity for clarification.

With the difficulties of securing public understanding of an *ideology* so apparent, the specific appeals made to the voters of the Granite State were welcomed by people in all 50 states. It is largely through the individuals' interpretations that we come to understand theories.

Conservatism as an abstraction impressed New Hampshire Republicans and other Americans less than the interpretations of the concept that were provided by Goldwater himself. What conservatism, Republican style, did or did not consist of in 1964 was largely determined, in the minds of the voters, by the style of his personal campaigning.

Nelson Rockefeller

The archrival of the man from Arizona was Nelson A. Rockefeller, multi-millionaire, governor of New York, and representative of the Eastern, long-dominant wing of the Republican Party. Rockefeller was an established internationalist, a liberal, and a man who recognized the needs for, as well as the limitations of, big government. By anybody's evaluation, he was left of Goldwater on vital questions of foreign affairs, business, labor, social responsibilities of government, civil rights, and so on. If Goldwater was to be stopped in his drive for the nomination, Rockefeller would have to affect his course in New Hampshire.

Outwardly gregarious and bubbling, "Rocky" had many advantages. Youthful in appearance, vigorous, extremely wealthy, and determined to fight hard for his principles, he seemed to be a very likely contender. However, the divorce from the first Mrs. Rockefeller and the subsequent marriage to "Happy" were pronounced liabilities, much played up by all segments of the press. Rockefeller on the one hand decried what Goldwater stood for and, on the other, tried to rally the public away from its concentration on his own personal life.

Henry Cabot Lodge

Reportorial attention also turned to Saigon, where Henry Cabot Lodge, a Kennedy appointee, was established as Ambassador. Extensive commentary in the press, on radio, and on television revolved around this dark horse, but Lodge refused to say anything significant about domestic politics. After all, it was explained over and over, the Foreign Service regulations forbade such talk by him. A volunteer organization organized a write-in campaign on his behalf, but he could not even indicate approval or disapproval of their efforts, according to those regulations! Despite his long and distinguished public career, which included service in the U.S. Senate, a period as Ambassador to the United Nations, and the Saigon assignment, Lodge was not given much chance by the political sages. He was a New England favorite son and an internationalist, but his role as Nixon's running mate in 1960 had not endeared him to all Republicans. Many considered Lodge too much a gentleman for the rough and tumble of active campaigning.

However, in this television age, his face appeared on the screens frequently. Television's tendency to play up the drama of his situation proved that a distance of several thousand miles did not necessarily detract from his image. Then again, because he did not say anything to Hampshiremen, he did not make any mistakes. There he was, far away, aloof and doing his duty.

Overexposure versus the Silent Treatment

One of the most valid appreciations of what happened in New Hampshire is given by Theodore H. White, who relates how fully Goldwater managed to alienate segments of the registered Republicans. Much of what transpired was brought to the nation, day by day, by television. Hampshiremen and Oregonians, Arizonians and Virginians, New Yorkers and Missourians watched and pondered the meaning of what they saw and heard.

Supporters and detractors alike were surprised to find that Goldwater was not a good stump speaker. His public rally performances also tended toward flatness. Rockefeller, the irrepressible enthusiast, came over as expected, and his appraisals of public policy only tended to confirm earlier impressions gained through the mass media.

For Goldwater, the tone and depth of the public's questions on domestic and foreign issues were revelations. Audiences on streets and in stadiums confronted him with their concern over foreign policy, the bomb, civil rights, and the federal budget. These matters were popped to him wherever he traveled in the state. According to White (whose views are backed up by numerous other sources and by my own personal recollection), Goldwater's opinions often frightened people. "Goldwater was grotesquely overexposed." White summarizes the effects:

> In New Hampshire, Goldwater would say exactly what he thought, as he had always thought it—then shake with fury at its quotation in the newspapers, then at its analysis, its re-examination, its full-blown elaboration in the national columns and commentaries. He was offering New Hampshire the gospel of the true faith, hard money and individual rights. Here if anywhere, it should get sympathetic hearing. And yet, day by day when he read of himself in the papers, it was another Goldwater he was reading about, a wild man seeking to abolish Social Security and go to war with Russia.[6]

As the two leading contenders fought deeper into the preprimary election period, Goldwater's pronouncements divorced him more and more from the traditional Republican sentiments of the party faithful. Rockefeller did not necessarily look better to the registered Republicans in the audiences, but Goldwater looked progressively worse. Each day's "Goldwaterisms" were soon public property all over New Hampshire, via newspapers, radio, the television.

It was increasingly evident that, with the turn in voter appreciation, Goldwater, while still expressing all outward signs of confidence, became ill at ease with the press corps and was particularly bothered by television coverage of his appearances. Rockefeller was unfailingly and almost unnaturally warm and cordial to all in his public appearances and able to take advantage of any peering television eyes.

When they cast their ballots on a very wintery March day, more New Hampshire Republicans turned to the silent man in Saigon than to either of the two most active solicitors. We have good reason to speculate whether such a situation would have been possible before television! We may be witnessing a new kind of politics. A hard-bitten, practical politician might in the future advise, "Don't battle for their votes—find yourself a privileged sanctuary and play it safe with the mass media."[7]

A ROAD OF THORNS

Looking back on the primaries of 1964, one wonders whether there are not legions of potentially good leaders who will be driven away from politics because of the massive intrusions of television. Transferring state primaries so fully from the local constituency to the national constituency has its virtues, but very serious problems are also produced. A serious, competent, and experienced potential candidate may not be willing to embark on the endurance contest, the road of thorns, that stretches from the idea of holding office to the practical realities of being exposed to massive news coverage as an active candidate. From state to state the hopeful solicitors are pursued. Nowhere are they truly given the chance to talk to local people and have their appeals restricted to the immediate audience. Men who may have all the talents required to do a good job in public office may not be able to master the art of handling television.

If a candidate starts off weakly in the first primary, the national electorate is negatively impressed with his initial efforts, and from then on he must defend himself. In the old days, before television, initial mistakes could be offset as he went along the campaign trail. Today, the first wounds never heal, but the first successes are still perishable. True, Goldwater got the nomination despite New Hampshire, but that was because his major efforts were aimed at party workers across the nation. New Hampshire's primary did not affect the Goldwater nomination drive appreciably, but it did point up his difficulties in rallying voter support.

Primary contests are overrated. Buildups and mass media coverage are so intense that the emphasis is placed on the search for a winner; if we look at the results of primaries, however, we cannot say that they always predict winners and losers in the races for nomination. For example, Lodge won the New Hampshire primary in 1964. And when Goldwater and Rockefeller clashed head-on in California's primary, Goldwater achieved only a very slim majority. Why then, was it so widely touted that Rockefeller had *lost?* Did the slight difference hang on the arguments of each man, or was it determined by the last-minute impact of the birth of a Rockefeller heir—an event that reminded voters of Rockefeller's divorce and remarriage?

Hypotheses and Opinions

Too much fever is whipped up by these primaries. Having said that, I remind the reader to appreciate the virtues of television in the totality of the election process. We strive for a balanced judgment! Former Republican Chairman Leonard Hall may have been right when he said, in 1956, that television made it impossible for special interests to deliver votes in blocs because elections are now won or lost in the living rooms of the voters.[8] Still, special interests are not intrinsically *bad*. Aside from the bloc-voting problem, the appeal to interest and idea groups is part and parcel of our American tradition.

J. G. Blumler, an astute British student of television, asks us to look at commentaries about relationships between mass culture and social realities. He worries about the "escapist hypothesis," which, in the words of Raymond Williams, holds that "majority T.V." is a "substitute for the world of actual experience and conflict which is both too painful and too obscure." There is also a "reassurance hypothesis" built on the theme that what is seen has been designed "not to trouble but to reassure." Reality is not accurately reflected; the designers "rearrange its elements into something we can bear." Finally, there is the "replacement hypothesis" that persons seen on television represent reality— "what human beings normally, primarily are."[9]

Are the candidates accepted or rejected on the basis of what they themselves do or say? The impartiality of the press is a myth, even though reporters may honestly try to be as objective as they can. A survey of editors and broadcasters taken by the widely respected professional journalism magazine, *The Quill*, produced interesting results, as reported in August 1964. A random survey, in which 139 questionnaires were mailed and 89 returned (63 per cent), included the question, "Do you feel that the attitude of the candidate toward the press has any bearing on his treatment by the press?" Eighty-four per cent of those polled said that it did, while 16 per cent responded negatively. Another question was, "Do you feel there is any cause for real concern in the regular challenges to the 'impartiality' of political reporters?" Fifty-two per cent of the respondents replied in the affirmative, and 48 per cent in the negative.[10]

Reviewing the 1964 primaries, can we say that the electorate has become more politically mature due to television? Professor Angus Campbell, the director of the Survey Research Center at the University of Michigan, is doubtful.

> If there is one dependable law in the world of mass communication, it is that those most likely to seek information are already the best informed. Thus we find that the people who follow the elections campaigns most closely on television are precisely the same ones who read the most about them in the newspapers and magazines.
> It is among those at the other end of the scale, the quarter or third

of the population that is generally uninvolved and uninformed, that television might have hoped to have its greatest impact. But this group, alas, is very incurious about politics; its demand for information is exceedingly modest. Its members can apparently be induced to watch an occasional "spectacular," like the conventions or the debates, but their detachment from political matters is undisturbed.[11]

CERTAIN POST-NEW-HAMPSHIRE DEVELOPMENTS

The pattern established in New Hampshire by the television industry was elaborated upon for other key contests. A major difference between New Hampshire's primary and the others was that other states provided more involved problems of coverage. Time available to the candidates was greatly compressed after New Hampshire; electorates in the areas to be handled were less compact. As summer drew closer, interest tended to shift from the state scenes to the upcoming national conventions.

Rockefeller's organization turned more and more to the purchase of television time on local stations as the campaign progressed. In California, for example, radio and television stations up and down the state were offering messages by him and on his behalf. One item was a five-minute television condensation of the biographical film "The Rockefeller Story." On television prime time, spot announcements cost $1,333 if a big-city station carries them for a short period. It is said that the Rockefeller outlay for radio and television in California was at least ten times as great as the Goldwater organization's expenditure.[12] Goldwater relied "wholly on TV and radio to reach the uncommitted voter"; his public appearances were before well-organized rallies "attended almost exclusively by his own precinct workers."[13]

George Wallace

"Backlash" was the word used by economic columnist Eliot Janeway to describe the possible peril of automation combining with an economic recession to "squeeze" factory job opportunities. Under such a threat, he said, the white employees might fight Negro competitors for the available jobs.

George Wallace used the civil rights situation of 1964 to attempt to secure social "backlash" votes from anti-Negro and upset electors. He entered primaries to popularize the sentiment against Negroes in order to kill the civil rights bill then before Congress and as a part of his over-all effort to rally support for his undemocratic stands on the race question. To a significant degree, he appealed directly to blue-collar, working-class people in the Democratic primaries in Wisconsin, Indiana, and Maryland and drew, respectively, 34 per cent, 30 per cent, and 43 per cent of the votes in those contests. Fighting integration down the line, Wallace aggressively pushed himself into the primaries in order to secure heavy attention from the mass media. That was his right, of course, and few would advocate that an ardent segregationist should be denied democratic privileges, provided he stays within the bounds of the Constitution.

Theoretically, men enter the presidential primaries to attract attention to their qualities as presidential timber or to protect the interests of a major contender who, for one or another reason, does not choose to enter his name. Under the latter circumstances, it is the usual procedure that the voters are made very well aware of whom they are truly asked to support. President Johnson, for example, did not choose to enter primary battles and, on several instances, had his champions defend Administration interests.

Practically, Wallace saw in the primaries a marvelous opportunity to whip up voters to his anti-integration cause. What better way is there to get massive press attention than to determine where the press will be preoccupied and then to move in front of their view?

Ostensibly contesting for the Presidency as a Democrat, Wallace was actually fighting against the national party organization and deprecating political affiliations. Here was a man anxious to further a social (or antisocial) cause. He was not interested in traditional politicking for office; he wanted to deprecate the serious candidates or to force them to recognize his power over a segment of the electorate. Barry Goldwater recognized that power and shifted his tactics accordingly. When the gadfly Wallace had completed his work in the primaries, there was considerable speculation as to the magnitude of his accomplishment. Until the votes came in the following November, there was no reliable indication as to the true size of the "backlash" vote. As it turned out, what loomed large in the primaries boiled down drastically in the general election results.

Such degeneration of the theoretical purposes of presidential primaries will likely continue in the future. At this writing, no solutions to the problem appear tenable. Television follows where politics leads! If television is to concentrate on the serious contenders, some way will have to be found to better control the primaries; but since a minor candidate in any given primary could, conceivably, win nomination at a tied-up convention, the method of democratically dealing with the problem is presently obscure. Wallace not only fought for anti-Negro "backlash" votes; he also magnified a dilemma for the television industry and for the nation.[14]

If Senator Brewster of Maryland was correct in his comments in a television interview during Maryland's preprimary days, about 10 per cent of the voters are permanently aggrieved and will, in any election, support "any nameless, faceless man" who offers himself in total opposition to recognized authority, local or national.[15]

> The deplorable thing about Wallace is not just that most people fully understand his racist pitch but that a lot of them are stepping into voting booths and, in a privacy which apparently excludes even their own consciences, are signifying their approval of it. Though he is by no means a candidate for the presidency, Wallace is using the Demo-

cratic presidential primaries of various states to add his own voice to those who are attacking the civil rights bill in the Senate.[16]

Speaking on the nationally televised CBS program *Face the Nation* when he withdrew as a candidate in July of 1964, Wallace observed, "I was the instrument" through which "the high councils of both major political parties" were "conservatized."[17]

CONVENTIONS 1964

Preconvention Mass Media Effects

The mass media, say Paul T. David, Ralph M. Goldman, and Richard C. Bain in their valuable study, *The Politics of National Party Conventions,* have several basic functions in the course of a presidential campaign. First, by virtue of their reports, the public learns "during the early period" who the likely candidates are, at a time when the leaders of the parties are reluctant to deliver public comment on the subject. Second, these media classify "the relative standing of candidates," providing "useful guidance in the often foggy state of public opinion" at a stage when the field of the possible many is being reduced to the probable few. It is pointed out that candidates who are not taken seriously by the newsmen face a most difficult problem.

These authors feel that the function "most open to question is the transmission to the conventions of what purports to be the final popular mandate on the nominations."[18] They are concerned about the traditional dilemma that constantly faces reporters—the question of whether they are being objective or partisan. In 1964, newsmen's preconvention analyses of what the California primary results signified or of the relative standings of Nelson Rockefeller and Barry Goldwater likely had telling effects on the outcome of the Republican convention. Delegates are as impressionable as other citizens who view events in the light of mass media interpretations, but the effects of the reporters' analyses on the 1964 delegates have not yet been studied adequately. Indeed, now that the hour has passed, it may not be possible to secure satisfactory facts. Nevertheless, the general implication is clear—if a candidate goes to the convention with the mass media reporting that his bandwagon is rolling along gaining support, he holds a considerable advantage over the candidate who learns, via the mass media, that his bandwagon has stalled or fallen apart.

Perfect Setups for Television

National political conventions are perfectly set up for television. Most of the major action is concentrated in one city; virtually all the candidates are there; hundreds upon hundreds of delegates are available for "spectacular" scenes; and there is one single roof under which all sorts of dramas take place.

Commentators for each network, acting as "anchor men," serve to focus the efforts of teams of reporters, cameramen, and technicians. The proceedings draw representatives of all segments of the press from both domestic and foreign bases. There is a well-planned procedure, established by the party organizations, that the press can follow step-by-step; there is always the promise of unexpected drama that will be enacted within camera range; and there are the inevitable big moments that will be brought to living rooms around the nation. National political figures share the forum with interesting and colorful local celebrities; and infamous characters (in the opinions of many viewers) are always present. There are tangible results when the tallies are taken. Finally, there is the opportunity to show off the winners in all their glory and the losers in all their crestfallenness.

Add to all of this opportunity the hoopla and shenanigans of the bands, the pretty girls, and the delegates themselves as they cavort, and you can see why the television industry likes conventions. They give public service broadcasting a reputation which can be milked by the industry's publicity departments.

No less consequential to the television industry is the fact that it shines, in the public view, when it reports the conventions. Put the abilities of television staffs in conjunction with the exceedingly high popular interest that has been built up, and the efforts of the sight and sound crews win double appreciation.

Television Has Changed Conventions!

In the days when radio monopolized on-the-spot, direct reporting to the public, demonstrations on the convention floor were aimed primarily at the delegates and the others present in the hall. Today speeches and demonstrations are mainly directed to the national audience and only secondarily to the men and women who actually cast convention ballots. Introduction of "the man who" has become a cherished bit of Americana. A new tradition is for presiding officers to constantly remind the delegates that they are on television. "America is watching us today" will soon be recognizable as a folk phrase.

Examples of other changes in convention routines are readily available. Campaign managers can now direct operations on the convention floor, utilizing an elaborate communications system. In 1960, the Kennedy group had a communications network headquartered in "the house," a command post near the convention hall. The director, Hy Raskin, was able to keep in touch with floor situations via six "telephone positions" maintained in friendly delegations and seven roving walkie-talkies in the hall. It was claimed that any delegate could be contacted within seconds. All of the 13 contacts on the floor could be assembled on one line for a conference. We have a fine photograph showing Raskin, Robert Kennedy, Larry O'Brien, Ken O'Donnell, and Pierre Salinger in the command post, watching a bank of three television sets, each tuned to a different network. When something popped up as a problem, decisions were quickly relayed to the floor of the hall. Soon, one of the Kennedy representatives would be at work.

Chet Huntley, one-half of the famed television news team of Huntley-Brinkley, boasted about the effective liaison between the anchor men in the NBC convention booth and the network's reporters who covered floor happenings on the spot.

> Suppose one of our reporters—say, Herb Kaplow—is on the floor (and on camera) with a fellow from Pennsylvania, and there's a particular question I'd like him to put to the delegate. Is it difficult for me to get through to Herb from our booth? Nope. I do it by letting Reuven [Reuven Frank, the NBC producer] know I'd like my mike opened. At a hand signal from me, an audio man opens the mike—and I'm now able to ask Kaplow to ask the delegate about the something I want to know. Of course, it's happened that Herb has reacted to my request with a *"You* ask him"—taking off his earphone and putting it against the delegate's ear. Then, suddenly, the delegate and *I* are on the air. But all of this happens, literally, within moments.[19]

So television is but one medium for electronic communication! Since the proceedings that it shows are capable of being adroitly manipulated by persons removed from the publicly displayed scenes, there is, perhaps, a need for more television coverage of command centers. The modern versions of the smoke-filled rooms, these control centers direct the activities on the convention floor so efficiently that some delegates would probably enjoy themselves more and be more implicated in the goings-on if the leaders of the major parties would ban the communications gadgets that allow such long-distance manipulation. That is, of course, an unthinkable idea in a nation where symbols of *progress* are often more appreciated than are analyses of the social, economic and political ramifications which are more important.

New portable television cameras permit network people to squeeze right into convention floor huddles. The result is that candid camera work and downright snooping are sometimes indistinguishable from one another.

In booths high over the heads of the delegates sit the "anchor men" of each network, who are themselves television celebrities. Far too often, the commentators loom larger than the convention itself. Usually this happens because of one of the difficulties faced by television men: despite the adaptability of television to political conventions, there are many long stretches in the course of three or four days of proceedings when nothing of consequence is happening. The commentators often report that nothing at all is evident to them as they peer down on rows and rows of empty chairs or on sleeping delegates. To the credit of the industry, a spade is usually called a spade. But it is not unknown for the millions of viewers to witness events that are literally concocted by reporters who have been ordered to drum up some trade. Much of this drummer work is not a serious problem. However, in 1964, the viewers of the

Democratic convention were offered entirely too much loose talk about civil rights, pro and con, from persons—delegates and otherwise—who were happy to be pushed in front of the cameras.

For instance, Eugene ("Bull") Connor, the strident segregationist police leader of Birmingham, Alabama, had little to offer, but there he was, traveling from network booth to network booth, saying it over and over and over. In his off moments, the men with the portable cameras and microphones sought him out. He made a little news when he refused to take the oath of allegiance to the Democratic Party and was expelled from the floor under most mysterious proceedings. He had made himself into a notorious public figure with his lamentable work in Birmingham, and this gave the reporters good reasons to aim their equipment his way, but his popularity as an impromptu floor speaker depended more upon the lack of other events than upon his abilities as a mover of men, a delegate, or a critic of civil rights history. Finally, Connor had had enough publicity. "Pursued by officers, the quarry of a merciless pack of reporters and television men, he fled like a hare from the chase, harassed and frightened, trying to protect his little grandson from the jostling."[20]

Because a quiet stroll out on the floor of the convention by a well-known person has become impossible under the circumstances described, the leaders of the party do far less open campaigning than they did in past decades. Their retreat to the cloistered conference situation has become something of a rout.

Many observers feel that the convention organizers should work harder to accommodate television's responsible roles because of the need to protect the viewing public's interests. Some advocate shorter conventions; others want the dull periods removed from the agenda. To be sure, there is some virtue in the criticisms, but as a political scientist, this writer wonders whether the critics could not ultimately secure excellent television while the convention system as a viable political device fell apart. Like seniority in the Congress, the convention system is not perfect, but it has seemed better than alternatives.

THE REPUBLICANS CONVERGE

The Republican convention was set to convene on July 13, to be followed by the Democrats' assemblage on August 24. By early May, an Associated Press poll of delegates headed for San Francisco showed that Goldwater appeared to have 209 first-ballot votes, of the 655 needed for nomination. Other potential nominees, namely Lodge, Nixon, and Scranton, were far behind, with little opportunity left to secure delegate support.[21] However, for all his delegate strength, Goldwater was not conceded victory by Lodge, Scranton, and Rockefeller.

In early April, Governor Scranton had made it known that, while he did not want to run, he was still open to an "honest" draft.

Considerable speculation centered around the possible influence that former

President Dwight Eisenhower might exert on the presidential nomination. With typical sincerity and good will, Eisenhower addressed himself to the issue— which only gave rise to more speculation. He urged, on May 24, the selection of "a man who will uphold, earnestly, with dedication and conviction, the principles and traditions of our party." He wanted an exponent of "forward-looking Republicanism," a man who would be capable of advancing "true Republicanism" by "spotting new needs, sizing them up, and acting decisively when their national nature and scope require it." In that statement, Eisenhower stressed the issue of civil rights, his concern for human dignity, and his support of the United Nations.[22] His remarks, made just prior to the California primary, were interpreted by a majority of newsmen as a rebuff to Barry Goldwater. But true to form, the Arizona Senator declared that Eisenhower's opinions were "most timely and most welcome."[23]

After a June 6 meeting with Scranton at Gettysburg, it was reported that Eisenhower had urged Scranton to remain free for possible nomination and that the former President had hopes of an open convention. Scranton, the winner in the Republican primary in his own state, Pennsylvania, declared himself an active and announced candidate on June 12. However, it seems that his bid came too late. The Sunday preceding his announcement, he had appeared at the annual National Governors' Conference in Cleveland with a statement that would put him in the race ready for national television. A sudden telephone call from Eisenhower changed his plan at the last minute. He was told that the former President wanted no part of what was being played up in the press as a cabal against Goldwater. Scranton did get through the telecast, but he seemed confused. He even said that he would not oppose Goldwater.

Nixon reportedly followed up on the aborted Scranton "boomlet" by trying to get Governor George Romney of Michigan to take hold of the anti-Goldwater movement. When Goldwater heard of the Nixon efforts, he said, "I think he [Nixon] has talked his way out of running. He is sounding more like Harold Stassen every day."[24]

Goldwater had just voted, along with only five other Republican Senators, against the successful motion for closure on the civil rights debate that had lasted three months.

When the Republicans arrived at San Francisco, Goldwater was still far ahead in estimated delegate strength but far from uniting the party or its leadership. Goldwater was on the brink of confirming a nomination he had secured at the precinct and state levels of the organized Republican Party and had defended by holding off, in an adequate manner, those who threatened him in the primaries.

Goldwater's opponents were grim as they headed for San Francisco. For one reason or another, they had been unable to stop his drive, and as the convention drew closer, he seemed more and more a threat to what they advocated for the party and the nation. To cap it off, on Friday, June 19, the Senate passed the civil rights bill by a vote of 73 to 27, with 21 Democrats and six Republicans opposed. Goldwater had voted against the bill.

THE REPUBLICAN NATIONAL CONVENTION

Television performed three major functions at the Republican convention. It covered the public places connected with that meeting (the convention hall, hotel headquarters, and so on) and described the scenes verbally. Second, it brought the dramatic highlights and sidelights to the great audience that peered at the proceedings from afar. Third, a sense of the historical significance of the *total event* was conveyed to that audience.

By opening day, July 13, the Associated Press, in an "unofficial" poll, gave this breakdown of the likely delegate strengths of the contenders. Of the 1,308 delegates, Goldwater was conceded 736, or 81 more than the 655 needed for a first-ballot nomination; Scranton 162; Rockefeller 99; others 110; uncommitted 201.[25] There were other polls that showed that Governor Scranton and President Johnson had a wide lead over Goldwater in *popularity*. Representative William E. Miller, the Republican National Chairman, appeared on the television program *Issues and Answers* and discounted the latter polls. Miller was not alone before the network cameras on such programs. Each of the possible contenders and a host of others appeared, repeatedly on special programs, and on news and public policy programs when they did or said something special.

All the polls were treated as matters of considerable importance in television coverage of the convention. Thus, the citizenry was well aware of the Goldwater bandwagon's progress. Delegates to the convention watched too, and one wonders how much they studied the television accounts to get a bigger story than the one available from their seats.

Scranton Moves

Of particular interest were the moves made by the man who tried to stop the Goldwater bandwagon—William Scranton, the scrappy dark horse. Scranton went through the motions, looking for a while like a possible winner, and then went down for the count. Goldwater was floating on a tidal wave of delegate support. Goldwater forces and opposition groups displayed much bitterness toward one another in the course of the proceedings. That bitterness became public property through television's very direct reportage.

Beginning his preconvention drive so late, Scranton had come to San Francisco with a surprisingly strong record as one who deplored Goldwater and what he stood for. In large measure, the full television coverage of Scranton's belated move accounts for the fact that a man, little known nationally only 90 days before the convention, thought he had a chance at all.

Scranton, one feels, counted too much upon television. Television is a powerful instrument, but it has limitations. It cannot give people instant memories of a man, even if it can give people a sudden and sweeping introduction to his past and his present. Wherever Scranton went to campaign in that rush effort, television followed. By and large, however, the commentary stressed the futile quality of the Scranton appeals. Television could not get the vital delegate votes. Scranton could warn the nation that the tidal wave was coming, and he could make many worry about the way they would be sucked in. But even those who warmed to his arguments realized that Scranton was more the weather vane than the weathermaker.

So-called moderates were wondering as of early June whether Scranton would stick his neck out. On June 7, during the Governor's Conference in Cleveland, the Republicans were said to have accepted the inevitability of a Goldwater nomination despite George Romney's forecast of "suicidal destruction of the Republican Party." Rockefeller was annoyed because, at two press conferences, Scranton did not take the opportunity to speak up for the moderate cause.

Scranton declared himself firmly on television about a week later. On June 12, he traveled to the Republican state convention, at Baltimore, to make his announcement in an arena that gave him a setting of crowds and noise and lively spirits. He was the keynote speaker who appeared, on only 24 hours' notice, to address what had been a routine affair to pick delegates to the national convention. When Scranton finished his speech to those delegates with, "I come here to announce that I am a candidate for the Presidency of the United States," there was a ringing demonstration by a noisy, cheering, jumping crowd of enthusiasts. Were they enthusiastic about the man, or did they merely welcome the media attention suddenly thrust upon their previously routine proceedings?

Lodge returned to the United States and, on June 29, stated why he had given up the diplomatic post in Saigon. He favored Scranton because the governor was "prudent" and "not impulsive." The former floor manager of Eisenhower's successful bid for the Republican nomination in 1952 added his voice to those who pushed the belated Scranton effort.

On June 15, Scranton, commenting on his offer to debate Goldwater on television, said that his rival's refusal was "unfortunate for the American people." He went on, "I can't understand why he won't face me. I am ready to meet face to face with him any time so the people can see the differences in our views." It is not difficult for students of television to appreciate why Goldwater refused to debate on television and thereby elevate the status of Scranton's last-hour effort!

What were television and the other mass media reporting to the public during this struggle? Primarily, they communicated Scranton's attacks on Goldwater's fitness. Scranton charged that, if Goldwater were successful at San

Francisco, the Republican Party would have to "write off the very states in which our party must win." Many candidates, said Scranton, had begun "as a matter of survival" to plan independent campaigns (June 12). In Iowa (June 15), he hit at what he called "dime-store feudalism" and "extreme reactionaries." He told a Fargo, North Dakota, audience that Goldwater's stand on civil rights could cause violence if the Arizonian won the nomination (July 3).

Arguing shortly in advance of the platform committee's meetings in San Francisco, Scranton partisans proposed a plank condemning the John Birch Society and other extremist groups. Rockefeller urged that the party's platform affirm that the recently enacted civil rights bill was Constitutional (July 7). That would have meant that Goldwater's stand against the bill, based on his announced concern over whether certain sections were Constitutional, would have been clearly rejected in the party platform. On July 10, Scranton told the platform committee that, if the platform were truly Republican, major planks would be in opposition to Goldwater opinions on civil rights, the John Birch Society, Social Security, medical care, federal housing programs, poverty, and farm policy. "Certainly," said Scranton in a long statement, "I hope with you that the day has not come when we are little else than the guardians of reaction."

Scranton's team planned a fight over platform issues on the convention floor. Another item they wanted to urge on the delegates was opposition to Goldwater views on Presidential control over nuclear weapons. Scranton wanted that control reaffirmed. Setbacks to the Scranton forces occurred when Eisenhower refused to support their proposals for platform changes, and when Senator Dirksen of Illinois and Representative McCulloch of Ohio spoke up for the original platform plank on civil rights. (Dirksen and McCulloch had led the Republican forces that helped the passage of the civil rights legislation of 1964.) Then, even more steam went out of the Scranton drive when his address to the delegates was pitched into late hours for Eastern television viewers because the convention managers rescheduled a party-unity speech by Eisenhower to precede it.[26]

The last straw for the Scranton drive came on the night before the convention officially convened. A letter was delivered to Goldwater headquarters from Scranton headquarters. Scranton did not sign the letter before delivery, but he took responsibility for it. That letter ended with a challenge to Goldwater to debate Scranton on the floor of the convention, suggesting that, if Goldwater refused, the people would assume that "you no longer have any regard for the opinions of uncommitted delegates or the American public." The letter became high-level news material instantly when Goldwater's advisors, recognizing a classic mistake when they saw one, released it to the press. They ran off 4,000 copies for distribution to all the delegates and major Republicans and attached to each copy a memorandum from their chief. "I am attaching a copy of a letter

I received from Governor Scranton. I consider it an insult to every Republican in San Francisco. Barry." Excerpts from that Scranton letter will suffice.

> As we move rapidly toward the climax of this convention, the Republican party faces continuing struggle on two counts.
> The first involves, of course, selection of a candidate.
> Here the issue is extremely clear. It simply is this: Will the convention choose the candidate overwhelmingly favored by the Republican voters, or will it choose you. . . .
> With open contempt for the dignity, integrity and common sense of the convention, your managers say in effect that the delegates are little more than a flock of chickens whose necks will be wrung at will. . . .
> Goldwaterism has come to stand for nuclear irresponsibility. . . .
> Goldwaterism has come to stand for being afraid to forthrightly condemn right wing extremists . . . for refusing to stand for law and order in maintaining racial peace.
> In short, Goldwaterism has come to stand for a whole crazy-quilt collection of absurd and dangerous positions that would be soundly repudiated by the American people in November.
> Meanwhile, we have tried as best we can in the rigged situation engineered by your organization to articulate another point of view.[27]

Goldwater's organization controlled the convention's machinery; he maintained a margin of delegate strength sufficient for victory; and he trounced the moderate wing of the party when it dared show defiance. After Scranton had fired his last shot and it had ricocheted back in his face, all of the goals of the Goldwater group were to become realities, with the exception of the one goal that every Republican hopeful aspired to: the Presidency of the United States!

The convention gave Goldwater the nomination but, with the intraparty feuding common knowledge, he was seen, more and more, as an undemocratic victor. That was a legacy of San Francisco that the Goldwater group had to assume. Goldwater had won the battle but he was on his way to losing the war. In the pretelevision era, much of what transpired would have been buried in the welter of press news. Even radio would not have been able to convey the truth of the situation. Television did. Delegate strength is one thing; but mass impressions are also vital. The losers sulked and left with their bitterness undiminished; the winners strutted but faced the nation as the nominal heads of a very much divided Republican Party. The effects were soon apparent—even before the convention adjourned!

Eisenhower

Only one man had the power and the reputation to change the course of convention history. Eisenhower arrived in the city by the Golden Gate on July 12, the day before the convention opened. He was *under contract as a television commentator for the American Broadcasting Company,* an assignment that is most dubious for a former President going to the national convention of his own party. On July 14, he addressed the convention. It was a peak moment, in terms of public interest. Ike gave a good talk emphasizing what was on everyone's mind, while refusing to endanger his own popularity by translating idealistic phraseology into concrete political recommendations. He inveighed against demagoguery; spoke about great Republican traditions; suggested that strength was found in unity; asked for a fight against radicalism, which was bad for America; rejected intolerance; stood for fiscal integrity in national affairs; and urged the search for "better ways" to bring the truth to the public. Eisenhower was disturbed at the press reactions to the convention. "So," he admonished, "let us particularly scorn the divisive efforts of those outside our family, including sensation-seeking columnists and commentators, who couldn't care less about the good of our party and our entire economic structure."[28] He failed to appreciate the fact that most of the sensationalism was manufactured not by newsmen, but by politicians.

Reaction to Rockefeller

If the nation was disturbed by what it saw, the convention delegates were equally troubled. Divided in allegiances and set against one another by ideological strife, the delegates resented the effect the proceedings were having on the television audience and looked about for scapegoats. The Goldwater partisans appeared to be the most angered of all. The anger of the other delegates was tempered by the fact that, being in the minority, they felt less responsible for the spectacle.

After the howling demonstration that followed the Eisenhower address, the convention calmed down a bit to hear a 90-minute reading of the platform. Then, after prime television time in the East, Rockefeller was given permission to rise to defend three minority resolutions. As he rose, there was a smattering of applause, soon drowned out by raucous booing. The booing, interspersed with shouts of "we want Barry," was accompanied by all sorts of clangs and bangs and toots and hoots from a great variety of delegates with noisemakers of one type or another. Nelson Rockefeller was seen as a man in the camp of his enemies. Some order was restored, and Rockefeller went on into his five-minute exposition. It was more and more difficult to get the frenzied galleries to act civilized. Television cameras panned over a sea of hate.

Rockefeller shined at that moment. He took the jeers and taunts in stride and hit back at the angry assemblage, lacing his prepared remarks with comments such as, "This is still a free country, ladies and gentlemen." To the even more stirred-up convention, he went on, "These things have no place in America, but I can personally testify to their existence. And so can countless others who have also experienced anonymous midnight and early morning telephone calls, unsigned threatening letters, smear and hate literature, strong-arm and goon tactics, bomb threats and bombings." In the teeth of the storm, he went on, "Infiltration and take-over of established political organizations by Communist and Nazi methods." Then, "Some of you don't like to hear it, ladies and gentlemen, but it's the truth."

Theodore H. White, who was there and who saw the television reports as well, says, "As the TV cameras translated their wrath and fury to the national audience, they pressed on the viewers the indelible impression of savagery which no Goldwater leader or wordsmith could later erase." He credits the Goldwater organization with the attempt to squelch the demonstrations but reports that they could not. Later, White advises, "This was a new thing in American conventions—not a meeting, not a clash, but a coup d'etat."[-9]

Elmo Roper, the distinguished pollster, was also on the convention floor. Earlier, when Eisenhower mentioned the press in derogatory language, he saw delegates rise, cheer, and shake their fists at the NBC, CBS, and ABC booths above them. Roper was wearing an NBC badge as he stood in the aisle next to the alternate delegates from Alabama. Five of them pointed to his badge and singled him out for their boos for a full minute. Roper says that, had he been wearing a badge reading "pollster," he would have been no better off, because antipollster sentiment also "ran deeply through the Goldwater contingent."[30]

What Followed

What followed was as expected by the Goldwater team. On the first ballot, we saw on television tallies that South Carolina, in casting its 16 votes for the Arizonian, gave him 663 votes—eight more than needed for a first-ballot nomination. At the final count, Goldwater reached 883.

Later, the convention accepted his choice of William E. Miller for the vice-presidential nomination. Apart from his effort to achieve the presidential nomination, Goldwater's choice of Miller was his first major decision. Goldwater took no compromise man, no well-known national Republican leader. He took Miller from the post of National Chairman and rewarded him with the greatest gift he had to bestow. As if that were not enough, Goldwater next accomplished what was least to be desired. He delivered an acceptance speech that created more havoc at home and abroad. That, too, was grist for the television mill. He ended the address with words that tore another seam of party unity.

> Anyone who joins us in all sincerity, we welcome. Those who do not care for our cause, we don't expect to enter our ranks in any case. And let our Republicanism, so focused and so dedicated, not be made fuzzy and futile by unthinking and stupid labels.
> I would remind you that extremism in the defense of liberty is no vice!
> And let me remind you also that moderation in the pursuit of justice is no virtue!

This Party, its good people, and its unquestionable devotion to freedom will not fulfill the purposes of this campaign which we launch here now until our cause has won the day, inspired the world, and shown the way to a tomorrow worthy of all our yesteryears.[31]

About half of the New York delegation, led by Senator Kenneth Keating, walked off the floor. *The Times* of London had a special correspondent watching. He wrote, "The Goldwater camp will no doubt deny that he meant what his listeners thought he meant, which was an open refusal to protect the party from extremist groups and instead to welcome them within its ranks." And, "the fact that he chose to speak in this fashion after the shameful treatment of a respected representative of the Old Party (a reference to the display during Rockefeller's speech) disturbed more people than the New York delegation."[32]

Lessons for the Television Industry and for Politicians

The television industry learned much in the process of covering the convention. Primarily, the convention demonstrated that all of the fine talk about television being so instrumental in a democracy is based on truth. If the cameras and the reporters cover a sordid event and do an honest job, those who come out badly in the reportage are more likely to denounce the industry than they are to change their own ways. For example, it was not in dispute, before San Francisco, that newsmen and cameramen had rightful access to the convention floor, so long as they did not interfere. When police escorted NBC newsman John Chancellor from the floor and an attempt was made to eject CBS correspondent Mike Wallace, a strong challenge was made to that privilege. The Republican sergeant at arms took the actions, allegedly to clear the aisles. Both networks filed formal complaints, and after a meeting between industry representatives and convention officials, a working arrangement was agreed upon.[33]

This writer was in England during the Republican convention and was impressed with the reactions of many Britishers to the trans-Atlantic views and filmed reports of the meetings. Their often-repeated comment was that the affair, at crucial moments, had something of the aroma of fascism. It was said that part of the anger of the delegates was due to the fact that they knew that television was bringing their convention to the attention of national and world audiences. A wry story circulated at the time. One delegate supposedly turned to another and said excitedly, "Do you know that, at this very moment, we are being carried *live* to Europe on the Telstar satellite? What do you think of that?" The other delegate replied, "Shoot the damned thing down!"

Speaking before the Republican National Committee, on June 28, 1965, former President Eisenhower raised the question of how conventions should be run. He speculated on the subject of popular reactions to the 1964 affairs, saying that the American people had been "horrified" by what they saw.

Eisenhower urged the Committee to take steps to change the television viewer's "picture of confusion, noise, impossible deportment and indifference to what is being discussed on the platform." He proposed "a strong, permanent chairman, with dictatorial powers"—aided by tough sergeants at arms, preferably 6 feet, 4 inches in height, with background in the police, the Army, or the Marine Corps.

Eisenhower took another swipe at "sensation-seeking columnists and commentators" and suggested that cameramen and reporters be barred from the floor of the convention during its business sessions.

He urged a reduction in the number of delegates, advising that the total be limited to a maximum of 1,070—twice the number of electoral college votes.

He also reported to the Committee that his niece and the wife of a speaker had been molested by hoodlums on the floor. His niece was a page at the convention.[34]

To be sure, the Eisenhower opinions raise questions as to the basic roles of national political conventions in this television environment. One hopes that both National Committees will investigate the problem seriously, in time to effect changes for the 1968 meetings.

In the days before television, the long, drawn-out conventions did not antagonize the citizenry at large because most of their information came secondhand. Political scientists have long argued for substantial changes in format and procedures, but their opinions rarely went beyond audiences of their students and fellow scholars; working politicians pointedly ignored major criticisms. Under the present circumstances, the national audience receives its impressions firsthand and is distressed at the apparent clumsiness of the proceedings that it sees. The very commentators attacked by Eisenhower have furthered public education by pointing out these shortcomings.

The "dead" periods of the conventions of past decades could be overlooked because no one was watching. Most of the delegates occupied themselves, between the important sessions, by seeking whatever entertainments the convention city afforded. Today, the reporters repeatedly refer to the rows and rows of empty seats; to the steady drone of sound from the document readers; to the inane demonstrations for individuals who have no apparent chance of securing the nomination; to the chants from the galleries; and to the seemingly interminable histrionic nominating speeches.

The television audience has learned that most demonstrations are carefully prepared and well-subsidized productions, put on by legions of performers who are paid by the hour to shout the glories of a candidate they do not know and care little about. In Eisenhower's words, any demonstration "over five minutes is a spurious demonstration of unwarranted enthusiasm" that the presiding officers should abort.[35]

Reactions to the Eisenhower proposals came in quickly from executives of the television industry and from party leaders. Elmer W. Lower, president of

ABC News, cautioned against the proposal to bar reporters from the floor. It was not a "surefire cure," he said. A spokesman for the Democrats was reported as suggesting that Eisenhower's goals could be achieved if a more rigorous system of accreditation were enforced to limit reporters' access rights to the convention floor and to curb the movements of roving politicians. John Bailey, the Democratic National Chairman, agreed that a good look ought to be taken at reporting procedures during the conventions, since the growth of news media involvement in the past three conventions had been tremendous. Also, he observed that he had heard complaints from many delegates about the platform erected for the cameras having covered the rostrum at the 1964 Democratic assembly; this platform had blocked the view of many delegates.[36]

If political leaders want to prepare seriously for convention reforms, they should recognize that better procedure is not attained simply by making attacks upon the mass media. Hopefully, the political chieftains will confer with the leaders of the printed and electronic media about such reforms. It may be that the removal of the press representatives from the convention floor would have some merit. However, the press has not produced the major problems; it has only made the general public aware that these problems exist! Glossing over the central predicaments that lead to curbing the public's right to know will only produce greater dilemmas than have already been exposed. The former President should, in all honesty, admit that the events of his party's convention of 1964 were shaped not only by the organizing and reporting procedures then current, but also by the dogmatism of the clique that seized power in San Francisco. That clique was determined to flex its muscles and trounce its opponents. The issue of convention reform involves fundamental matters of political behavior as well as political procedure.

THE DEMOCRATS' NATIONAL CONVENTION

In contrast to the Republican convention, the Democrats' convention seemed all sweetness and light. First, no one who traveled to Atlantic City in August had cause to wonder about who the standard-bearer would be. President Johnson had managers who controlled every aspect of the proceedings. As for the vice-presidential nominee, he would be the man most acceptable to the President. The convention met to certify the candidates and not to argue about who they would be. It was more a coronation than a convention.

Southern delegates, who had had the power in previous conventions to raise havoc over the civil rights issue, were in a most awkward position. Johnson was a Southerner, and if they became too outspoken in their opposition to him, he could later retaliate, assuming that he won in the general election. So, while there was considerable rumbling, publicized through the mass electronic media largely because reporters wanted something to report, the Southern delegations simmered but did not boil over.

Of course, the image of John F. Kennedy hovered over the whole affair. Johnson had a problem to contend with, in that the showing of a eulogistic film about the late President could, possibly, have set off a wave of sentiment for the nomination of Robert Kennedy as Vice-President. The convention managers were accordingly told to postpone showing the film until after the nominations.

Having the sordid spectacle of the Republican convention behind them, the managers of the Democratic convention were determined to display a better picture to the public. Every effort was made to play up the differences between the two conventions. Speaker after speaker reminded the assemblage that, in contrast to the carnage of July, the August gathering was downright pleasant. Russell Baker reported on the opening day, August 24, that the convention was a "family party staged for television."

> The object is to leave the television audience with that good warm feeling that used to result from watching "I Remember Mama."
> Appropriately, the old patriarch in the White House has all his family gathered at the seashore, eating fudge and butter crunch, riding the ferris wheel and playing skee ball. . . .
> The worst spoilsports so far have been Gov. George Wallace of Alabama and Joseph L. Rauh, counsel to the Mississippi Freedom Democratic Party and chairman of the District of Columbia delegation. Yesterday for example, Mr. Rauh produced a parade of witnesses in the Credentials Committee who told the television audience what he called "a story of terror and tragedy in Mississippi."[37]

When real problems came up, such as the problem of what to do with those delegates from Alabama who refused to sign a pledge binding them to support the ticket, every attempt was made to avoid television showing people being ejected from the convention floor. Long wait-out maneuvers were devised by the Chairman and the sergeant at arms (for example, they had the chairs of the rebellious delegates removed whenever they left the floor). The heated battles between rival Alabama and Mississippi delegations were temporarily smoothed over, and displays of discord on television were avoided at all costs.

The issues were real, and the actions of the credentials committee were tangible, but why fight? After all, stirring floor battles of the past were preludes to strong campaigning for or against potential nominees or over platform planks. With the selection of nominees a problem out of delegate control and with the platform a mirror of Johnson's wishes, the party's convention managers quickly spread oil on whatever troubled waters they found. Antagonists could not really engage each other in battle as they slipped and slid through the administrative ooze.[38]

Fifty-five hundred newsmen and technicians were hard pressed to squeeze stirring news out of the doings of 5,260 delegates and alternates.[39] Aside from the coverage of the dramatic speeches, the important comings and goings of

Johnson, and the game of suspense that Johnson made out of the business of conferring the vice-presidential nomination on Hubert Humphrey, there were surprisingly few good stories.

One story came into view in the hearing room of the credentials committee, when Mrs. Fannie Lou Hamer of Ruleville, Mississippi, testified how she and other Negroes were brutalized by police when they tried to register to vote in Senator Eastland's and Senator Stennis's home state. Mrs. Hamer's direct rendition of an awful story provided millions of viewers with a most dramatic mix of the personal and public aspects of the convention. Other credentials committee hearings over the seating of delegates provided good feature material for the nation. Those hearings of the platform committee that were on public view were tedious, under the circumstances of the convention.

The great moments of the convention were a remarkably dynamic speech by Senator Pastore of Rhode Island, who brought the convention to life with his fiery keynote address; the showing of the Kennedy film, which caught the emotions of the assemblage—as did the remarks of Robert Kennedy that followed; and the acceptance speeches of Senator Humphrey and President Johnson.

Convention sidelights were also brought into the homes of the land. For example, television viewers saw street demonstrations by civil rights groups and by the American Nazi Party, which uses almost any convenient public occasion to seek publicity for its sick ideas.

Democratic Battle Cries

The three major speeches, those by Senator Pastore, Senator Humphrey, and President Johnson, set the tone for the coming campaign from the Democratic point of view. In those addresses the nation was alerted to the major issues that the party's national standard-bearers would press home. Pastore stressed the issue of responsibility, as faced by the President in a nuclear age, and the need for a reasonable, sensible leader. He also hammered on the social-welfare theme, asking whether the Republicans meant, by their "clear choice," to "change the social security system" or "to repeal the minimum wage law or to weaken the unions in America." Turning to international affairs, he challenged the opposition as to whether they proposed a withdrawal from the Atlantic Alliance or from the United Nations.

Hubert Humphrey, in his acceptance speech, said that those "shrill voices" that had laid claim in the past weeks "to the great spirit of the American past" longed "for a past that never was." He also warned that the Presidency was not the job

> . . . for a man who is impetuous at one moment and indecisive the next. Nor is it a place for one who is violently for something one day and violently opposed to it on the next. Nor is this an office where

statements on matters of major foreign policy are so confusing and so contradictory that neither friend nor foe knows where he stands.

Then he undertook the task for trying to separate Barry Goldwater from the mainstream of political thought adhered to by, in Humphrey's opinion, Republicans and Democrats alike. Calling the Republican leader "the temporary spokesman of the Republican Party," Humphrey began an almost rhythmic chant that highlighted the areas where most Democrats and Republicans had agreed. After each point he shouted out, with bitter satire in his voice, "But not Senator Goldwater!" Soon the assembled delegates joined him on that phrase, chorusing it throughout the hall. Their vice-presidential nominee argued that, in the past three and one-half years in the United States Senate, most Democrats and Republicans had voted for the civil rights bill, for "an expanded medical-education program," for the National Defense Education Act, and to help the United Nations carry on its peace-keeping work. After each point there was the punctuation "but not Senator Goldwater" or "but not the temporary Republican spokesman."

Humphrey also urged the Republicans who "put our country above their Party" to vote for the Democratic ticket in November. Of course, in his view, they were the "responsible and forward-looking" members of the opposition party.

President Johnson was almost beatific in Atlantic City. When he appeared on television screens, it seemed that a monarch was visiting. In accepting the nomination, he engaged in almost above-the-battle philosophizing about the "great society." After promising to rededicate the nation to the goals of his predecessor, he expounded upon the higher ambitions of our people.

> Weapons do not make peace; man makes peace. And peace comes not through strength alone, but through wisdom and patience and restraint.
>
> Every American has the right to be treated as a person. He should be able to find a job. He should be able to educate his children. He should be able to vote in elections and he should be judged on his merits as a person. . . .
>
> This nation, this generation, in this hour has man's first chance to build a great society, a place where the meaning of man's life matches the marvels of man's labor. I am determined in all the time that is mine to use all the talents that I have for bringing this great lovable land, this great nation of ours together. I believe some day we will see an America that knows no North or South, no East or West, an America that is undivided by creed or color and untorn by suspicion or class.[40]

The stage was set for the head-on clash between the Goldwater-Miller and the Johnson-Humphrey tickets. After the two major-party conventions, the nation and the candidates took a breather. Then, in late summer, the final race of 1964 speeded to the hours of decision at the ballot boxes.

FOOTNOTES

1. Theodore H. White, *The Making of the President, 1964* (New York: Atheneum Publishers, 1965), p. 98.

2. John H. Fenton, "Electronic Plague Hits New Hampshire," *New York Times,* March 8, 1964. For analysis of the New Hampshire primary, see also Gene Shalit and Lawrence K. Grossman, *Somehow It Works: A Candid Portrait of the 1964 Presidential Election by NBC News* (New York: Doubleday & Company, Inc., 1965); John Skow, "Sweepstakes in the Snow," *The Saturday Evening Post* (March 14, 1964), pp. 17–21; William S. Ellis, "As New Hampshire Goes, So Goes Who?" *New York Times Magazine,* February 2, 1964.

3. See James M. Perry, *A Report in Depth on Barry Goldwater* (Silver Springs, Md.: The National Observer, 1964), p. 85.

4. See Phyllis Schlafly, *A Choice Not an Echo* (Alton, Illinois: Pere Marquette Press, 1964), pp. 78–85.

5. Barry Goldwater, *The Conscience of a Conservative* (New York: Macfadden Books, 1963); John A. Stormer, *None Dare Call It Treason* (Florissant, Missouri: Liberty Bell Press, 1964); Edwin McDowell, *Barry Goldwater: Portrait of an American* (Chicago: Henry Regnery Co., 1964); Arthur Frommer, *Goldwater, from A to Z* (New York: Pocket Books, 1964); Fred J. Cook, *Barry Goldwater: Extremist of the Right* (New York: Grove Press, Inc., 1964).

6. Theodore H. White, *The Making of the President, 1964,* pp. 104–105.

7. See comments of Richard H. Rovere, *The Goldwater Caper* (New York: Harcourt, Brace & World, Inc., 1965), p. 55.

8. Helen B. Shaffer, "Television and the 1956 Campaign," *Editorial Research Reports* (September 6, 1955), pp. 615–632.

9. J. G. Blumler, "British Television," *British Journal of Sociology* (September 1964), p. 230.

10. "Campaign Coverage, '64," *The Quill,* Vol. 52, No. 8 (August 1964), p. 13.

11. Angus Campbell, "Has Television Reshaped Politics?" *Columbia Journalism Review* (Fall 1962), pp. 10–13.

12. Gladwin Hill, "G.O.P. Candidates Press Campaign in California," *New York Times,* May 24, 1964.

13. "Goldwater vs. Rockefeller," *New York Herald Tribune,* June 3, 1964.

14. Theodore H. White, *The Making of the President, 1964,* pp. 233–236.

15. Richard H. Rovere, "Letter from Washington," *The New Yorker* (May 16, 1964), pp. 193–198, especially p. 194.

16. Loudon Wainwright, "Huckster for a Hot Summer," *Life,* Vol. 56, No. 19 (May 8, 1964), p. 21. Also, for other background, see Ben A. Franklin, "Hate Groups Back Wallace Bid," *New York Times,* May 14, 1964.

17. "Wallace Gives Up Presidency Race: Denies Any Deal," *New York Times,* July 20, 1964. For pertinent learned commentary on the relationships than can be developed by television, see Seymour Feshbach, "The Effectiveness of Aggressive Content in Television Programs upon the Aggressive Behavior of the Audience," in Leon Arons and Mark A. May, editors, *Television and Human Behavior* (New York: Appleton-Century-Crofts, 1963), pp. 83–97.

18. Paul T. David, Ralph M. Goldman, and Richard C. Bain, *The Politics of National Party Conventions* (New York: Vintage Books, 1964), pp. 26–27.

19. For the Kennedy team's talents, see "How the Kennedys Beat Party Pros," *Life,* Vol. 49, No. 4 (July 25, 1960), pp. 23–24; for the NBC abilities on the floor, see

Chet Huntley, "The Way It Is," in the NBC News brochure, *Huntley-Brinkley, NBC Convention & Election Almanac* (New York: NBC, 1964), p. 7.

20. Theodore H. White, *The Making of the President, 1964*, pp. 169–170.

21. "Goldwater Gains Delegates," report on Associated Press poll, *New York Times*, May 4, 1964.

22. Dwight David Eisenhower, see statement in *New York Times*, May 25, 1964.

23. Charles Mohr, article on Goldwater reaction, *New York Times*, May 26, 1964.

24. See "The News of the Week in Review," *New York Times*, June 14, 1964.

25. See "Convention Opens Today; Goldwater Victory Seen; Platform Backs His Views," *New York Times* (International edition, Paris), July 13, 1964.

26. For the background to Governor Scranton's opposition to Goldwater, see Joseph A. Loftus, "G.O.P. Governors Foresee Victory for Goldwater," *New York Times*, June 8, 1964; "Transcript of Scranton Talk" and "Pennsylvania Aristocrat" and Cabell Phillips, "Scranton Saves Baltimore Show," *New York Times*, June 30, 1964; Richard H. Parke, "Scranton Asserts Goldwater Stirs 'Havoc' in Nation," *New York Times*, June 14, 1964; Joseph A. Loftus, "Scranton Begins Drive in Midwest," *New York Times*, June 16, 1964; "Scranton Scores Goldwater Vote on Civil Rights," *New York Times* (International edition, Paris), July 4, 1964; "Scranton Aides Ask G.O.P. Fight on Extremists," *New York Times* (International edition, Paris), July 10, 1964; "Republicans: Some Facts of History," *Time*, Vol. 84, No. 2 (July 10, 1964), especially pp. 13–17.

27. Harold Faber, editor, *The Road to the White House*, pp. 58–59.

28. "Text of Eisenhower's Talk to the G.O.P. Convention," *New York Times*, July 15, 1964.

29. Theodore H. White, *The Making of the President, 1964*, pp. 200–202.

30. Elmo Roper, "The Meaning of San Francisco," *Saturday Review* (August 22, 1964), pp. 17, 36.

31. See Gene Shalit and L. K. Grossman, editors, *Somehow It Works*, p. 93.

32. "Senator's Open Invitation to Extremists," *The Times* (London), July 18, 1964.

33. See "Much Time Used but Little News," *Broadcasting* (July 20, 1964), pp. 37–38.

34. David S. Broder, "Eisenhower Asks Convention Curb," *New York Times*, June 29, 1965.

35. *Ibid.*

36. Warren Weaver, Jr., "G.O.P. Votes to Study Eisenhower's Convention Reforms; Democrats Indicate Interest," *New York Times*, June 30, 1965.

37. Russell Baker, "Democrats Too Placid for Palmistry," *New York Times*, August 24, 1964.

38. For some background, see the section on the Democratic convention in G. Shalit and L. K. Grossman, editors, *Somehow It Works*, pp. 103ff.

39. Theodore H. White, *The Making of the President, 1964*, p. 276.

40. G. Shalit and L. K. Grossman, editors, *Somehow It Works*, pp. 106, 131–135.

9 / The Best and the Worst of Times

OF PROPOSALS AND DISPOSALS

According to some eminent political prognosticators who divined the over-all meanings of the primaries, the conventions, and the nominees' philosophies in late August 1964, there was every sign of a great ideological struggle ahead.[1] Americans would be asked to choose between the socialistically inclined Johnson-Humphrey ticket and the expounders of rugged, individualistic conservatism. A classic contest based upon philosophies of government would be a sharp break from the usual personality clashes, common since Franklin D. Roosevelt's first presidential victory. No Tweedledum-Tweedledee choices in 1964! No hair-margin finish similar to the 1960 outcome was in the offing, they said. Barry Goldwater and William Miller would truly offer a clear choice to the electorate. Like it or not, the voters seemed destined to be party to a European-type rivalry.

It did not work out that way, although the race did start as advertised. The campaign grew increasingly banal and vicious and ended in the most lopsided victory in modern American history. Choice turned out to be a major factor, but it was not a choice between philosophies. Ballot-casters in November were forced to choose between a Republican team out of touch with the majority sentiments of the GOP, and the Democratic nominees, who were able to present themselves as the only reasonable alternatives to bitter, frustrated men who seldom proposed ideas and who usually concentrated on attacking the end results of a long period of bipartisan action. The final election tallies showed that the one issue that attracted a hard core of Goldwater loyalists was the race issue. If we will recall all of the talk about economics and social welfare that Goldwater and his partner indulged in, the most lamentable aspect of the election campaign is that, for many Southern voters, so much of conservatism evolved into "Wallace-ism."

Another surprise was that, as the campaign reached its midway mark, Goldwater seemed to grow tired of his own enterprise and left much of the hard swinging to Miller. With that development, Miller, who was comparatively unknown even with the massive publicity that he was able to trigger, was seen as the real infighter. This, of course, alienated even more of the traditional Republicans, who were already somewhat upset by Goldwater and his propositions. Important Republican leaders displayed a marked reserve about the titular leader's efforts and, in some cases, were openly antagonistic. Kenneth Keating, George Romney, Nelson Rockefeller, John Lindsay, and Dwight D. Eisenhower gave only lip service or separated themselves from Goldwater and his works altogether. Keating announced that he was an independent Republican who would be fighting for a New York Senate seat on his own record alone. John Lindsay ran for the House of Representatives in a New York City district on the same theme. Romney urged Michigan voters to consider him for the governorship by concentrating on state rather than national problems. Rockefeller disdained to work for the national ticket, although he was willing to *greet* Goldwater in Albany. Having such friends, Goldwater had little need for enemies. Richard Nixon campaigned for Goldwater, but he managed to maintain a most meaningful position as an advocate of party unity—above all. Eisenhower, the only great Republican vote-getter since the Depression, kept his usual above-the-battle stance.

Johnson and Humphrey were able, in direct proportion to Goldwater-Miller backsliding, to look better and better. They stressed the social-progress theme that was so evident at their party's placid convention. The outstanding Democratic victory can easily be interpreted as an outstanding Republican defeat, which the man from Texas and the man from Minnesota only helped along. In assessing how fully Goldwater contributed to his rivals' success and how little valid ideological campaigning took place, one is reminded of the apocryphal tale about the deathbed scene of Gertrude Stein. A worshipful disciple smitten almost beyond salvage by the sight of her idol slipping from life, blurted out, at the last possible moment, "Oh, Miss Stein, Miss Stein, what is the answer, what is the answer?" If we are to believe this well-worn story, Miss Stein pushed her head up with that final bit of strength and inquired, "What was the question?"

Goldwater's main complaint was that Americans had been driven by the Democrats and their fellow travelers into the worst of times. Johnson argued that his opponent was at least a century out of touch with reality and that it was the best of times. The majority of voters accepted the latter view.

Sad to say, the outcome of the election did not signify mass enthusiasm for the winners. Both major parties offered much less, for historical and sociological reasons, then they had in 1960.

There were very real problems before the country during the campaign. President Johnson and Hubert Humphrey were not always specific as to how they would handle those problems, but they were able to convince a majority of the electorate that their approaches were sound and reasonable. Goldwater and company, perhaps unfairly at times, were tagged as the ones with the radical or eccentric ideas.

Extremism: Illustrations

We have already observed that Goldwater's thoughts about extremism, in his acceptance speech at San Francisco, did not sit well with many sober-minded people. His position on the major federal civil rights legislation of that election year also tended to put him into alliance with segregationist groups. On the subject of crime and its prevention, Goldwater advanced the view that much crime was stimulated by "welfare statism," while underplaying the other, deep-rooted causes of crime.

The Goldwater thesis that left-wing domination of government had produced most of the ills of our society made him popular with extreme right-wing groups, like the John Birch Society and the Minutemen, who were also achieving reputations for radicalism.

On foreign affairs, the Republican nominees propounded sweeping and drastic solutions that were largely anti-United Nations and that offered cures of an inherently radical and dangerous nature for the problems of the North Atlantic Treaty Organization, China, and Vietnam.

Meeting with reporters at his Texas ranch on July 19, the President opened his remarks on the civil rights question. He chided Senator Goldwater by name and deplored "all hate organizations by whatever name they mask and produce and spread this venom. I am not one who believes the end justifies the means." Asked whether he agreed with Governor Rockefeller's opinion that certain statements by Goldwater encouraged extremist groups to violence against Negroes, the President said that he condemned anyone's "playing upon the prejudices of the people of this country."[2]

On August 16, Johnson attacked Goldwater for his idea that battlefield commanders should be allowed to use nuclear weapons in retaliatory attacks on North Vietnam. Goldwater had, a few days before, suggested the President's implied permission for such use of nuclear arms. Johnson snorted, "Loose charges on nuclear weapons without any shadow of justification by any candidate for any office, let alone the Presidency, are a disservice to our national security, a disservice to peace and, as for that matter, a great disservice to the entire free world." That retort was delivered at a news conference in the White House rose garden.[3]

TELEVISION ENTERPRISE: THE CRISIS FACTOR

During a Presidential campaign, the television industry, largely through the enterprise of the networks, performs several major functions. First, there is the function of following the candidates around the country and arranging for the appropriate coverage of their activities and pronouncements. That function attracts the most attention in that it has to do with the overt processes of political solicitation, by the specific candidates, for specific offices of government.

Television's second function—covering the general news at home and abroad —is often as consequential to the election as are the speeches and other traditional trappings. During the 1964 campaign period, this second major element of television work often provided the public with more important election stories than the activities and speeches of the candidates themselves could provide.

There appears to be a strong connection between specific electioneering every four years, and the actions taken by individuals and groups anxious to impress the public or to force governmental change on matters of domestic importance. Governor Wallace's 1964 "candidacy" in several Democratic presidential primaries was one example. Likewise, the results on November's election night were not the only targets of those who where pressuring for or against civil rights, for or against extremist groups, or for or against "morality."

A general election stirs society to reshape itself more quickly, in part because a mood of agitation is inherent in the specific political contest. Emphasis is constantly on problem-raising and problem-solving. No matter which way the election goes, the citizenry tends to associate the word "election" with the idea of reform. The seeds of change sown by rival candidates—particularly by challengers anxious to expose the abuses of the incumbent group—take root and flower during election years. Elections are societal crises!

Our conclusion is by no means a novel one. The point is simply that a people accepting television almost as a political staff of life should also be aware of its potential side effects; without belaboring the power of television to cover and display events so vividly, it is possible to foresee a normal timetable of agitation, specifically set to election crises, that tells us when the public is to be stirred up as few publics, before television, could have been stirred up.

RACIAL VIOLENCE

We had a long, hot summer in 1964. In major cities across the land social disturbances over racial issues ranged from peaceful picketing to bloody riots. In mid-July, ugly rioting took place in New York City's black ghettos—Harlem and the Bedford-Stuyvesant section of Brooklyn. Rochester, New York, had a full-scale race riot.

In August, a six-week search by federal agents and forces produced grisly results in Mississippi. The bodies of young civil rights workers Andrew Goodman (20 years old), Michael Schwerner (24 years old), and James Chaney (21 years old) were found buried in a cattle-pond dam. Goodman and Schwerner were two white boys from New York who had set out to promote Negro voter registration. Chaney was a local Negro who worked with them, in and about their base in the town of Philadelphia. Evidence uncovered pointed to the strong possibility that the three were brutally murdered by white racists.

The Ku Klux Klan was growing; in Biloxi, Mississippi, three Negro children became the first of their race to desegregate Mississippi public schools below the college level (mid-August); in Paterson and Elizabeth, New Jersey, Negro youths rioted on three successive nights (mid-August); in the Chicago suburb of Dixmoor, 70 persons were arrested after a two-day racial outbreak caused by a liquor store proprietor's accusations against a Negro woman (mid-August). He accused her of stealing a bottle of gin.

On September 26, a report to the President on the racial disturbances in nine cities over the country was made public by the Federal Bureau of Investigation. Item number 10 of the "Conclusions" (about what caused the troubles and what aggravated the situations in cities as far apart as New York City and Seaside, Oregon) was as follows:

> 10. The arrival of large numbers of reporters and television cameras at the riots provided an opportunity for self-seeking individuals to publicize wild charges on television and radio and in the press. These circumstances provided additional incitement to the rioters and served to attract others to the scene.[4]

KEEPING RACIAL TENSION DOWN

A Suggestion, a Meeting, and Communique

Barry Goldwater, at a news conference on July 20, urged that the "tension that exists" over civil rights be excluded from the campaign. "I don't want to see any words of mine or anyone connected with me touch anything off." That same day, Johnson asked Congress for an additional 13 million dollars to implement the civil rights law.

That Goldwater suggestion about removing tension was connected to the thought that he and the President might join together in opposing further racial inflammation. The two men met in the White House on July 24 for 16 minutes. When Goldwater left, he avoided reporters and photographers and made no personal statement. A cryptic communique, agreed to by both men, was made available. "The President met with Senator Goldwater and reviewed the steps he had taken to avoid the incitement of racial tensions. Senator Goldwater expressed his opinion, which was that racial tension should be avoided. Both agreed on this position."

A Televised News Conference

Perhaps Goldwater was a victim of "one-upsmanship." Two hours prior to his appointment with Goldwater, the President had held a televised press conference. According to *Newsweek*, the President had had his press secretary, George Reedy, "plant" a question with Edward T. Folliard of the *Washington Post*. Folliard asked whether Johnson was going to have a "pact" with Goldwater to take the civil rights issue out of the campaign. Johnson replied:

> I believe that all men and women are entitled to equal opportunities, so that they can be judged according to their merits and not according to some artificial barrier. Now, to the extent that Senator Goldwater differs from these views, or the Republican Party differs, there will, of course, be discussion. I propose to discuss and debate the hard and difficult issues . . . on the assumption that the American people are willing to listen, and are intelligent and are unafraid. . . . If Senator Goldwater and his advisors and his followers will follow the same course that I intend to follow, and that I expect the Democratic Party to follow, which is a course of rebutting and rebuking bigots and those who seek to excite and exploit tensions, then it will be most welcome [and] a very fine contribution to our political life in America.[5]

ISSUES BANDIED ABOUT DURING THE CAMPAIGN

Precious little orderly debate occurred after the campaign opened, following Labor Day. There was a great deal that could have been argued through, but most of the topics were raised and analyzed in polemical manner. Pugnacity was a more noticeable trait than sagacity in the candidates. Once Johnson began on his "President of all the people" theme and Goldwater began his fundamentalist emotionalizing, almost all hopes for enlightening public debate on the issues were dashed.

The President's strategy was to *ignore* Goldwater. Certainly, the Rooseveltian disciple Johnson was well aware of how studiously FDR had ignored Thomas E. Dewey in the campaign of 1944. On the other side, Goldwater's natural bent toward emotionalism and exaggeration increased when he found Johnson unwilling take the bait and argue with him directly. Thus, each man talked his way through his own version of the 1964 race without unduly bothering the other.

After a few weeks of touring in September, Johnson became certain that he had analyzed the fighting tactics of his opponent. Goldwater's inability to inject any great surge of enthusiasm into the ranks of his followers was surprising. In time, it became apparent to all that he was making grave mistakes. The very directional appeal for Southern support and the related loss of almost all of the Negro vote across the nation was one. As others followed, it was explained that Goldwater was an honest man who said exactly what he thought. Theodore White says that a "vast incoherence" was observable in the Goldwater effort.

> The campaign in September had begun in confusion; a speech on crime in peaceful St. Petersburg, Florida, whose retired elderly wanted to hear about Social Security . . . ; a speech scoring Johnson's anti-

poverty program in stricken West Virginia; an anti-reapportionment stand in under-represented Atlanta; a swift and unsatisfactory reference to TVA . . . in Tennessee.[6]

Goldwater soon complained that he was misunderstood. Sometimes he *was* misunderstood, or misquoted, or maligned; but most of the time he was losing potential votes because he was *understood*. Richard Rovere, writing for publication on November 1, 1964, expressed the opinion that Goldwater's views about domestic politics were "pre-industrial" and his views on foreign policy, "pre-atomic."[7]

Despite the platitudinous character of the campaign, Rovere suggests that we, as a people, got a clear picture on a clear choice. That is true, but how abundantly beneficial it would have been if Johnson had been shaken out of his father-image role and really forced to answer his challenger on the subjects of foreign policy (China, the bomb, NATO), war policy (Vietnam), economic questions, Medicare, Social Security changes, and the like. All these topics were cited by the candidates, but a careful study of the daily reports on the speeches indicates that Goldwater and Miller failed to "draw blood" with their arguments. For the Republican nominees, the only absolutely surefire oratorical line was an allusion to the Bobby Baker scandal.

CAMPAIGNERS' CHARACTERISTICS
AND SIGNIFICANT CAMPAIGN EVENTS

Aside from the major Johnson television appearance on October 18 to discuss leadership changes in the Soviet Union, the President did not bother to exert himself before the cameras during the 1964 campaign. He and his advisors reasoned that the campaign's more than ample television coverage of Johnson wading into crowds of admirers and giving short talks, or shouting out to crowds along a parade route, "Come on now, let's all go to the speakin'," was more valuable than formal television appearances.

Mrs. Johnson, on October 6, began an eight-state, 1,800-mile, 48-speech tour of the South in support of her husband's candidacy. Her staff and her daughter Lynda accompanied her on a whistle-stop jaunt unique in American history. Television went along, and at every stop, the cameras ground out her adventures as she stressed the national implications of the election as seen by a gracious Southern "Lady Bird."

Between October 7 and October 13, the President managed to appear before hundreds of thousands of persons in 15 states and to millions via the press coverage he attracted. The next three days were filled with events of immediate and long-range political consequence. Of immediate attention was the personal tragedy of Walter W. Jenkins, special assistant to the President. It was revealed, on October 14, that he had been arrested by Washington police on a morals charge involving what were described as "disorderly [indecent] gestures." This sad story was widely played up in the press, and many commentators on politics remarked that, if Goldwater wanted to, he could take political advantage of this personal disaster striking at the inner chambers of the White House. However, FBI and other reports convinced Goldwater that the tragedy was one that troubled the Jenkins family to a greater extent than it implicated the Administration. It was made clear that national security was not violated. To his credit, the Republican nominee did not play up the affair. Had he chosen to, especially in an era of electronic mass communications, the results might have utterly destroyed Jenkins while winning voters to the Republican ticket. Barry Goldwater displayed admirable restraint in this instance.

President Johnson was much distressed by the news of the Jenkins difficulties. The two men had worked together for some time. It was said that the President was visibly shaken when his advisor's breakdown was brought to his attention. Still, he went on and campaigned even more vigorously. One speculates that Lyndon Johnson took renewed confidence from the subsequent warm receptions he received on his tours.

Goldwater was less familiar with crowds, not an extraordinary crowd-pleaser at rallies of his supporters (except when he called out the name of Bobby Baker), and less than spectacular as a television personality. Only when he appeared on purchased time to discuss the meaning of his campaign with a few well-chosen representatives of the public did he shine. In a living room setting, Goldwater was at ease and cogent; in the rally situation, he disappointed followers by not striking those resounding blows they were expecting and by repeating so much of his material from place to place that his remarks fell flat with those who had heard them before. He did not have that charismatic quality that is the mark of most successful politicians. William Miller, his running mate, drew more enthusiastic receptions with his quick, sharp, angry, and satiric interpretations of the Administration in Washington. The success of the vice-presidential nominee as a bantam contender drew cheers from hopeful Republicans of the right wing, but it did not attract new voters to the ticket.

The candidates traveled extensively. By the midpoint between Labor Day and election day, Johnson had gone some 15,000 miles and made 20 appearances; Goldwater had gone some 20,000 miles and stopped 67 times.[8] The President alternated between White House duties and campaign obligations. At home or on the road, his publicity was excellent. After all, the nature of most of the campaigning allowed him the freedom for speeches that were a mixture of Andrew Jackson and modern evangelism. Then again, when he was in Washington, his duties as President attracted much attention—he saw to it that they did.

It could well be that, by the midpoint of the campaign, Goldwater could not have won the election. Perhaps a slashing attack on his opponents, couched in specifics, could have taken Goldwater off the downgrade. But Johnson chose to be general, and Goldwater did not seem able to do what he most needed to do.

Incredible as it was, the Republican nominee, on October 6, told 350 editors and publishers of United Press International, at their annual conference, that he would not discuss "nit-picking issues" or offer solutions to specific problems. Neither, he said, would he tailor his remarks to the areas of the country in which he campaigned. "I don't have any desire or particular interest in getting down to what will make this particular district or that particular district respond to me."[9]

He should have developed such interests, if the barometer of editorial press support was meaningful. By the middle of October, *Editor and Publisher* noted that, since its editorial-support poll had begun in 1932, Johnson was the first Democratic presidential candidate ever to have a majority of the decided newspapers in his favor.[10]

GOLDWATER ON TELEVISION

A study of the itinerary of the Republican nominees shows that Goldwater appeared frequently on television. A good guide is provided by surveying the press releases of the Republican National Committee, which announced those appearances or contained the texts of the programs.

> September 14—Goldwater's television debut of the campaign; a five-minute message (2:25–2:30 P.M., Eastern Daylight Time) on why the Administration "does not understand the nature of the threats to the peace, the nature of the enemy who threatens the peace. . . ."
>
> September 18—The first half-hour television program, carried nationwide by more than 200 CBS stations (9:30–10 P.M., EDT). "Peace for you, for your children—and my children. Peace with honor and Justice. Lasting, permanent peace. . . . That is my goal, my prayer, and my pledge to you."
>
> September 22—An appearance with Dwight Eisenhower entitled "Conversation at Gettysburg—Dwight D. Eisenhower and Barry Goldwater." (9:30–10 P.M., EDT; NBC.) At the conclusion of the program, actor Raymond Massey appealed for money to sustain Goldwater's television appearances. He said, "If you agree with me that the Goldwater story needs to be told, put your money where your heart is—send a check to T.V. for Goldwater–Miller, Box 80, Los Angeles 51, California. . . . Support the Goldwater crusade. In Your Heart, You Know He's Right. Thank You."
>
> October 2 —Announcement by the Republican National Committee that at least five 30-minute, nationwide telecasts featuring the Senator would highlight the final month of the campaign. (October 6, 9:30–10 P.M., EDT—NBC network; October 13, 9:30–10 P.M.—NBC network;

October 20, October 29, and November 2, all beginning at 9:30 P.M., EDT).

October 6 — Half-hour address (9:30–10 P.M., EDT) over more than 180 stations of the NBC Network. The Senator answered questions on "America Asks Barry Goldwater." A member of Teamsters local #399, 37 years old and the father of two children, asked about the nominee's tax-reduction proposal; an executive secretary from Tulsa, Oklahoma, asked about the seeming rift between China and Russia. Goldwater replied, in part, "Just keep this in mind: No matter who wins that fight, we're still fighting Communists as our enemy in this world." Other questioners posed inquiries about Cuba; the desirability of a stronger stand towards Communists; Social Security; foreign aid programs; and antipoverty programs. Goldwater ended the session, which originated in the NBC studios in Washington, D.C., by stressing the public's right to get "straight answers, honest answers, and answers now before November 3rd." He jibed at Johnson for refusing "to debate me before the nationwide audience" and suggested that the refusal could be explained in two ways — "through fear of facing up to these issues or through contempt for the good sense of the American people, and for their right to know where candidates for offices of public trust really stand."

October 7 — Announcement by the Republican National Committee that 30 nationwide, five-minute telecasts covering nine top issues would feature Goldwater. "CBS will carry 17 . . . , NBC will broadcast 11, and ABC will air two of them," Dean Burch said.

October 9 — Richard Nixon appeared before and after Goldwater's address to discuss "The Real Job of the Presidency." Nixon expounded on the upsurge of Goldwater sentiment he found all over the country. He said, "People are beginning to listen. They're beginning to think, and, most important, they're beginning to learn the truth." Also, ". . . I'm sure that when you finish listening to him, you will say: here's a reasonable man, here's a calm man, here is a patriotic man. Above all, here is a great American who will make a great President."

Among other points, Goldwater, in his address, stressed his reasons for going into different sections of the country and, seemingly, speaking in an unorthodox manner. "I have gone into the heart of Appalachia . . . and there I have deliberately attacked this administration's phony war in poverty. . . . I will not attempt to buy the votes of the American people. . . . I will not treat any of you as just so many special interests. . . . I will not appeal to you as if you were simply pocketbooks . . . surrounded on all sides by self-serving concerns."

October 13 —Senator Goldwater was interviewed by NBC correspondent Ron Nessen. Nessen asked Goldwater, at one point, what had hurt him the most. The reply— "Well, I think the repetition of the outright lie I am trigger happy has hurt me more than anything." Nessen asked later whether Goldwater expected some sort of a "big break" before the election or whether "the current trend" would take him over 50 per cent! Goldwater commented, "I think we have had our big break, and, I think we are now moving up. The break would be no one specific thing—just a combination of things that a campaigner likes to see happen in a campaign."

October 23 —A "TV Brunch With Barry" on the NBC network (11:30–12:00 noon, EDT). Six women were featured with the candidate. They included the widow of a pilot shot down in Vietnam (he had sent letters revealing the use of obsolete equipment); a 68-year-old woman entirely dependent on Social Security; a housewife concerned about rising costs of living; a mother of three children, concerned about the school-bussing issue; a physician's wife worried about crime; a corporation lawyer to discuss women holding important jobs in business and government.

October 20 —Nationwide address of "Morality and Government" over the CBS network, 9:30–10 P.M., EDT.

October 21 —Nationwide address on "Soviet Shift and U.S. Policy" over the ABC network, 10:30–11 P.M., EDT.

October 22 —Nationwide address on "The Free Society" over the ABC network, 10–10:30 P.M., EDT. Here are two of the key paragraphs from his talk.

Where government presumes to control equality, forgetting that in its essential areas it lies with God's province and the laws of nature, there can only be conformity. Government must consider and treat all men equal in the areas of law and civic order. Otherwise, and in no other area, can it *make* men equal. . . .

Our aim, as I understand it, is neither to establish a segregated society nor to establish an integrated society. It is to preserve a *free* society.

October 28 —Announcement that a special five-minute *radio* "Goldwater Report" would be carried on more than 300 stations of the Mutual Broadcasting System, from October 28 through the Monday preceding Election day.

October 31 —A campaign rally speech, from Columbia Township Auditorium, Columbia, S.C., was carried by 87 TV stations in 14 Southern and Southwestern states (7:30–8:30 P.M., Eastern Standard Time). Goldwater asked,

"Don't you want a President who, above all, respects the Constitution—who respects the independence of other branches of government, and the rights of our sovereign states? Don't you want a President who opposes the forced bussing of children from their normal neighborhood schools—who opposes the principle of forced integration as well as forced segregation?"

November 1—Actor Ronald Reagan delivered an address entitled "A Time for Choosing" in support of the Senator (5 P.M., EST) on the NBC television and radio networks.

November 2—Election-eve campaign appearances of Goldwater and Miller and their families. CBS-TV Network, 9:30–10:00 P.M., EST.[11]

DEMOCRATIC TV COMMERCIALS AND A REPUBLICAN MORALITY FILM

Both parties hired advertising agencies to handle their advertising on television. Doyle, Dane, Bernbach, Inc., took on the Democrats' account, and Erwin Wasey, Ruthrauff & Ryan, Inc., a subsidiary of the Interpublic Group of Companies, Inc., worked for the Republicans.

It was announced that the Democratic ads would concentrate on the general theme, "take the record of this Administration to the American people." Twenty-second, one-minute, and five-minute "spots" were prepared for television. The Democratic National Committee reportedly had a budget of about $4 million for advertising, almost all of which was earmarked for television. Network television was to account for $1.7 million of that budget, with the remainder of the broadcast fund set aside for those television "spot" presentations.

The Republican National Committee, it was alleged, had about $4.8 million set aside to advertise their national candidates. All but $200,000 was assigned to national television. According to Erwin Wasey, the Republican advertisements were to cover issues of foreign policy, morality, and peace.

We have just surveyed the program developed by the Republicans for the display of Goldwater and Miller on half-hour and hour-long programs. The Democratic Party did similar organizing for the President and Hubert Humphrey. Both National Committees planned programs right through to election day.[12]

By-products of the over-all preparations were highly controversial. The Democrats took the lead on the controversy front on September 7, when one of their campaign "spots" interrupted NBC-TV's *Monday Night at the Movies* showing of "David and Bathsheba." In the course of the one-minute film, a little girl with windblown hair was seen picking daisies in a sun-swept field. The child starts to pick the petals of one daisy, and as she plucks each petal, she counts, "One, two, . . ." Behind her, the sound track provides a male voice counting the numbers backwards, from ten to zero. The man counts with "doom-filled cadence." When he intones, "Zero," there is a screen-filling scene of an atomic explosion. Then the voice of the President is heard saying, "These are the stakes. To make a world in which all of God's children can live, or go into the dark. We must either love each other, or we must die." The doom-voiced announcer picks up the thread at this point and urges viewers to vote for President Johnson on November 3—"The stakes are too high for you to stay home."

It is not surprising that the Republicans were up in arms after viewing the film. Three weeks after the first showing, Goldwater said, "The homes of America are horrified and the intelligence of Americans is insulted by weird television advertising by which this Administration threatens the end of the world unless all-wise Lyndon is given the nation for his very own." Prior to the Goldwater blast, Hubert Humphrey had already expressed his opinion that the commercial was "unfortunate."[13]

Dean Burch issued a statement on October 15, attacking the Democratic Party for a campaign based upon "slanted, biased, and fraudulent propaganda which is unparalleled in American political history." He did not aim solely at the aforementioned commercial. He was just as angered by the one that took off on a "Goldwaterism" occasioned by the Republican candidate's travails in New England early in the year. Goldwater had blurted out, "Sometimes I think this country would be better off if we could just saw off the Eastern seaboard and let it float out to sea." A television "spot" was prepared for the Democrats, showing a representation of the continental United States being sawed apart at about the Mississippi River. As the film displayed the Eastern seaboard floating off, the Goldwater sentiment was repeated by the announcer. Still another "spot" concentrated on a campaign poster showing Rockefeller's face and name. It called to viewers' minds, in no uncertain imagery, the San Francisco convention. The poster toppled onto a littered floor, and the announcer's voice said, "Remember him? Governor Rockefeller. He said Barry Goldwater's positions can spell disaster for the [Republican] party and for the country."[14] Other such inventive "spots" were presented during September and October.

Burch complained about the Democrats' offerings to Charles Taft, chairman of the Fair Campaign Practice Committee. Among other things, the Republican National Chairman said:

> We feel sure that these tactics will do the President more damage than good, but Senator Goldwater has no desire to benefit from a public revulsion. The dignity of democracy must not be permitted to suffer unduly in the heat of a political campaign.
> The fear and scare technique is not new in politics. But its use in the extreme sense to avoid an honest discussion of the issues should not be tolerated.[15]

Representative Charles A. Halleck, the House Republican minority leader, protested from the floor of that august legislative chamber on September 15. He asked his colleagues, "If the Democrats will stoop to these tactics to win an election what can the country expect next?"[16]

The next time the issue was raised, the Republicans were the offenders! One of Barry Goldwater's cardinal causes was furthering *morality*. To bring that cause to the American people, a half-hour documentary film was prepared for the Republican Party. It was designed to show how President Johnson was leading a society that was morally decaying; a group called the Mothers for a Moral America sponsored the film. When it was brought to the National Broadcasting Company, the officials of that network debated whether it could be screened without extensive editing. The film, entitled "Choice," was narrated by Raymond Massey. To show the need for a more moral America, it contained many scenes of *immorality*.

One staged portion had a speeding Lincoln Continental racing across the screen, with beer cans being tossed out of the driver's window from time to time. It was an obvious allusion to news reports of the previous Easter that the President had been drinking beer while driving his car near the LBJ ranch. The President was not mentioned by name. Other scenes showed violence and looting in city streets; gyrations of young people doing the "twist" with frenzy; shots of a young girl in a topless bathing suit being peered at by young men; "montages of pornographic magazines and book covers"; "the marquees of 'nudie' theaters"; shots of Billie Sol Estes, the legally loose Texas financier; and pictures of Robert G. (Bobby) Baker.

When Senator Goldwater saw the film, he urged the party to withdraw it and cancel bookings. He called it "racist" on the grounds that certain of its scenes dealing with Negroes and whites did not win his approval.[17]

The advertising campaigns of the Democratic and Republican Parties, to the degree that they included these overtly propagandistic offerings, should give all Americans cause for worry. There is no doubt that advertising men can so distort elections with their "creativity" that all semblance of rationality can be lost. In 1964, the campaign opened a Pandora's box, and out poured the hit-them-below-the-belt productions that demean democratic standards. In that campaign both major parties appear to have erred seriously. In politics, as in sports, it is not always whether you win or lose that counts; most important is how you play with peoples' emotions and sensibilities and capacities to reason. One hopes that the bad experiences of 1964 will lead to reforms. However, there is nothing presently on the horizon that gives the critical observer any cause for optimism.

POLLSTERS' CONCLUSIONS

Politicians find great sport in decrying the significance of public opinion polls. A favored theme in campaign speeches lampoons anyone who would rely on such polls. Popular election decisions are made at the ballot boxes, say contenders, not upon questionnaires.

For all that, it is difficult to find a political office seeker who does not diligently follow polling results that bear upon his campaign or upon the opposition's. When polling results appear adverse to a politician's chances, he ignores any public mention of them or makes known his haughty indifference to such surveys. If polling results show that he leads, he cheerfully accepts indications of the will of the people, even if he takes the precaution of emphasizing to his supporters that there is truth in the old adage "There's many a slip between the cup and the lip." When polls show a strong leaning to his cause, he feels it necessary to urge his people to do more work. Few political savants can forget the historical importance of that race in 1948, when the polls predicted a Dewey victory, and the populace selected Truman.

In 1964, both major parties relied upon polls to a greater extent than was admitted publicly. However, the *core* campaign leaders were loathe to equate reliance upon polls with confidence in polls because, among other things, politicians still had too much to learn about the net effects of television. They could not decide whether, for example, last-minute effects of television work could throw even the most reliable polls for a loop.

The major polling organizations, from Labor Day of 1964 on, consistently revealed that Johnson was leading Goldwater nationally. On July 23, the Gallup poll gave the President a 7-to-3 lead. When Goldwater was given the edge, it was often restricted to estimates of Southern thinking—as was the case in the Gallup poll of August 7, which held that Goldwater had the support of 51 per cent of the Dixie electorate, while his rival had 40 per cent.

Pollster Samuel Lubell was reported as saying that, as of mid-August, one of every seven persons who had voted Democratic in 1960 had shifted to Goldwater, while Johnson had picked up the support of one of every five individuals who had voted Republican four years before. By early September, *The New York Times* reported, "George C. Gallup puts the ratio at 68 to 32 in Mr. Johnson's favor; the survey of Elmo Roper finds it 67–28 with 5 per cent undecided; and Louis Harris . . . reports Mr. Johnson leading 62 to 38." A Gallup survey made public on October 18 gave Johnson 64 per cent and Goldwater 29 per cent, with 7 per cent cited as undecided. The final Gallup organization poll results forecast a Johnson sweep, with the President credited with 64 per cent of the popular vote to Goldwater's 36 per cent. Louis Harris, in his nationwide poll, offered the same conclusion. Samuel Lubell predicted a "Johnson landslide."[18]

THE VOTERS TURN OUT: TELEVISION REPORTS

When a hard-fought political campaign nears its conclusion and the electorate is preparing for the day when ballots will decide arguments, television functions in two ways to serve the people: getting out the vote and reporting results.

The Get-Out-the-Vote Promotions

Television performs a vital get-out-the-vote service with its drives to remind voters of their responsibility in a democracy. Unlike the newspaper and magazine industries, which have no statutory obligations, the television industry is expected by the Federal Communications Commission to provide such public service announcements as a condition for maintaining their licenses in good standing. In recent years, heavy reliance has been placed upon television to get people trooping to the polling booths. The industry, acting in association with private public-spirited and nonpartisan organizations such as the American Heritage Foundation and the Advertising Council, has prepared promotional campaigns that consist of one-minute, 30-second, and 20-second films designed to remind people to register and vote.[19] Individual television stations and networks are also active in preparing and presenting other promotional material to stimulate voting.

Reporting Election Returns

NETWORK ELECTION SERVICE

A heartening development in a highly competitive business took place in early June of 1964, when it was announced that the Network Election Service (NES) had been created by the three television networks, acting in conjunction with the Associated Press. NES was designed to streamline and speed up reporting of the returns. A three-man board was established to direct the combined operation. Each network had one director on the board—the AP was a nonvoting member. It was estimated that the organization would have the news supplied by some 100,000 reporters, who would feed reports into headquarters in the 50 states and in Washington, D.C. The 51 centers would, in turn, send returns to a television-industry tabulating complex in New York City. From the New York City complex, each network and the AP would feed its own vote-reporting organizations. Shortly after the establishment of NES, the United Press International organization joined. NES concentration was planned for the presidential contest and for gubernatorial and senatorial races at the state level.

The television audiences benefited because the major effect of the pool was to eliminate differences in incomplete vote results during the counting. At each stage, identical figures would be supplied to the television networks and to the press associations. Most of the expense for the pool coverage was carried by the networks, but the press associations also provided substantial funds.

The individual networks and press associations each reserved the right to predict the winner of any race, basing the prediction upon its own calculations and projections. Thus the door was left open for claims of superiority in news reporting.[20]

REPORTING THE LATE RETURNS

Because of time-zone differences that enabled voters in the Middle West and West to go to the polls after polling booths in the East had closed, there was some concern that network predictions about voting results could lead to voter reactions from citizens who had not yet cast their ballots. On November 1, Dean Burch, the Republican National Chairman, asked the networks not to *slant* "the import of early returns in Tuesday's elections as happened in 1960." He went on:

> In 1960, the TV industry performed a distinct disservice with the inaccurate interpretation of the early results. . . .
> The entire nation was misinformed. From almost the very outset it was made to appear that Sen. Kennedy was substantially ahead and that he would score a landslide victory. . . .
> At no time did the TV computer-prediction apparatus indicate that the election would be decided in a photo-finish. In fact, Mr. Nixon was repeatedly abused and ridiculed by TV commentators [for] not conceding early in the evening. . . .
> This was the poorest kind of reporting. And who can tell whether or not the false impressions given the nation by TV commentators and TV pollsters did not influence some of the voters in the Middle West and West who had not yet voted.[21]

We have precious little scientific evidence to affirm or deny the Burch allegations. It is too early to sound the alarm bells or the all-clear signals. It is possible that, in a future election, voters under the influence of election news broadcasts could swing a Presidential election one way or another by voting late (in California, for example). As voters become more aware of the power of late returns, they *could* act accordingly, although in 1964, it appears that they did not.

Gladys and Kurt Lang, in a paper presented at the 1965 Annual Conference of the American Association for Public Opinion Research and entitled "Ballots and Broadcasts: The Impact of Expectations and Election Day Perceptions on Voting Behavior," found little by way of startling voter shifts. They concentrated primarily on a sample of 364 registered voters in the East Bay area of California. From their study, we learn that reports of the Johnson sweep that were given early on election day "were sufficiently unambiguous to dispel most doubts." As for late-election-day slack, or the reduced motivaton to vote, they reported, "Our data indicate that neither the broadcasts nor the perceptions they induced were influential in causing the abstentions." Finally, they observed, "Our study found clear-cut broadcast-induced slack only in the case of one single Goldwater supporter, who as a result of what he heard lost all interest in voting."[22] The Lang study of a small group of California voters is valuable but was obviously not intended to be a definitive study of the larger problem.

As a footnote to the problem, it should be noted that the Columbia Broadcasting System announced on October 20 that, in order to allay any criticism, it had instructed its staff not to declare a winner in the Johnson-Goldwater race until one or the other had achieved, clearly, the necessary majority of 270 electoral votes. Fred W. Friendly, president of CBS News, said, "We will speak of 'indicated winners,' 'apparent winners' or 'probable winners' until both our analysis of the vote and the vote itself leave no doubt of the result."[23]

NETWORK VARIATIONS

Each of the networks touted the virtues of its own procedures for reporting returns swiftly and accurately. CBS had what it called "vote profile analysis." VPA was a system of carefully analyzing selected voting precincts in each state with the objective of setting up political "models." Each model consisted of between 32 and 60 well-chosen precincts. The precincts chosen formed a cross section of the electorate. An enormous amount of data about the precincts was programmed into computers "which compare the actual statewide vote in previous elections with the total vote from the model precincts in those same elections. The model as a whole must accurately reflect the political behavior of the state, and research goes on until it does." Ethnic, age, education, and status data are also fed into the computers. Altogether, CBS prepared 108 Vote Profile Analyses—"49 for the Presidential contest, plus 25 Gubernatorial and 34 Senatorial elections." Regional and national reports, combined with the sagacity of the network's experienced reporters, filled out the VPA picture. CBS worked with the Louis Harris political research team and the International Business Machine organization to accomplish its objectives.[24]

The American Broadcasting Corporation boasted about the twin Burroughs B 5500 computers that it had installed in its New York City studios to analyze "nationwide voting patterns on November 3, and provide the network with an advance look at the outcome of the 1964 Presidential Election."

ABC developed a scheme similar to the VPA by feeding "volumes of historical data from past elections" into the computers and comparing the data with the "latest information from national public opinion polls being collected by Oliver Quayle Associates."[25]

The National Broadcasting Company worked in conjunction with Radio Corporation of America, its parent company, to put together a computer system for election-day reporting. It, too, was similar to the CBS effort. NBC had what it labeled its "Electronic Vote Analysis System."

All in all, it was estimated that the networks expended about 7 million dollars to cover the story of election day.[26]

THE BIG STORY OF ANOTHER BEGINNING

Human beings love a story that has a clear beginning, a good plot, and a definite conclusion that leads them on to another story. The presidential election of 1964 was such a story. After much public controversy and personal soul-searching, the voter stepped into the voting booth. By pulling on plungers of an electric voting machine or by filling out his paper ballot and casting it into a box, he declared his views and defended his heritage.

When all the votes were counted, the result was as indicated by the pollsters —a Johnson victory by a substantial margin. The President garnered 43,126,218 votes (61 per cent) to overwhelm Goldwater, whose candidacy was approved by 27,174,898 voters (38.5 per cent). The electoral-college vote was 486 to 52. Goldwater carried (by .04 per cent) his own home state of Arizona and five states of the Deep South—Mississippi, Alabama, Georgia, Louisiana, and South Carolina—by decisive margins.

On November 4, 1964, even before the dust settled, the campaigns for Congress of 1966 and for the Presidency of 1968 were beginning, however faintly, to take shape. Even for a Republican party battered by the returns of the previous day, there would be another chance.

LESSONS AND SUGGESTIONS

The presidential campaigns are too long. Six weeks of active soliciting by candidates, aided and abetted by the mass media, would be reasonable. Campaigning would certainly tend to be more educational and less tedious for the public. Nominees would find the process more attractive if they were not forced to wear themselves out both physically and mentally. Interparty debate would probably be less repetitious and more profound if office seekers and campaign managers did not have to concentrate so much on *lasting out* the campaign. A Gallup poll taken after election day of 1964 found that there was much public criticism of the whole process of selecting a President of the United States. Objections were widespread on "mudslinging" and on the length of the campaign. A majority opinion, it was reported, supported the idea of having the candidates restrict most of their efforts to television and radio appearances in lieu of traditional approaches.[27]

Some major reform is necessary to offset the financial problem that faces aspirants to all public offices in this country. On the eve of election day 1964, *Broadcasting* magazine compiled an estimate of the television and radio costs of the election from the convention days through to November 3. That estimate, based on information supplied by "unofficial but authoritative sources," did not include production costs or the millions of dollars spent on the primary campaigns. Amazingly, it was found that costs had jumped almost three times above the 1960 expenditures—from $14.2 million in 1960 to the record total of approximately $40 million in 1964. Half of the 1964 total was for the presidential contest, and half was part of the television and radio campaigning for state and local candidates.[28]

Perhaps it is time for us to think seriously about establishing two national presidential primaries, to be held under the same general regulations that have been developed for the general election in November. Each party's candidates would thereby avoid the tiresome business of jumping from state primary to state primary. This idea may have serious flaws, however, and the proposal should be argued at length. There are virtues to the present system. The principal one is that it stresses the importance of local and regional reactions to the candidates. Again, the present arrangement allows the arguments of the contenders to mature over a period of time.

It is conceivable that there would be no loss to democracy if the federal government, in conjunction with the networks, provided an established amount of program time for the nominees selected by the conventions—so many hour-long programs, so many half-hour programs, and so on. Of course, since such a scheme should be a product of Congressional legislation, the major political parties would have to see the benefits to be derived.

The Federal Communications Commission, in conjunction with other appropriate federal agencies, should regulate the advertising material prepared for the campaign, to the sole end that the more distressing products of 1964 do not become historical precedents for even worse preparations. It must be emphasized here that this suggestion is not intended as an opening wedge for censorship. There are limits to public endurance, however, and fearmongering must be curbed before it increases.

If the two major parties and the minor parties were required to hold their conventions during the last week in August and the first week in September, we would have less tiresome campaigns. Under that arrangement, active campaigning would not begin until the third week of September. The idea of a six-week campaign would be made practical. No one would be allowed a head start.

These suggestions and others that have been made by serious students are lessons taken from recent experience.

TELEVISION, EDUCATION, AND POLITICS

Civic responsibility does not increase in proportion to the quantity of television programming on political subjects; it increases only in proportion to the quality and the pertinence of the presentations.

We are on the verge of a television environment that will lead future observers to comment that we conducted politics in a rather primitive fashion. Commentators of decades yet to come will probably resolve that the pattern of today and of the recent past was far too disorganized and freewheeling. They will note that, when network television first flowered, the political trend was to highlight the novelty and the powers of the medium, with insufficient attention paid to the necessity for restraint.

We can now just see the beginnings of global television made possible by satellite communications systems. Let us hope that we do not suffer from mass communications. Above all, we are required, if our free society is to continue and to prosper, to exert ourselves to keep ahead of the machinery that science produces.

FOOTNOTES

1. For an example, see Walter Lippman, "A Realignment of Parties?" *Newsweek* (July 20, 1964), p. 15, for his opinion that Goldwater would probably work hard to effect splits in both major parties. He would, said Lippman, endeavor to do so to win after 1964 by creating a "coalition of the Goldwater anti-Federalists . . . with the irreconcilable segregationists and White supremacists in the South and other states."

2. Cabell Phillips, "Johnson Chides G.O.P.'s Nominee on Ties to Allies," *New York Times,* July 20, 1964.

3. Tom Wicker, "Johnson Assails Goldwater View on Atomic Weapon," *New York Times,* August 17, 1964.

4. "Text of F.B.I. Report to President on Summer Riots in 9 Cities over Country," *New York Times,* September 27, 1964; for another view on background to riots, see Ralph Ellison, "Harlem Is Nowhere," *Harper's Magazine* (August 1964), pp. 53–57.

5. For Goldwater proposals, see "Goldwater Asks Truce on Rights," *New York Times* (International edition, Paris), July 21, 1964; for President's news conference statements, see "Civil Rights: The White House Meeting," *Newsweek* (August 3, 1964), p. 15.

6. Theodore H. White, *The Making of the President, 1964,* p. 335.

7. Richard H. Rovere, *The Goldwater Caper,* p. 167.

8. Harold Faber, editor, *The Road to the White House,* p. 217.

9. Warren Weaver, Jr., "Goldwater Maps Ideological Drive." *New York Times,* October 7, 1964.

10. "Johnson Picks Up Fresh Support in Endorsements by Newspapers," *New York Times,* October 17, 1964.

11. The author thanks the Republican National Committee, and especially its news editor (at headquarters during the campaign), Mr. James L. McKenna, for providing him with a complete file of the Committee's news releases on the Goldwater television effort. The following news releases are referred to in the text. "Present Administration Doesn't Understand Threats to Peace, Sen. Goldwater Says in First GOP Television Message" (September 14, 1964); "First Nationwide Television Address . . . by Senator Barry Goldwater" (September 19, 1964); "America Asks Barry Goldwater" (October 6, 1964); "Senator Goldwater to Speak to Nation Five Times for Half Hour on Television during Last Month of GOP Presidential Campaign" (October 2, 1964); "30 Five-Minute Telecasts . . . Discussing Issues to be Presented on Nationwide TV . . ." (October 7, 1964); "Dick Nixon to Appear on TV . . . with Senator Goldwater . . ." (October 8, 1964); "The Real Job of the Presidency . . ." (October 10,

1964); "Interview . . . by Ron Nessen of NBC . . ." (October 13, 1964); "6 Women Who Will Join Sen. Goldwater for 'TV Brunch with Barry . . .'" (October 16, 1964); "Nationwide TV Address on 'Morality and Government' over the CBS Network . . ." (October 20, 1965); "Nationwide TV Address on 'Soviet Shift and U.S. Policy . . .'" (October 21, 1964); "Nationwide TV Address on 'The Free Society' . . ." (October 22, 1964); "5-Minute 'Goldwater Report' . . ." (October 28, 1964); "Campaign Speech at the Columbia Township Auditorium, Columbia, S.C. . . ." (October 31, 1964); "Ronald Reagan's Address Supporting Sen. Goldwater . . ." (October 31, 1964); "Election Eve Campaign Appearances . . ." (November 2, 1964).

12. Leonard Sloane, "Advertising: Democrats, G.O.P. Woo Voters," *New York Times,* September 27, 1964.

13. Pete Hamill, "When the Client Is a Candidate," *New York Times Magazine,* October 25, 1964.

14. *Ibid.*

15. News release, "GOP Chairman Files Official Protest about Democrats' Commercial with Fair Campaign Practices Committee," Republican National Committee, Washington, D.C., September 15, 1964.

16. News release, "Representative Halleck Reports He Has Received Protests Deploring Democrats' Campaign Commercial," Office of Representative Charles Halleck, Washington, D.C., September 15, 1964.

17. For commentary on "morality" and on the film, see Nan Robertson, "G.O.P. Film Depicts 'Moral Decay,'" *New York Times,* October 21, 1964; William Buckley, Jr., "The Campaign, the Film and Morality," *Boston Globe,* November 2, 1964; Richard L. Strout, "Morality Issue Gets New Impetus," *Christian Science Monitor,* October 16, 1964; Charles Mohr, "Campaign Issues—V," *New York Times,* October 29, 1964.

18. See the following news items: "Gallup Poll—Johnson 7, Goldwater 3," *New York Herald Tribune,* July 23, 1964; George Gallup, "Goldwater Leads Johnson in South," *New York Herald Tribune,* August 7, 1964; "Voter Shifts Found to Favor Johnson," *New York Times,* August 19, 1964; Earl Mazo, "If the Polls Are Right," *New York Times,* September 11, 1964; George Gallup, "LBJ Tops Barry by 64%–29%," *Boston Globe,* October 18, 1964; George Gallup, "Personal Appeal Dips in Campaign," *Boston Globe,* October 25, 1964; Earl Mazo, "A Johnson Landslide Predicted in the Final Polls," *New York Times,* November 3, 1964.

19. William A. Glaser, "Television and Voting Turnout," *Public Opinion Quarterly,* Vol. 29, No. 1 (Spring 1965), p. 73.

20. "NETS, AP Pool Forces for Nov. 3 Elections," *Radio-Television Daily,* Vol. 94, No. 112 (June 10, 1964); "UPI Joins Election Pool Coverage Plan," *Radio-Television Daily,* Vol. 94, No. 114 (June 12, 1964); Jack Gould, "100,000 To Gather Election Returns," *New York Times,* June 10, 1964; "TV Pool: New Core of U.S. Election Coverage," *Broadcasting* (June 15, 1964), pp. 78, 80.

21. News release, "GOP Chairman Asks TV Networks Not To 'Slant' Early Returns as in '60," Republican National Committee, Washington, D.C., November 1, 1964.

22. Gladys Engel Lang and Kurt Lang, "Ballots and Broadcasts: The Impact of Expectations and Election Day Perceptions on Voting Behavior," paper presented at the 1965 annual conference of the American Association for Public Opinion Research, May 14, 1965.

23. Jack Gould, "CBS Will Delay Forecasts Nov. 3," *New York Times,* October 21, 1964.

24. *Vote Profile Analysis: A New Tool for Election Night Reporting,* Brochure prepared by the Columbia Broadcasting System, 1964, 11 pages.

25. News release, News Bureau, *Burroughs Corporation,* Detroit Michigan, n.d.; see also, news release, "Politics 1964," American Broadcasting Company, October 15, 1964.

26. "Fast Count, Accurate Calls and It's Over," *Broadcasting* (November 9, 1964), pp. 38–39; also, Edwin H. James, "The Trouble $2,475,000 Can Buy," *Television,* Vol. 21, No. 12 (December 1964), pp. 72–73.

27. "Gallup Poll Finds Most Voters Would Be Happier with Shorter Campaigns," *Boston Sunday Globe,* November 22, 1964.

28. "Campaign Radio-TV $40 million," *Broadcasting* (November 2, 1964), p. 23.

Index

Alsop, Joseph and Stewart, 34
American Civil Liberties Union, 64, 106
Army-McCarthy hearings, 14–16
Aubrey, James Thomas, Jr., 7, 8
Aware, Inc., 7
Bailey, John, 140, 168
Bain, Richard C., 155
Baker, Robert G. (Bobby), 123, 180, 181, 187
Baker, Russell, 45, 46, 53, 54, 56, 169
Baker, Warren E., 10
Barnett, Ross, 87
Bell, Jack, 111
Birch, John, Society, 5, 6, 162, 176
Blackwood, George, 51
Blumler, J. G., 152
Bolton, Oliver T., 128
Bow, Frank T., 128
Brewster, Daniel B., 144, 154
Brinkley, David, 122
Brown, Edmund G. ("Pat"), 23
Brown, John Mason, 11
Brownell, Herbert, 79
Browning, James R., 72
Bundy, McGeorge, 89
Burch, Dean, 131, 140, 186
Burns, James MacGregor, 76, 77
Campbell, Angus, 152, 153
Carroll, Joseph F., 92
Casey, Ralph D., 31
Cater, Douglas, 46, 47, 54
Central Intelligence Agency, 89
Chambers, Whittaker, 11
Chancellor, John, 166
Chaney, James, 177, 178
Chotiner, Murray, 35
Cleveland, Grover, 75
Columbia Broadcasting System, 7, 8, 136, 137 (See also Frank Stanton)
Combs, George Hamilton, 30
Communications Act of 1934, 8–10 passim
  Section 315 (See Equal time rule)
Connally, John B., 69
Connor, Eugene ("Bull"), 158
Cooke, Alistair, 54
Coolidge, Calvin, 32, 75, 76
Cornwell, Elmer E., 74, 84
Costello, Frank, 12
Craig, May, 85
Cronkite, Walter, 95, 118
Crown, James Tracy, 86
Cuban missile crisis, 89–93
Cushing, Richard Cardinal, 72
Cushman, Robert E., 9
Daley, Richard J., 26
Daly, Lar, 26, 27
David, Paul T., 155
Debates (See Political debates)

Democratic National Convention (See Political conventions)
Dewey, Thomas E., 1, 21, 23, 147, 179, 188
De Gaulle, Charles, 69
Douglas-Home, Alec, 122
Dulles, John Foster, 79
Early, Steven, 77
Edwards, Donald, 128, 129
Eisenhower, Dwight David, 21, 26, 32, 71–74 passim, 86, 95, 96, 175
  activities at 1964 Republican Convention, 163, 164, 165
  approach to voters, 32
  convention reform proposals, 166–168
  influence on 1964 Republican presidential nomination, 158, 159
  1952 presidential campaign, 33, 34, 35
  peace trip, 96
  press conferences, 74, 75, 77, 78, 81, 84, 85
  use of television, 78, 79
Equal time rule, 20, 24–28, 64, 138–140 passim
  attempted suspension, 62, 63
  and minority parties, 63, 64
Erhard, Ludwig, 122
Estes, Billie Sol, 119, 187
Fairness doctrine, 138, 139
Faulk, John Henry, 7
Federal Communications Act (See Communications Act of 1934, Equal time rule, Fairness doctrine)
Federal Communications Commission, 8–10, 26, 29, 138, 140, 193
Fenton, John, 146
Folliard, Edward T., 179
Ford, Gerald R., 130
Fortas, Abe, 114, 115
Friendly, Fred W., 191
Funston, Keith, 114
Gallup, George, 188
Glaser, William, 4
Glenn, John H., 94
Goldenson, Leonard H., 64
Goldman, Ralph M., 155
Goldwater, Barry, 49, 121, 124, 131, 132, 138, 140, 150, 151, 154, 155, 159, 160, 162, 171, 174, 175, 186, 187
  1964 presidential campaign
  campaign activities, 178–181
  extremist views, 176
  nomination acceptance speech, 165, 166
  preconvention support, 158
  presidential primaries, 144–146
  television appearances, 182–185
  television coverage, 147, 148

Goodman, Andrew, 177, 178
Gould, Jack, 99
Gromyko, Andrei, 89
Gruening, Ernest, 129
Guihard, Paul, 87
Hagen, Harlan, 128
Hagerty, James Campbell, 78, 79, 81, 85, 86
Hall, Leonard, 32, 152
Halleck, Charles A., 186, 187
Halpert, Saul E., 60
Hamer, Fannie Lou, 170
Harding, Warren G., 75, 76
Harrington, Alan, 60
Harris, Louis, 188, 191
Harrison, Benjamin, 75
Hartnett, Vincent W., 7
Hennock, Frieda B., 10
Henry, E. William, 131
Herman, George E., 95
Hiss, Alger, 11, 36
Hoover, Herbert C., 32, 75, 76
Hughes, Emmet John, 19
Hughes, John, 92, 93
Humphrey, Hubert H., 22, 49, 129, 170, 171, 174, 175, 185, 186
Huntley, Chet, 157
Janeway, Eliot, 153
Jenkins, Walter W., 180, 181
Johnson, Claudia ("Lady Bird"), 104, 180
Johnson, Lynda, 180
Johnson, Lyndon Baines, 48, 104, 110, 139, 140, 144, 153, 154, 168–170 passim, 174–176 passim, 185, 186, 192
  domination of television, 118–121
  first days as president, 114, 115
  personality, 116
  prepresidential political record, 110–113
  press relations, 85, 116–118
  1964 presidential campaign
    campaign activities, 178–182
    nomination acceptance speech, 171
    preconvention press coverage, 121–124, 125
    press conferences and equal time rule, 138
Katzenbach, Nicholas, 87, 99
Keating, Kenneth, 91, 92, 93, 166, 175
Kefauver, Estes, 16, 21, 26, 143
  crime investigation, 10–12
Kelley, Stanley, Jr., 30, 31
Kennedy, Edward M., 23
Kennedy, Ethel, 71
Kennedy, Jacqueline, 70, 104, 107
Kennedy, John Fitzgerald, 27, 48, 60–62 passim, 65, 100, 110–113 passim, 121, 124, 125, 143, 144, 169, 170
  assasination, 69, 70, 104–109, 148
  Cuban missile crisis, 89–91, 93
  cult, 94
  European trips, 97

Kennedy, John Fitzgerald (continued)
  inauguration, 71–74
  intervention in Mississippi, 87, 88
  1960 presidential campaign
    convention communications network, 156
    debate with Hubert Humphrey, 22
    debates with Richard Nixon (See Kennedy-Nixon debates)
    election victory, 70, 71
    religious issue, 36, 37, 38
    views on presidency, 43
  personality, 46–48, 116
  press conferences, 74, 80–86
  televised interviews, 95, 96
Kennedy-Nixon debates, 1, 18–20, 50, 51, 64, 86
  appraisals, 51–53, 60
  audience size, 19, 49
  background, 20–22
  content, 48–50 passim, 53–59 passim
  effects, 18–20, 22–24
  formats, 50
  impact, 51
  press reactions, 53–60
  proposal of, 49
Kennedy, Robert, 18, 71, 73, 87, 89, 99, 122, 123, 156, 169, 170
Khrushchev, Nikita, 46, 96, 97
Kilduff, Malcolm, 117, 118
Kintner, Robert, 106
Krock, Arthur, 31, 32, 55
Ku Klux Klan, 178
Lang, Kurt and Gladys, 138, 190, 191
Larson, Arthur, 5, 6
Lawrence, William H., 95, 122
Levin, Michael, 34
Lewis, Fulton, Jr., 55
Lewis, Ted, 84, 100
Lindsay, John, 175
Lippman, Walter, 85
Lodge, George, 23
Lodge, Henry Cabot, 61, 124, 125, 144, 145, 149, 151, 158, 161
Longworth, Alice Roosevelt, 33
Lowe, Jacques, 71
Lower, Elmer W., 167
Lubell, Samuel, 188
Lucy, Autherine J., 98
McAndrew, William, 106, 140
McCarthy, Joseph R., 12–16
McCormack, Edward, 23
McKinley, William, 75
MacMillan, Harold, 97
McNamara, Robert S., 92, 93
Managed news, 84, 97–100
Marshall, Burke, 87
Mass media functions, 155
Massey, Raymond, 187
Mazo, Earl, 19
Meredith, James, 86, 87
Merton, Robert, 31
Michener, James A., 58

Miller, William E., 160, 165, 174, 175, 180, 181, 185
Minority parties
rights to equal broadcast time, 63, 64
Moody, Blair, 20
Moore, Robert L., 27
Morton, Thruston B., 22
Mothers for a Moral America, 187
Multer, Abraham J., 130
Mundt, Karl E., 14
National Council for Civic Responsibility, 5–7
National Educational Television
political programming, 137
Neustadt, Richard E., 121
Nixon, Patricia, 35, 71
Nixon, Richard M., 27, 47, 48, 71, 124, 125, 144, 145, 146, 158, 159, 175
Checkers speech, 34–36
debate with Edmund G. Brown, 23
1960 presidential election campaign
debates with John F. Kennedy (See Kennedy-Nixon debates)
personal appearances, 37
telethon, 61
views on presidency, 44
views on religious issue, 36, 37
personality, 44–46
Nizer, Louis, 7
Oppenheimer, J. Robert, 69
Oswald, Lee Harvey, 106
Paar, Jack, 27
Page, Sister Mary Paul, 94
Pastore, John, 170
Penty, George P., 86
Pettit, Tom, 106
Phillips, Cabell, 47, 79
Political broadcasts
costs, 131–134 (tables)
Political campaigns
reforms needed, 192, 193, 194
(See also Presidential election campaigns)
Political conventions, 154–171
biasing effects of television, 155–158 passim
1960 Democratic National Convention, 156
1964 Democratic National Convention, 168–171
1964 Republican National Convention, 160–166
reform proposals, 166, 167
theatrical quality, 155, 156
Political debates, 20–24, 29, 31
1964 campaign proposal, 70
presidential participation, 65
(See also Kennedy-Nixon debates)
Presidential election campaigns
1960 campaign
issues, 48, 49
religious issue, 36, 37
role of television, 62
(See also Kennedy-Nixon debates,

Presidential election campaigns
(continued)
John F. Kennedy, Richard M. Nixon)
1964 campaign
issues, 174
pollsters predictions, 187–188
(See also Barry Goldwater, Hubert H. Humphrey, Lyndon B. Johnson, William E. Miller)
Presidential primaries, 22, 131, 143, 151, 152, 153
backlash vote, 153, 154
1964 New Hampshire primary, 145–151, 153
Presidential press relations, 74–79
Preston, Dickson, 117, 118
Quarles, Donald A., 80
Quayle, Oliver, Associates, 191
Racial problems in U.S., 177–179
Radical right broadcasting, 6
Radio
impact on politics, 37
FDR's use, 33, 77
Raskin, Hy, 156
Reedy, George, 117, 118, 179
Republican National Convention (See Political conventions)
Reston, James, 32, 53, 55, 58, 117
Rockefeller, Nelson, 23, 70, 121, 124, 150, 153, 155, 158, 161, 162, 175, 176, 186
candidate in 1964 presidential primaries, 144, 145, 149, 151
speech at 1964 Republican convention, 164, 165
Romney, George, 23, 144, 159, 161, 175
Rooney, Fred B., 130
Roosevelt, Franklin Delano (FDR), 32, 110, 111, 179
1944 election campaign, 23
press relations, 75, 76, 77
radio talks, 33, 77
Roosevelt, James, 128, 129
Roosevelt, Theodore, 75, 76
Roper, Elmo, 3, 4, 165, 188
Rossiter, Clinton, 74, 75
Rovere, Richard H., 46, 180
Ruby, Jack, 106
Rusk, Dean, 89
Salant, Richard S., 136
Salinger, Pierre, 58, 71, 81, 82, 86, 95, 96, 129, 156
Sarnoff, Robert, 20, 27, 49, 50
Schafly, Phyllis, 147
Schwerner, Michael, 177, 178
Scranton, William, 70, 125, 144, 158, 159, 160–163
Seldes, Gilbert, 37
Sevareid, Eric, 33, 59, 122
Siepmann, Charles A., 8
Simpson, Milward L., 129
Smith, Alfred E., 32, 37
Smith, Howard K., 50, 131

Smith, Margaret Chase, 144, 145
Smith, Merriman, 106
Sorenson, Theodore, 90, 114
Stern, Philip M., 60
Stanton, Frank, 20, 27, 70, 136, 138
Stassen, Harold E., 144, 145, 159
Stein, Gertrude, 175
Stevenson, Adlai, 20, 21, 33, 34, 70, 90, 143
Sullivan, John Paul, 139
Sullivan, Mark, 33, 75
Sylvester, Arthur, 100
Symington, Stuart, 49
Taft, Charles, 186
Taft, Robert A., 26
Taft, Robert, Jr., 127
Television
  as a news source, 3–4
  as incitement to riot, 178
  blacklisting, 7
  cabinet meeting, 79
  campaign coverage problems, 134, 135
  controversial broadcasts, 5, 6
  cost of air time, 131–134 (tables)
  in courtroom, 119
  coverage of Army-McCarthy hearings, 14–16
  coverage of Kefauver crime investigation, 10–12
  coverage of Kennedy assassination and funeral, 105–109
  Defense Department briefing on Cuban missiles, 91–93
  Defense Department press conference, 79
  Editorializing, 29, 138, 139
  effect on election results, 189, 190
  effect on political conventions, 154–158, 167
  effect on U.S. political life, 1–3
  effect on voter turnout and behavior, 188–190
  impact on viewer, 32, 33
  impact on electorate, 152, 153
  influence on politics, 127–130

Television (continued)
  minority party problems, 23–24 (See also Equal time rule, Fair play doctrine)
  1960 presidential campaign coverage, 62
  1964 presidential campaign coverage, 136, 137 (See also Political campaigns, Kennedy-Nixon debates)
  persuasive power, 4
  political advertising, 33, 34, 38, 185, 186
  political functions, 176, 177
  prediction of election results, 191
  presidential domination, 118–121
  presidential press conferences, 74, 78, 79, 80–86
  quiz show scandals, 7
  value in news coverage, 93, 94
Thomson, Charles A. H., 25, 26
Tower, John G., 129
Truman, Harry S., 1, 33, 57, 58, 77, 188
University of Alabama crisis, 98, 99
United Nations, 5, 11
Valenti, Jack, 117, 118
Vanocur, Sander, 55, 95
Walker, Edwin A., 87
Wallace, George, 98, 99, 131, 155
  backlash vote, 153, 154
  primary campaigns, 144, 153, 154
Wallace, Mike, 166
Warren, Earl, 72
Wasilewski, Vincent, 138
Welles, Orson, 11
Welsh, Joseph N., 15
White, Theodaoe H., 18, 52, 146, 150, 165, 179, 180
Wicker, Tom, 46
Williams, Raymond, 152
Willkie, Wendell, 147
Wilson, Charles E., 79, 80
Wilson, Woodrow, 75, 96
Xerox Corp., 5
Yarborough, Ralph W., 28, 69
Zablocki, Clement J., 130